NEW DIRECTIONS IN SCANDINAVIAN STUDIES

TERJE LEIREN & CHRISTINE INGEBRITSEN, *Series Editors*

Cw141

NEW DIRECTIONS IN SCANDINAVIAN STUDIES

This series offers interdisciplinary approaches to the study of the Nordic
region of Scandinavia and the Baltic States and their cultural connec-
tions in North America. By redefining the boundaries of Scandinavian
studies to include the Baltic States and Scandinavian America, the series
presents books that focus on the study of the culture, history, literature,
and politics of the North.

Small States in International Relations
EDITED BY CHRISTINE INGEBRITSEN, IVER B. NEUMANN,
SIEGLINDE GSTOHL, AND JESSICA BEYER

Danish Cookbooks: Domesticity and National Identity, 1616–1901
BY CAROL GOLD

Danish Cookbooks

DOMESTICITY & NATIONAL IDENTITY,

1616–1901

CAROL GOLD

UNIVERSITY OF WASHINGTON PRESS, SEATTLE

MUSEUM TUSCULANUM PRESS, UNIVERSITY OF COPENHAGEN

THIS PUBLICATION IS SUPPORTED BY A GRANT FROM
THE SCANDINAVIAN STUDIES PUBLICATION FUND.

Published in the United States by
University of Washington Press
P.O. Box 50096, Seattle, WA 98145 U.S.A.
www.washington.edu/uwpress
ISBN-13: 978-0-295-98682-1 (pbk. : alk. paper)
ISBN-10: 0-295-98682-4 (pbk. : alk. paper)

Published in Europe by
Museum Tusculanum Press
126 Njalsgade, DK-2300 Copenhagen S, Denmark
www.mtp.dk
ISBN 978 87 635 0608 3

LIBRARY OF CONGRESS CATALOGING-IN-PUBLICATION DATA
CAN BE FOUND AT THE BACK OF THE BOOK.

The paper used in this publication meets the minimum requirements of
American National Standard for Information Sciences-Permanence of
Paper for Printed Library Materials, ANSI Z39.48-1984.

COVER IMAGE: *Kitchen Interior with Reading Girl*, painting by Jens Juel, 1764.
Statens Museum for Kunst, Copenhagen, KMS 7100

To the memory of my parents

LILLIAN AND AUGUST GOLD

who taught me to love both
cooking and reading

MENU

ACKNOWLEDGMENTS

A S HISTORIANS, WE MAY LIKE TO THINK THAT we work alone. Of course, we do not. We depend on colleagues, friends, family, and other support networks to help us in our research and writing. Without this support, we probably would not be able to finish our projects, and I certainly would not. So, it is with much gratitude that I thank the following people for their continued and unstinting help, advice, and support.

To John Heaton and Tim Pursell, colleagues in the History Department at the University of Alaska Fairbanks, thanks for providing an environment, and occasional competition, in which good historical research could take place.

To the group of Danish teachers in North America who met with some irregular regularity for the past several years, many thanks for ongoing enthusiasm for my project. Although not historians, you listened with interest and asked probing questions

which often forced me to leave my comfortable historian's box and view my work from a new perspective. And many thanks to the Danish Ministry of Education for their generous funding of these meetings and their willingness to include "non-Danish Danes."

To longtime friend and sister historian Adda Hilden, to Ole Hyldtoft of the History Department at the University of Copenhagen, and to Michael and Susan Whyte of the Anthropology Department at the University of Copenhagen, my thanks for taking the time to read earlier versions of this manuscript in much detail and to spend many hours discussing it with me. Your thoughtful comments are highly appreciated and all remaining faults are mine alone.

To Dixon Jones, graphic artist and cartographer; to Dipika Nath, copyeditor; and to Mette Olwig, indexer—the sous chefs who work behind the scenes—my deep appreciation for your professional work. Without your help, the soufflé would fall.

To my longtime friends Sheri Layral of Fairbanks and Myra LeWinter of Copenhagen, innumerable thanks for constant prodding and support; and with special thanks to Myra for help with the title. It helps immeasurably when other people believe in you as well.

appetizer

FRONTISPIECES

PLATE 1. Cookbook: Containing one hundred necessary pieces / about brewing/baking/
cooking/preparing snaps and mead / which are useful for housekeeping, etc. Which have not
previously been printed in our Danish language. Printed in Copenhagen by Salomone
Sartorio, 1616.

Koge=Bog:

Jndeholdendis

et hundrede fornødene stycker/
Som ere / om Brygning / Bagning/
Kogen/ Brendeviijn oc Miød at bere-
de/ saare nyttelig vdi Huß-
holding/ etc.

Som tilforn icke paa vort Danske
Sprock vdi Tryck er vdgaaen.

Prentet I Kiøbenhaffn/
Aar 1637.

PLATE 3. *The Royal Danish and in respect of all manner complete Cooking, Baking and Preserving Book, or seven hundred and ten instructions arranged for Noble and Aristocratic Families, as well as for everyone, according to which can be prepared expensive and ordinary dishes, and how to dry and preserve many fruits, together with 52 rules about sweets. All, after many years of his own experience, sincerely and without personal interest, offered by Marcus Looft, Master Chef in Itzehoe.* Fourth improved edition. Copenhagen, 1804.

Den Kongelige Danske
og i Henseende til alle Slags Maader
fuldstændige
Koge=, Bage=
og
Sylte = Bog,
eller
syv hundrede og ti Anviisnings=Regler,
indrettet for
Herskaber og fornemme Familier,
saavelsom for
alle og enhver især,
hvorefter der kan tillaves saavel kostbare, som ordinaire
Retter, saa og hvorledes endeel Have=Frugter skal
tørres og indsyltes,
samt
52 Regler om Confiturer.
Alt efter mange Aars egen Erfaring oprigtig og uden al
Interesse lagt for Dagen af
# Marcus Looft,
Mester = Kok i Itzehoe.

Fierde og forbedrede Oplag.

Kiøbenhavn, 1804.
Trykt i det Kongelige Vaisenhuses Bogtrykkerie
af C. F. Schubart,
og tilkiøbs i Rothes Boghandling No. 8 paa Børsen.

drick sc:

Kogebog

for

mindre Huusholdninger, indeholdende over 100 Anviisninger til paa en billig og nem Maade at tillave god og velsmagende Mad.

Priis 12 Skilling.

Kjøbenhavn.

Jul. Strandbergs Forlag.

Faaes i Bog= og Papirhandelen Holmensgade 18, Stuen.
Trykt i Lund & Jensens Bogtrykkeri.

1867.

PLATE 4. *Cookbook for smaller households, containing over 100 recipes for preparing good and well tasting food in a cheap and easy manner. Price 12 Sk. Copenhagen: Jul. Strandbergs Press. Can be bought in the bookstore, Holmensgade 18, ground floor [1867].*

DET DANSKE KØKKEN

AF

CARL GINDERUP.

ERNST BOJESENS

FORLAG 1888.

PLATE 5. *The Danish Kitchen* by Carl Ginderup. Ernst Bojesens Press, 1888.

PLATE 6. Laura Adeler, *Illustrated Cookbook for Town and Country, with over 600 recipes for cooking, baking and preserving.* Copenhagen, 1893.

FRØKEN JENSENS
KOGEBOG

KØBENHAVN
DET NORDISKE FORLAG
BOGFORLAGET: ERNST BOJESEN
1901

PLATE 7. *Frøken Jensens Cookbook.* Copenhagen: The Nordic Press. Bookpublisher: Ernet Bojesen, 1901.

first course

COOKBOOKS AS HISTORICAL
SOURCE MATERIAL

COOKBOOKS, AS DO ALL BOOKS, TELL STORIES. Yet, anyone who has spent any time delving into cookbooks knows that very few people actually read them. And only a small group uses very many of the recipes. Why then do people buy cookbooks? The pictures, these days, are attractive; if the books are from foreign places we dream of traveling there or relive past travels. We salivate over fancy dishes or consider living in styles that we cannot afford. And, occasionally, we use the recipes to try out new dishes or to re-create food we remember from our childhood. Cookbooks, in the words of Nicola Humble, are "documents of desires, fears, and hopes."[1]

Cookbooks, however, rarely convey what people actually eat; recipes for common, everyday foods often do not appear in cookbooks. Perhaps the rationale is that everyone knows how to make the daily staples, so there is no need for a detailed recipe. Bread,

for instance, the staple carbohydrate of the Danish kitchen prior to the advent of potatoes in the nineteenth century, never shows up in early Danish cookbooks. Professional chefs, for whom these books were written, either knew how to bake bread (or at least how to supervise the baking of it) or, more likely, never made it themselves, preferring to buy from professional bakers or have servants make it. The absence of bread recipes, therefore, does not mean that no one ate bread; rather, it was too common to require a place in a cookbook.

Why then research old cookbooks, if they do not accurately depict the culinary habits of the day? Even if they do not tell us about everything that people ate, cookbooks can explain several other things. Literacy levels, for example, because one needs to be able to read in order to use them. They speak to numeracy, or at least to the presumed level of the reader's ability to manipulate numbers. Cookbooks may tell us something about household size. How large are the portions? Are the recipes intended to feed six to eight people or are there sections, indeed entire books, with meals for singles? Cookbooks may also suggest something about ingredient availability or, at least, about the contemporary level of knowledge of various ingredients. Chances are, there will not be recipes for pineapples in Siberia or for moose stew in the Sahara. Sample menus from specific places and time periods probably come the closest to discussing what was actually available, and possibly even eaten. Like other prescriptive literature, cookbooks relate what their authors expect from their readers—what they ought to be eating and how they ought to eat, if not necessarily what they do eat.

As with all prescriptive literature, a dialectic process takes place between the writers of cookbooks and the societies for which they claim to be writing. This book is concerned with some of the most obvious changes in Danish cookbooks—the growth of a bourgeois consciousness, the analogous development of domesticity, and the evolution of nationalism and a specific Danish national identity. Of course, the change in cookbooks parallels changes that we know are taking place in the social and political world, both within families and households as well as outside them, as a bourgeois domesticity develops inside the home

and the country modernizes and encounters the rest of the world from within the boundaries of the new Danish nation state.

Cookbooks, while they certainly reflect changes in society, also themselves constitute these changes. According to Arjun Appadurai, "cookbooks appear in literate civilizations . . . where cooking is seen as a communicable variety of expert knowledge. . . . [They] represent the culinary expression of a dynamic that is at the heart of the cultural formation of [the] new middle class."[2] As society changes, as new middle classes evolve, cookbooks capture the changes and, in so doing, help the changes along. In this, of course, cookbooks are no different from any other form of prescriptive literature, but their prescriptive role is not always recognized.

To say that cookbooks are markers of social change is to say that changes in dishes, recipes, ingredients, or menus are indicators of changes in the larger society. So, for instance, when recipes for bread baking begin to show up in Danish cookbooks, when there had been none previously, one can assume that something is going on in the social and cultural spheres. Or when, starting in the late eighteenth century, Danish cookbooks begin to be filled with instructions on how to manage a good household or with injunctions to eat homegrown Danish products, whereas earlier books had contained little beyond recipes, something has changed. The change may be as simple as the development of new technology, such as the introduction of enclosed stoves with ovens, which would obviously simplify the process of baking bread at home, or it might reflect something more dramatic, such as changes in women's roles or in the nature of the state. Whatever the explanation, changes in cookbooks serve as flags and it is up to the historian to decipher what these flags mean.

This book is an attempt to decipher some of these flags in cookbooks published in Denmark between 1616 and 1901. What can and do cookbooks tell us about the society in which they were written? What messages are being sent out through this medium and how can they be interpreted? Thus, this study is not about food or recipes or how to prepare and eat food; rather, it is about the *societies* in which food is prepared and eaten. Obviously,

to the degree that we are what we eat, the two are inseparable, but the main focus of this study will be on what we are rather than what we eat; the latter will be treated as a product of the former.

Cookbooks not only provide access to recipes but, in writing down recipes, they demystify and concretize dishes, making them infinitely repeatable and even common. In *Cooking, Cuisine and Class*, Jack Goody contends that

[the middle class's] concern with status was greatly aided by the use of printed books, manuals of domestic behavior including the ubiquitous cookbook. . . . These manuals helped them to breach the hierarchical organisation of cuisine, since the "secrets" of rich households were now revealed.[3]

As cookbooks reveal "secrets" and make them reproducible, upper-class dishes become more commonplace, enabling middle-class households to emulate upper-class behavior. As this leveling phenomenon spreads through society, it eventually goes in both directions; thus, the newly independent Danish farmers take their food with them as they move into the political sphere and up the socioeconomic ladder.

Joseph König believed that in addition to providing directions, cookbooks also provided moral guidance. In a cookbook translated from German into Danish, he wrote:

It is historically striking that in some areas of Germany people put almonds and raisins in this [crayfish] soup, precisely because people in these areas also have a moral need for something sweet. Thus in a thousand instances, it is confirmed that people are no different than what they eat.[4]

Germans, König believed, needed "moral sweetening," so they added fruit and nuts to their soup. Few authors are quite so frank about the connection between food and society but it is a thread that runs through many of the cookbooks.

About 150 cookbooks were published in Denmark between 1616, the date of the first published cookbook, and 1901, the date of Kristine Marie Jensen's very popular *Frøken Jensens Kogebog*

(*Miss Jensen's Cookbook*). Handwritten collections of recipes, however, go back to the thirteenth century. Half of the published
cookbooks were written by women; the other half divides fairly
evenly between men and anonymous authors who did not give
away their gender. Somewhat more interesting, however, is the
fact that of the twenty-one books published between 1616 and
1795, only two were written by women, and those two were published very early on, in 1648 and 1703. Thus, early cookbooks
were written by men, although what is probably the first cookbook originally written in Danish (not a translation) was written
by a woman; Anna Elisabeth Wigant's *En Høy-Fornemme Madames
Kaagebog* (*An Aristocratic Lady's Cookbook*) was published in 1703.[5]
Of the twenty-one books published between 1795 and 1837,
women wrote six and men wrote ten; however, after 1837, the
cookbook authors are overwhelmingly female. This reflects a
parallel shift in the presumed audience for cookbooks—from
professional chefs, who could be male or female (indeed the earliest cookbook printed a frontispiece with a woman cook), to
housewives and housekeepers, who were, according to cookbook
titles, mostly female.

Danish cookbooks were apparently quite popular in the time
period examined. Of the ones printed between 1616 and 1901,
at least thirty-seven came out in more than one edition, and
twenty-two, in more than two editions. Madame Mangor's
Kogebog for Smaa Huusholdninger (*Cookbook for Small Households*),
arguably the most popular of these, came out in forty editions
between 1837 and 1910, and a sequel, *Fortsættelse af Kogebog for
Smaa Huusholdninger* (*Continuation of Cookbook for Small Households*), came out in twenty-nine editions between 1842 and 1901.
But Mangor was not the only bestseller. C. Jacobsen's *Nye Koge-
Bog* (*New Cookbook*) came out in nine editions between 1815 and
1866; Christiane Rosen's *Oeconomisk Huusholdnings-Bog* (*Economic Housekeeping Book*) came out in three editions with four
volumes from 1818 to 1832; and H. V. Nielsen's *Allernyeste Kogebog indeholdende Anviisning til at lave saavel alle simple i en borgerlig
Huusholdning brugelige Retter* (*Newest Cookbook, with Instructions
for Making . . . Useful Dishes in Bourgeois Households*) was issued in
five editions between 1823 and 1836. Sørine Thaarup's *Kogebog*

for *By- og Landhuusholdninger* (*Cookbook for Town and Country Households*) went through twelve editions between 1868 and 1891. Laura Adeler's *Illustreret Kogebog for By og Land* (*Illustrated Cookbook for City and Country*) reached nine editions between 1893 and 1923. And *Frøken Jensens Kogebog*, first published in 1901 (and the one older cookbook all Danes know about today), was published in at least forty-four editions by 1975 and was reprinted in a special anniversary edition in 2001. Jensen's popularity probably equaled that of the early-twentieth-century cookbook author Fannie Farmer (*The Boston Cooking-School Cookbook*)[6] or of the later Irma Rombauer (*Joy of Cooking*).[7] The extensive reprinting of cookbooks indicates that there was obviously a thriving market for them, and publishers, at least, thought cookbooks were good business. Another mode of book publication and sales was through prepaid subscriptions; Christiane Rosen (1767–1847), for instance, sold most of her books before they were written, and this, too, indicates significant popularity.

There is little change in the physical appearance of the books over the three centuries. The early books present their recipes in a prose format, weaving ingredients, amounts (when given), and processes into a single narrative. It is not until the twentieth century that ingredients are listed separately, in the format that is familiar to us today. Pictures also are scarce; the early cookbooks have none. Sometime in the late eighteenth century, diagrams start appearing—first of place settings, later of cooking implements and the process of cutting up meat. None of the early cookbooks has pictures of finished dishes. Today's pictures are probably a result of better photography and a cheaper printing process.

Danish cookbook titles, however, do change over time. The earliest cookbooks are simply called "Cookbook," or some variation on the theme, such as *A Good and Very Useful Cookbook*[8] or *New Complete Cookbook*.[9] From 1785 to 1800, nine of the twelve books published use "woman" somewhere in the title. And starting in 1837, with Madame Mangor, the most common words are "housekeeping" and "households," which, rather than any specific reference to women, appear in some form or another in half the titles.

Read in chronological order, the Danish cookbooks in this study break down into three groups, each with a different audience and a different agenda.

❖ From the early seventeenth to the mid-eighteenth century, Danish cookbooks written primarily by men address themselves to professional chefs, probably for large, wealthy aristocratic households. The recipes here presume a high degree of culinary experience and ability, and mostly serve to remind the cooks of possibilities, both in terms of dishes and ingredients.

❖ The second group, from the mid-eighteenth century to the mid-nineteenth, is radically different from the first. Written by both men and women, these books address themselves to housewives and housekeepers, mostly women. They are extremely didactic; they preach at their audiences, telling them not only how to prepare individual dishes but also how to keep house, train servants, and generally maintain a positive domestic environment. They seem to be addressing cooks who are not as comfortable in the kitchen and contain many more specific references to women in their titles.

❖ The last group, from the mid-nineteenth to the turn of the twentieth century, comprises books written mostly by women addressing themselves to small and large *households*, rather than to cooks per se. Still addressing women, these books assume the reader's familiarity with cooking and are much less didactic. Indeed, several of the books from this time are simple listings of recipes, without any prescriptions at all.

These dates are obviously approximations and there are certainly overlaps among the cookbook authors. However, the mere fact of the changes and the fuzziness around the edges of the changes acts as a marker for the historian, indicating that the society is changing in some way.

One way to mark this change is to examine the audiences that the cookbooks addressed, and literacy would, of course, be a part of this equation. Could the intended audience read? Here we have to distinguish between different audiences at different times. We have no way of knowing if the professional chefs for

whom the first group of cookbooks was written could read. Did the chefs read the books themselves or did someone else—the lady of the house or a professional housekeeper—read the recipes aloud or remind the chefs of the necessary ingredients? Were these books even meant to be used in cooking? Were they, rather, written in order to divulge "secrets," to use Goody's term, or to show off the author's intimate knowledge of the upper classes?

These are not immediately answerable questions. However, what we do know is that by the time of the first published cookbook in 1616, Denmark was a Lutheran country, with a Lutheran state church. In order to attain civil personhood and one's majority, one needed to be confirmed in the church, and in order to be confirmed, one needed to be able to read (or, at least, to memorize) Luther's *Small Catechism*. A recent book by Charlotte Appel establishes a high level of functional urban literacy in Denmark as early as the seventeenth century.[10] There is no reason to suppose that this literacy fell off in the succeeding centuries. Indeed, the 1739 School Law, which mandated education for *all* children, emphasized the teaching of Christianity and from that followed an emphasis on learning to read. Ingrid Markussen's study, *For the Honor of the Creator, Service to the State and Our Own Good*, confirms that students in the eighteenth century attended school anywhere from "hardly at all" to "every other day," but that learning to read was expected of all.[11]

The 1814 School Law reiterated the emphasis on literacy. It again mandated education for all children, male and female, from age seven until confirmation: "Religion, writing and arithmetic, as well as reading . . . [and] proper deportment shall be taught in the schools."[12] Neither the 1739 nor the 1814 School Law distinguished in any way between boys and girls; both were expected to attain the same level of literacy. Markussen asserts, "we must conclude that women in rural districts must have attained literacy at least as quickly as men."[13]

As for middle-class women, for whom the second group of books was written, there is good reason to presume that they could indeed read. There were at least 150 private schools for girls in Copenhagen in the late eighteenth century, and no reason to suppose that there were not similar schools in other urban

areas of Denmark as well. At a bare minimum, these schools taught girls to read, knit, and embroider.[14] In her autobiography, Christiane Rosen talks of starting school in Køge (a small town on the island of Sjælland in Denmark), and learning to read at the age of three and a half years; this was in 1770. Her father later taught her writing and arithmetic.[15]

Lending libraries flourished in Copenhagen from the turn of the eighteenth to the nineteenth century. These libraries regularly printed and circulated lists of their holdings. Dozens of books specifically targeting women—handbooks, ladies' books, New Year's gifts, journals, "collections for women," women's histories, behavior manuals—appear on the libraries' lists. Several of these were of the "gift book" variety, such as *Library for the Beautiful Sex, Women's Library, Monthly Magazine for Women, New Year's Gift for Women, Philosophy for Ladies,* and *A Lady's Friend.* Some targeted new wives and mothers, such as *Advice for Marriageable and Newlywed Women, A Medical Diet for Newlyweds, Gynecology or Maidenhood, Intercourse and Marriage,* and *A Handbook for Mothers.* People in the publishing and book distribution trade obviously believed it worth their while to print and circulate books of all sorts addressed to women. Since the mass market for cookbooks, starting in the middle period, comprised middle-class women and since schools and educational possibilities had been available from at least the mid-eighteenth century, there was probably an available literate audience for cookbooks.

Although literacy among rural women has been less well researched, reports from clergymen in rural areas to the local school boards document their concerns about parishioners who were unable to read and thus were not eligible for confirmation.[16]

Female literacy was a public and acknowledged fact. This is perhaps not so surprising in a Lutheran country that emphasized individual access to the Bible, but the extent of literacy beyond the Bible is perhaps worth noting. Publication of books directed specifically at women, such as those mentioned above, implies a general awareness of female literacy as well as the existence of a market large enough to make their publication economically feasible; it should come as no surprise, therefore, to find cookbooks addressed to women.

Cookbook titles are also an indication of the presumed audience. From 1616 to 1785, with one exception in 1703, the titles of the books are basically just variations of "cookbook" such as *A Good and Useful Cookbook* (1648), *A Small Tested Cookbook* (1740), and *A Nice Little Cookbook* (1733). As they address themselves primarily to professional chefs, the titles of these volumes reflect their audience. From 1785 to 1830, starting with Carl Müller's *Nye Koge-Bog for den retskafne Huusmoder* (*New Cookbook for the Respectable Housewife*), thirteen of twenty-four titles include some form of feminine address in the title. They address themselves to housewives, housekeepers, and young women; *The Danish Housewife* (1793), *Education for Young Women* (1795), *The Experienced Advisor for Domestic Women* (1796), *New Original Danish Cookbook for Women* (1806), and *The Danish Housewife's Kitchen Catechism* (1801) tactfully combining the religious and the domestic necessity for reading.

Reflecting still another change in audience, starting with Madame Mangor's book in 1837, cookbooks now claim to be for "households," both large and small, rural and urban. Women continue to appear in titles, although with much less frequency. *Cookbook for Rural Households* (1846), *Cookbook for Small and Large Households* (1848), *Cookbook for Large and Small Households* (1851), *Practical Cookbook for Every Household* (1855), *Cookbook for Rural and Urban Households* (1857), *Cook- and Preserving Book for Young Women Who Wish to Manage their Own Households* (1860), *Concise Cookbook for Every Household* (1861), *Cookbook for Smaller Households* (1864), *Common Cookbook for all Classes and Especially for Housewives and Expectant Housewives* (1866), *Sensible Cooking and Housekeeping* (1866), *Complete Cookbook for Smaller Households* (1868), *Cookbook for the Danish Housewife* (1871–1872), *The Danish Kitchen* (1888), and finally, in this list, *Frøken Jensens Cookbook* (1901). This is just a sampling, but it paints the general picture.

With books printed for women, addressed to women, often in several volumes or editions, there is no reason to assume that women could not read these books. The language is not terribly difficult; although it is not particularly simple either. The intro-

duction to a 1798 cookbook, *Education for Young Women*, notes that "[t]hose who understand housekeeping only seldom have time to acquire many books or to read those that deal with the job of keeping house. This book is meant for those people."[17] Although the women to whom this book is directed may not have the *time* to read, there is an obvious assumption that they *could* read.

Christiane Rosen goes so far as to tell her public that they need to learn reading and mathematics. "It is a necessity for every young housewife and housekeeper to be able to read and figure, in order to compare their expenses with their incomes." There is no sense here that she is advising anything unusual; rather, she is explaining why such skills are necessary. She goes on to add that "[t]hey must know exactly what to expect of every product," promoting the idea of knowledgeable housewives and housekeepers.[18]

The anonymous author who wrote *Education for Young Women* in 1798 goes a step further and assumes a writing ability with a section in the book "on preparing pens to write with." The use of goose quills for writing is discussed, as well as how to pull them from the geese or collect those that have fallen out. Even if these pens are being prepared for someone else, perhaps for the man in the house, there is a sense of familiarity with and understanding of the process involved.

A further indication of these women's literacy is the level of numeracy assumed by the recipes themselves. Reading was taught before either writing or arithmetic[19] and the cookbooks presume a fairly high level of numerical manipulation ability. If readers had the functional numeracy to use the recipes, they surely had the literacy to read them. The introduction of specific amounts— one-half pound, one-and-a-half pots—implies that the readers also had a basic understanding of how to weigh and measure. "Five-quarters" is a fairly common measurement in the recipes, reflecting perhaps that it is a common Danish phrase (*fem kvarter*) but one which nonetheless implies a certain level of arithmetic understanding.

A 1703 recipe for cinnamon cakes introduces some quite specific measurements, along with some nonspecific estimations:

Take a pound of wheat [white] flour, a half pound of sugar, saffron, eight egg yolks, a pail of rose water, one *lod* of cinnamon, a little grated coriander, melted butter, a little cold water. Make a batter from this and bake over a good fire.[20]

Some of these measurements remain vague—"a little grated coriander" or "a little cold water"—but there is also a specificity to other measurements, such as "a pound of wheat flour, a half pound of sugar," which supports the assumption of some level of numeric ability. A pail was a quarter of a liter, and a *lod* was a specific measurement that would equal 15.6 grams or 1/2 ounce today, but it would have been found as an individual weight for scales in eighteenth-century kitchens.

A chocolate cake recipe from 1766 called for twenty-four to thirty eggs (eggs were much smaller then), one and one-half pails of milk, one pound of butter, a half pound of sugar, a half pound of ground almonds, twenty-four egg yolks, a half pound of finely grated chocolate, two spoonfuls of lemon juice, and twelve stiffly beaten egg whites. At the end of the recipe was the advice: "If you do not want the cake so large, then you can just take *half* of everything" (emphasis added).[21]

Just how sophisticated is the concept of dividing something in half? And how many cooks, even today, can easily divide one and one half in half? It seems obvious that as early as the beginning of the eighteenth century, Danish cookbooks were addressing cooks who were functionally numerate as well as literate.

In contrast, a recipe from the mid-nineteenth century in America stated, "Let the molasses drip in as you sing 'Nearer My God to Thee.' When it's raining, sing two verses" (molasses flows more slowly in the rain).[22] American cookbooks remained fairly innumerate until the end of the nineteenth century, although note the presumption that everyone knows *Nearer My God to Thee*, or at least one verse of it; one could always repeat the verse in the rain. Although not all American cookbooks were innumerate and in fact several assumed functional numeracy, no Danish cookbook assumed innumeracy on the part of its readers.[23]

The earliest cookbooks, addressed to professional chefs, were directed to an upper-class clientele. These recipes were meant

for huge households with money and many people to feed either on a daily basis or for special occasions. They tell little if anything about average households. However, once the cookbooks begin to address women and smaller households, we can assume that the social level of the audience changes. Authors are now addressing middle-class households. Certainly, the family would have to have enough money to be able to afford to buy books or, perhaps, to know people who could afford to buy books to give as presents.

An analysis of the changing frontispieces of cookbooks (see examples at the front of the book) shows quite clearly the change in times as well as in the presumed audience. The frontispiece from the 1616 *Cookbook* shows a well-dressed woman cooking over an open fire in a well-stocked kitchen.[24] A second edition, from 1637, has shifted the emphasis from food preparation to food consumption and portrays a well-dressed couple partaking of food in a well-appointed bedchamber.[25] In earlier periods, it had been quite normal to receive visitors in bedrooms, the opulence of the bed indicating the stature of the host.[26] This is still quite a well-to-do family and the shift from the kitchen to the bedroom may well reflect a sense that the finished meal is of more importance than its preparation. In either event, the cookbook still addresses itself to wealthy, upper-class, aristocratic families. Marcus Looft's cookbook from 1766 (1804 reprint shown), still addressed to "noble and aristocratic families," also shows a large kitchen, with a female cook and a servant boy. Through the doorway can be glimpsed the "noble" couple waiting for their meal.[27]

One hundred years later, an anonymous *Cookbook for Smaller Households*, clearly portrays a smaller kitchen, with a female cook or housewife watching a pot on an enclosed stove.[28] She is still in charge of her space but the space itself is much smaller. Laura Adeler's *Illustrated Cookbook for City and Country* from 1893 moves the focus from the woman watching the stove, cooking, to a simply dressed woman *presenting* the finished product, with an enclosed stove and other cooking utensils in the background, which make it clear that the woman has prepared the food herself. In 1888, Carl Ginderup moves his women out-

side the kitchen; despite his title, *Det Danske Køkken* (The Danish Kitchen), his cookbook shows two women, one well dressed, the other with shawl and apron (perhaps the woman of the house and her cook), buying food from a local fishwife.[29] Finally, with *Frøken Jensen's Cookbook*, in 1901, cooking has been distilled to the smoke that issues from chimney pots during the process. Her frontispiece of urban rooftops can also be taken as a symbol of the advent of industrialization.[30] Obviously, we have moved a considerable distance, both physically and socially, from the premodern cookbooks.

As the cookbooks change in title, tone, and graphics, the social standing of the readers also changes to comprise mostly the middle classes. The obvious change in the visual presentation—from cooks preparing food for wealthy patrons to women doing their own food preparation—reflects the development of the middle-class "cult of domesticity," which located women in the sphere of the home and kitchen. Jensen's chimney pots might also be seen as representing the new urban industrial working class, and thus indicating a further shift in cookbook audiences away from the earlier upper-class households.

In the Danish context, the concept of middle class takes on an additional dimension. If "middle class" is defined as the social group that owns enough in terms of property or skill to be economically self-sufficient, and is not noble, then we must include in the category the new "self-owning" peasants (*selvejere*)—the independent farmers (*gårdmænd*) of the late eighteenth and early nineteenth century who now owned title to their land. This extends the concept of the middle class from the cities into the agricultural countryside.

During the reform era of the late eighteenth and early nineteenth century, the absolute Danish monarchy, supported by a group of very wealthy, progressive landowners, broke up the old communal strip farming systems, consolidated farms into individual geographically contiguous plots, and sold them to the peasants who had previously farmed them in a symbiotic paternalistic relationship with noble landlords. (This is dramatically different from the contemporaneous enclosure movement in England, which expanded landlord holdings at the expense of

peasants who were often forced off the land.) Roughly 40 percent of the peasants now received title to their own plots of land, thus becoming landowners themselves and moving into the middle class. Wealthy landlords benefited because they received cash payments for what had often been marginally productive land and also freed themselves from the tax burdens connected with these lands. Peasants who were able to buy their own land with the help of low-interest state loans benefited from their instant transformation into *selvejer*, or independent, farmers.[31] Of the roughly 60 percent of the peasants who were left out of this process, little was heard until the middle of the nineteenth century, when they started organizing their own political parties. Some of them will later show up in cookbook titles as "small households."

The development of these new middle-class households parallels the growth in domesticity which views women as being in charge of the private, domestic sphere, balanced by men's participation in the more public, business sphere. Cookbooks now assume somewhat smaller households, which are still fairly large by modern standards, as the housewife was still responsible for feeding the various nonrelatives who worked on the farm or in the house, that is, farm workers or apprentices as well as servants. As the farmer gains title to his land, his wife takes on the responsibility for her kitchen; as the land now belongs to the husband, the kitchen belongs to the wife. The shift in titles from some version of "cookbook" to "housewives" and "housekeepers" reflects changes in real estate as well as in culture.

Thus, as the world outside the kitchen changes—as peasants become farmers and move into political processes, as will be seen later—so too do cookbooks change. As prescriptive literature, cookbooks can be seen not only as mirrors of their society, marking and reflecting social change, but also as catalysts of these changes, as will be discussed in later chapters. Society, language, menus, dishes—changes in one reflect as well as facilitate changes in the others.

first intermezzo

MENUS

Carl Müller, *New Cookbook*, 1785[1]

DINNER WITH TEN DISHES, TWO REMOVES

....

FIRST REMOVE [OR SERVING]

Brown soup with chopped chicken

Soup á la Pompadur

Paté of wood snipe

Stuffed fish

Small crayfish

Oublié [stuffed surprise]

SECOND REMOVE

Roast wild pork

Roast ortolane

Artichoke custard
Abalone with oysters
Four round plates with condiments

AT THESE DINNERS, SERVE THE CAKES, JELLIES, COMPOTES, ICES, ETC.,
WITH DESSERT.

DINNER WITH EIGHT DISHES, TWO REMOVES

FIRST REMOVE
Soup á la reine
"Balloon" of turkey [stuffed turkey]
Profiteroles with veal

SECOND REMOVE, WITH DESSERT
Viennese tart
Roast snipe
Marinated fish
Spinach with crayfish
Ragout of rooster combs

NB. IF YOU CAN GET FISH, YOU DO NOT NEED THE RAGOUT.

Condiments
Plates with desserts

EVENING MEAL WITH FIVE DISHES [SERVED TOGETHER]

Roast wood snipe
Calves head with oysters
Small patés of cauliflower
Abalone in a pyramid
"Patience Bread" [cupcakes]
Condiments

EVENING MEAL WITH FOUR DISHES

Roast turkey
Hare

Minced snails
Compote with apples and jelly
Plates with desserts

Anon., *Education for Young Women*, 1795[2]

ON THE ACTUAL SERVICE

....

Here are dish suggestions for a good housewife when she wants to entertain a large party. I also include some drawings, which show where to place the dishes, according to the numbers, and in what order the dishes should be eaten.

Figs. 1 and 2 show a dinner service with two removes, and fig. 3, an evening meal with one course.

FOR DINNER SERVICE, THE FOLLOWING DISHES
WOULD BE APPROPRIATE.

....

The numbers refer to accompanying diagram, plate 8

White soup with noodles and parmesan cheese   1
Brown soup with meatballs   1
Platters with small patés of crayfish or oysters   2
2 platters with roulettes   3

NB! AFTER THE SOUP HAS BEEN EATEN, REPLACE IT WITH 2 LARGE DISHES,

FOR EXAMPLE

Roast venison with brown gravy and pickles   4
Ham or roast beef with cabbage or spinach   7
Meatballs with mushrooms (sorrels)   5
Beef tenderloin with small onions   5
Partridge with orange juice and grated orange peel   6
Capons with oyster sauce   6

NB! THE TWO SMALL ROUND DRAWINGS LABELED O AND E, WHICH ARE PLACED

ON EACH END OF THE MIRROR [SPEIL], ARE FOR OIL AND VINEGAR, PEPPER,

MUSTARD, ETC. SALT SHAKERS, AS WELL AS THE SALADS AND PRESERVES, SOUR

AND SWEET ACCOMPANIMENTS FOR THE ROASTS ARE PLACED HERE AND THERE
AMONG THE PLATTERS.

SECOND REMOVE

....

Roast turkey, hare, or whatever other roast one has

NB! AT EACH END OF THE TABLE

2 platters with fish, carp, pike, or whatever one has   1
2 platters with greens, asparagus, peas, or such   3
two compotes
two kinds of salad, or salmon or herring

AFTER THE GUESTS HAVE BEEN SERVED, THE FOOD IS REMOVED AND THE
DESSERT PLACED ON THE TABLE, SUCH AS CAKES, JELLIES, ICES, CRÈMES,
AND MERINGUES, AND CANDIES, SUCH AS BURNT ALMONDS, MACAROONS,
PASTILLES, FRUIT, AND MARMALADE.

EVENING MEAL SERVED TOGETHER (FIG. 3)

....

A warm paté of poultry with sauce   1
Veal fricassee with oysters   2
Cauliflower with veal or lamb cutlets   3
Chicken with mushroom sauce   4
Fish—carp, pike, bream, or whatever one has   5
A roast—either hare, turkey, venison, or whatever one has   6

NB! ALSO SERVE A COUPLE OF COMPOTES AND SALADS, WHICH ARE PLACED ON
THE FOUR CORNERS OF THE TABLE, AND ARE MARKED C AND S

Two tarts or cakes, as desired   7
Gelé or blanc mange   8

FRUIT IS PLACED AT EACH END, MARKED IN THE DRAWING F AND K. THE OTHER
DESSERTS ARE PLACED AROUND THE TABLE, BETWEEN THE PLATES, AS IN THE
DRAWING, MARKED D.

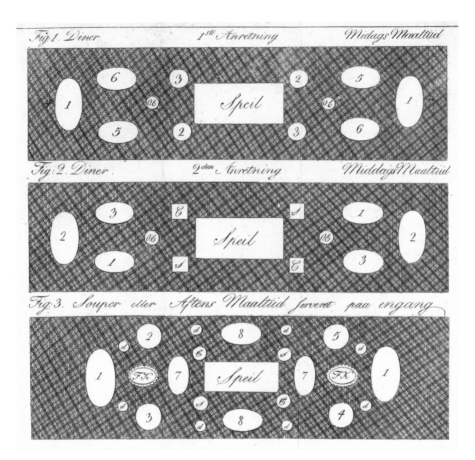

Fig. 1. Diner 1ste Anretning Midags Maaltiid

Fig: 2. Diner 2den Anretning Middags Maaltiid

Fig: 3. Souper eller Aftens Maaltiid serveret paa engang

PLATE 8. Table setting, end piece, Anon., *Education for Young Women* vol. 2
(Copenhagen, 1796).

FIG. 1. Dinner. 1st Service. Noon Meal. [Speil = mirror]

FIG. 2. Dinner. 2nd Service. Noon Meal.

FIG. 3. Supper or Evening Meal served in one course.

NB! WATER PITCHERS ARE PLACED BY THE OIL AND VINEGAR OR BY THE PLAT DE
MENAGER, IF YOU HAVE THEM, AND THE GLASSES BY EACH INDIVIDUAL SETTING.

Conradine Hasberg, *Cookbook for Rural and Urban Households*, 1857[3]

FOR HOUSEHOLDS WITH FOUR COURSES

....

Clear meat bouillon with white and green dumplings
Fish, boiled or fried

Roast venison with compote
Russian orange pudding

Potato soup with meatballs
Chicken with mushrooms
Roast beef
Waffle with whipped cream

Brown soup with fishballs
Paté with venison ragout
Roast turkey with ditto [venison ragout]
Fruit omelet

Giblet soup
Fried fish
Roast veal with compote
Parisian or other cake with vanilla cream

FOR HOUSEHOLDS WITH TWO COURSES

....

Meat soup with white and red dumplings
Roast, whatever you can get

Yellow pea soup with meatballs
Horseradish meat (from the meat cooked with the pea soup)

Rice pudding with beer or currant wine
Stuffed cabbage or meatballs with green beans or stewed potatoes

Chicken soup with rice
Cream puffs, pancakes, or something similar

FOR THE SERVANTS [ONE COURSE]

....

Soup with fresh or salted meat, with peeled potatoes, kohlrabi,
carrots, and dumplings
Buckwheat porridge with fried pork

Barley porridge with kohlrabi stewed in milk, sprinkled with pieces of pork and lung sausage

Dumpling milk (buckwheat is especially good for dumplings)

Maria Rasmussen, *Cookbook for Urban and Rural Households* 1864[4]

DINNER SERVICE
....

Brown soup with fish balls and white root vegetables
Fried turkey
Butter cake with gooseberry jelly

Clear soup with dumplings or meatballs
Boiled or fried fish
Roast veal
Wine jelly or cookies

Sweet soup
Veal cutlets
Princess pudding

Green pea soup
Smoked salmon with green beans
Roast chicken
Snowballs with whipped cream

Nielsine Nielsen, *The Housefriend's Cooking and Milking Book* 1885[5]

DAILY DINNER FOR WINTERTIME
....

SUNDAY
Rice pudding with either boiled pork or headcheese, and potatoes

MONDAY
Barley porridge and pancakes

TUESDAY
Veal soup with dumplings, or white cabbage and browned veal,
or pork soup with white cabbage

WEDNESDAY
Sweet pudding and fried pork with small potatoes

THURSDAY
Barley porridge with either fresh or dried fish, or boiled pork
with stewed potatoes, cabbage, or beets

FRIDAY
Green spoon cabbage, or yellow pea soup with meat

SATURDAY
Beer porridge with leftovers

Madame Ane Marie Mangor, *Cookbook for Small Households*, 40th ed., 1910[6]

WINTER WEEK IN A FINER HOUSEHOLD

....

SUNDAY
Beef soup with green beans, chopped roots, and white bread
Roast venison
Caramel pudding

MONDAY
Rice flour pudding
Boiled fish
Meatloaf with vegetables

TUESDAY
Wine pot
Venison ragout, with the leftovers from Sunday, with rolls
Fruit

WEDNESDAY
Fresh, boiled, warm, smoked ham with Brussel sprouts
Granade of chopped fish with chicken and mussel sauce

THURSDAY
Brown bean soup, made from the ham
Fricassee of veal breast, with oysters and chestnuts
Rum pudding

FRIDAY
Sweet (fruit) soup
Roast beef
Pancakes

SATURDAY
Eggcake (omelet) with topping or macaroni pie with ham
Boiled beef with sharp brown gravy and potatoes

WINTER WEEK IN A COMMON HOUSEHOLD

SUNDAY
Roast veal
Apple pudding with sheep's milk, cream, or cooked milk

MONDAY
Velvet pudding
Meatballs with veal shank

TUESDAY
Giblet soup, may also use bones from veal roast
Macaroni pudding with butter and parmesan cheese

WEDNESDAY
Porridge soup
Reheated roast veal from Sunday

THURSDAY
Yellow pea soup, eaten together with the salt meat with which it's cooked
Rusk cake

FRIDAY
Fish pudding
Calf's liver as beefsteak

SATURDAY
Beer pudding with herring
Boiled beef with stewed root vegetables

second course

HOW COOKBOOKS CHANGE

EVERAL ASPECTS OF DANISH COOKBOOKS CHANGE OVER the centuries, reflecting changes in the societies in which they were written. Among these are changes in procedures for preparing food, in the dishes included, and in suggested menus. There are also variations in the tones of the cookbooks, from description to prescription, and back. These changes, reflected also in cookbook titles and authors, break into the three groups discussed in the first course.

The earliest cookbooks can best be described as *aides memoires* for the chefs, who probably worked in large noble households. The recipes here are simple listings of ingredients with little emphasis on amount or detail. They are written in a narrative prose style, quite unlike the format for recipes with which we are familiar today. Such a recipe presupposes that the cook knows what the dish is and how it will turn out. Recipe number XCVII,

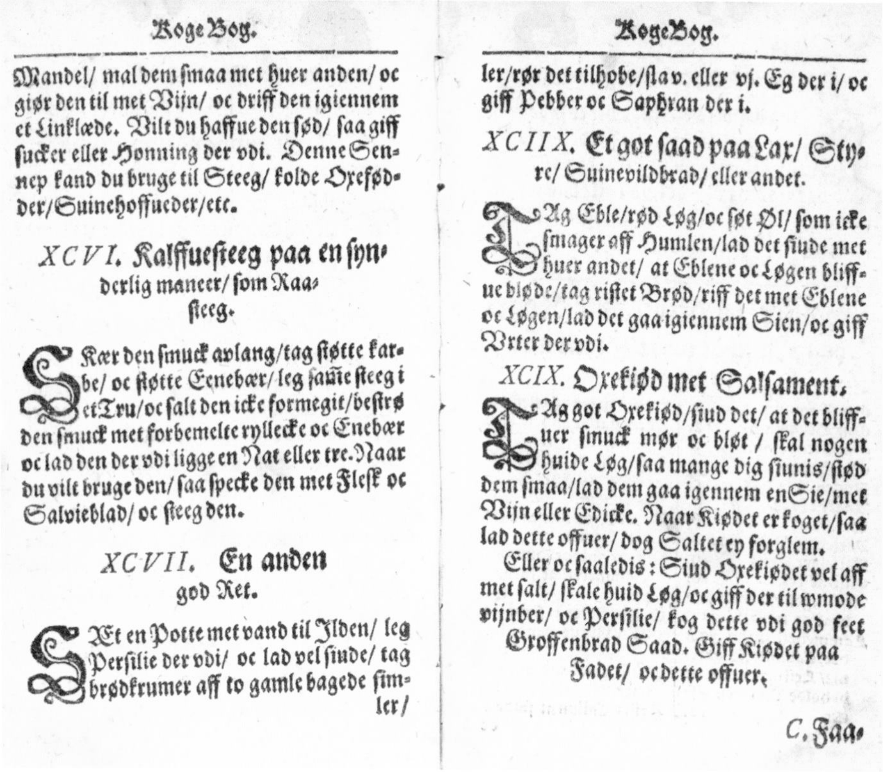
KogeBog.

Mandel/ mal dem smaa met huer anden/ oc giør den til met Vijn/ oc driff den igiennem et Linklæde. Vilt du haffue den sød/ saa giff sucker eller Honning der vdi. Denne Sennep kand du bruge til Steeg/ kolde Oxesødder/Suinehoffueder/etc.

XCVI. Kalffuesteeg paa en synderlig maneer/ som Raasteeg.

SKær den smuck avlang/tag støtte karbe/ oc støtte Enebær/ leg saiñe steeg i et Tru/oc salt den icke formegit/bestrø den smuck met forbemelte ryllecke oc Enebær oc lad den der vdi ligge en Nat eller tre. Naar du vilt bruge den/ saa specke den met Flesk oc Salvieblad/ oc steeg den.

XCVII. En anden god Ret.

SEt en Potte met vand til Ilden/ leg Persilie der vdi/ oc lad vel siude/ tag brødkrumer aff to gamle bagede simler/

KogeBog.

ler/rør det tilhobe/slav. eller vj. Eg der i/ oc giff Pebber oc Saphran der i.

XCIIX. Et got saad paa Lax/ Styre/ Suinevildbrad/ eller andet.

TAg Eble/rød Løg/oc søt Øl/ som icke smager aff Humlen/lad det siude met huer andet/ at Eblene oc Løgen bliffue bløde/tag riffet Brød/riff det met Eblene oc Løgen/lad det gaa igiennem Sien/oc giff Vrter der vdi.

XCIX. Oxekiød met Salsament.

TAg got Oxekiød/siud det/ at det bliffuer smuck mør oc bløt / skal nogen huide Løg/saa mange dig siunis/stød dem smaa/lad dem gaa igennem en Sie/met Vijn eller Edicke. Naar Kiødet er koget/saa lad dette offuer/ dog Saltet ey forglem.
Eller oc saaledis: Siud Oxekiødet vel aff met salt/ skale huid Løg/oc giff der til wmode vijnber/ oc Persilie/ kog dette vdi god feet Groffenbrad Saad. Giff Kiødet paa Fadet/ oc dette offuer.

C. Faa-

PLATE 9. Page of recipes, Anon., *Cookbook* (Copenhagen: Salomone Sartorio, 1616).

XCVI. Roast Veal in a different manner/as game.

XCVII. Another Good Dish.

XCIIX. A Good Plate of Salmon/Kidney/Wild Pork/or Other.

XCIX. Beef with Salt.

for example, from the 1616 *Cookbook* is titled, "Another Good Dish," and appears in the cookbook between a recipe for roast veal and one for salmon. The index lists it as "spoon food" (*søbemad*).[1] It is not at all obvious what the dish actually is, but a seventeenth-century cook would presumably have been familiar with it.

XCVII. ANOTHER GOOD DISH

Put a pot with water over the fire / put parsley in / and let it sit / take the breadcrumbs from two old baked rolls / mix it together / add an egg or not / and add pepper or saffron.[2]

This soup recipe from 1648 also assumes considerable familiarity on the part of the cook.

A SOUP OF FRIED FISH

Mix together a good portion of finely chopped onions in butter until brown. Add a glass of wine vinegar; add a little pepper, saffron, salt and a spoonful of raisins, as you wish. Let it cook together. When the fish is fried, first serve the soup and then lay the fish over it. Then it will be right and good.[3]

The recipe says nothing about how or when to fry the fish, what kind of fish, where the soup comes from, or even how one "lay[s] the fish over" soup. There is no specificity in the recipe; amounts are not given, even the ingredients are "as you wish." This is not to say that it is a bad recipe; indeed, if one is familiar with the dish, that is probably all that is needed, but it does assume a great deal of knowledge and competence on the part of the user.

However, by the eighteenth century, this was changing. Recipes were getting more specific. And although there still seems to be an underlying assumption that the cook knows what the end result will be (a feature of many cookbooks today), amounts, at least, get more specific. A recipe for "red pudding" (*rød grød*) from 1703 reads:

RED PUDDING

Take a half pound of rice flour, and one and a half pots of red wine. Add sugar, cardamom, cinnamon and finely chopped candied fruit. Let it cook until it is smooth and thick. Take 4 shillings worth of almonds, mince them and stir in and cook. You can put this in ceramic forms, if you wish, or you can put it in a dish.[4]

This is a more comprehensible recipe; one can envision the pudding. Not only does this recipe contain specific amounts, there is also an order to follow, what to look for ("smooth and thick"), and an explanation of how to serve the dish. Measuring scales must have been standard equipment in most kitchens,

since weights show up in many recipes. In 1800, Svendsen listed weighing scales as among the necessary utensils for a kitchen.[5] Whether "4 shillings" literally referred to the quantity that the amount would buy or whether the amounts had become standardized over time in such a way that "4 shillings worth" represented a specific amount, in either case, the recipe is quite precise.

Over time the recipes start to include much more specific preparation details as well. A beef recipe from 1799 actually mentions the length of time the beef should cook (three hours) and varies the sort of fire (first, "steady," then, "hotter") over which to cook it.

Cover it well and set it over the fire. When it begins to boil, take it from the fire, and put it over *a steady coal fire*, so that it just simmers. After *three hours*, check if it is tender enough, then put it over a *hotter fire*.[6] (Emphasis added)

Madame Mangor, in 1837, quite frankly admits that it is almost impossible to achieve a good roast beef the first few times.

The first times one roasts beefsteak, one can not expect to be successful, because it takes experience to watch the heat so that the meat can quickly achieve a crust without burning and can remain juicy inside, but not bloody.[7]

This is a departure from the 1616 *Cookbook*, which simply stated, "when the meat is cooked," assuming that the cook would understand.

Take good beef, pound it until it is beautifully soft and tender. Peel some white onions, as many as you think, chop them finely and put them through a sieve with wine or vinegar. When the meat is cooked, serve it, but don't forget the salt.[8]

The recipe reminds the readers to include white onions and salt, but otherwise leaves them pretty much on their own. By the mid-eighteenth century, the responsibility for knowing when "it

has cooked enough" still rests with the cook; however, many more ingredients are now listed in the recipes such as spices, bay leaves, thyme, salt, orange, lemon, although the concept of "spices" is still somewhat vague. But a cooking order or procedure has appeared.

ENGLISH BEEF

Take a piece of beef from the inner thigh, sprinkle with vinegar, wine, spices, bay leaves, thyme, salt, orange, lemon, and let it *stand overnight; roast it in the morning* on a spit, constantly drip it with the sauce in which it has stood; when it has cooked enough, put it in a pot, remove the juices with which it has been basted, cover well and put it on a mild fire, sprinkle with a little flour and a couple of chopped anchovies; you can also thicken with a little sweet cream.[9] (Emphasis added)

As one follows the progression of beef recipes alone, one can see a growing specificity of time, procedure, and ingredients. In 1818, Christiane Rosen's beef recipe says, "boil for 16 to 20 minutes. Remove it to another casserole."[10] And Madame Mangor has admitted how difficult the process can be. By the time Laura Adeler writes, at the end of the nineteenth century, her directions are exact and precise. She includes not only the specific spices ("ginger, pepper, cloves, allspice") but also the sort of smoked pork to be used ("half lean and half fatty"), along with its size ("a little finger"). How to cook the meat, what size pot to use ("not too large"), how much water to add (enough "to cover the meat"), and how long to cook it ("4 hours") are all included in her recipe (see recipe, chapter 7).[11] Little is left to chance, or to the cook's prior knowledge.

The growing specificity of recipes reflected here points to several possible causes. Most obviously, it would seem to reflect a belief on the part of cookbook authors that their readers were not as familiar with the cooking processes and with finished dishes as previous readers had been. They take much more care to lead the reader through the paths of cooking. This, in turn, may reflect the changing assumptions about women and housewives—that they are now much more responsible for the hands-on manage-

ment of their homes and kitchens—which, in turn, reflects the development of domesticity that accompanied the growth of the middle classes.[12] An additional effect of the specificity would have been to standardize dishes and make them infinitely repeatable. Anyone could cook now; it no longer took any special skill or training. Thus, all women could now be held responsible for providing their families with a certain quality of food.

In addition to changes in preparation details in the cookbooks, the dishes themselves change as well. Recipes for common, everyday foods such as bread begin to appear. There are several possible explanations for this. Perhaps the professional chefs to whom the early cookbooks were addressed did not themselves bother with anything so mundane as baking bread. Perhaps the servants baked the bread. But the middle-class women to whom the later cookbooks are addressed are now baking their own bread. Whether servants or professional bakers had previously baked the bread, earlier housewives and cooks had not needed this specific knowledge; but now, around the late eighteenth and early nineteenth centuries, housewives are presumed to exercise more oversight in their kitchens. Maybe there is a fear on the part of cookbook authors that the mother-daughter information line has been broken. The author of *Education for Young Women* explained that the book was being written for a friend whose mother had died when she was young, so, she had had no one to train her in housekeeping skills.[13] Although this would appear to be a very specific case, it is emblematic of a perceived change, since one would hardly publish a book for the individual case of a single orphan.[14]

The growing immiseration due to the 1813 bankruptcy caused by the Napoleonic Wars may also have forced more people to do their own baking. Buying readymade food may have simply been beyond the reach of greater numbers of people, including the middle classes to whom cookbooks were addressed. A philosophy of making do with fewer or lower quality goods would also have supported and been supported by the rise in women's domesticity, keeping more of these household chores within the home.

Technological changes could affect cooking patterns as well. Toward the end of the nineteenth century, enclosed stoves

became available for "modern" kitchens; this opened up both roasting and baking possibilities which, although they may have existed before, now became much simpler and thus more common. White bread and cakes could now be cooked in the ovens of the new stoves. For any or all of these reasons, we see a change in the cookbooks from the early nineteenth century on, and the possible explanations support a thesis that other sources also point toward—beginning in the early nineteenth century, Denmark witnesses a rise in domesticity that places women firmly in the kitchens, with new responsibilities for hands-on food preparation and for maintaining order within the home and in the nation.

The example of bread is instructive for tracing some of these changes. Bread makes an appearance in Danish cookbooks first in the nineteenth century and early discussions of bread talk about its benefits for health. In *Oeconomisk Sundheds-Kogebog* (*Economic Health Cookbook*, 1800) Svendsen writes:

I begin with bread, the most common, most indispensable, healthiest dry vegetable food. . . . I think it inappropriate to teach anyone bread baking here, since almost every servant girl is more or less experienced in this. . . . I will only speak of how healthy it is.[15]

Svendsen dismisses the actual baking of bread as beneath his notice, as something for servants, and concentrates on such matters as the health value of bread, the best kind of flour to use, and how hot the oven should be. Instead of giving specific recipes, he discusses the need to bake bread.

Because flour, even though it contains the essential element of growth, would be difficult to digest as it is, and additives such as butter and egg make it even worse, one seeks to open up the flour so that it is more acceptable to our strength and better suited to join with our juices.[16]

Svendsen wants to give scientific health reasons for consuming bread. Despite the fact that it is a staple of the Danish diet, he feels compelled to explain its importance. In this, of course, he is mirroring scientific attitudes reaching back to the European

Enlightenment, one of the main tenets of which was that everything was susceptible to rational explanation. Thus, one should
eat bread because it is healthy and bake flour in order to make
it easier to digest, not because one is hungry or grain is
available.

I will return once more to bread's ingredients. The coarser the flour is
ground, the heavier the bread will be. That's why the so-called "shop"
bread, without bran, is sweetened, but for many people this does not
taste as good as the finely ground, home-baked bread. Flour from grain
that is too fresh or too old is not as good as that which has sufficient dry-
ness, neither too fresh nor too old. The flour should be neither spoilt,
moldy, damp nor filled with worms; wheat flour from wheat which has
been burnt is also useless, as is rye which has weeds mixed in with the
grains. All of this can have harmful effects on the body.[17]

Here Svendsen combines a plug for homebaked bread with admonitions on staying away from bad flour. Interestingly, he gives no
indication as to whether the flour is bad because of poor supplies
or poor home storage. But the overall emphasis is on protecting
the body from "harmful effects." This is not surprising consider-
ing that he is writing a *health* cookbook "to make all possible
kinds of good-tasting dishes which will promote and maintain
health."[18]

Twenty years later, in her *Oeconomisk Huusholdnings-Bog* (*Economic Housekeeping Book*), Christiane Rosen devotes several pages
to a very detailed description of baking, including several different types of bread-rye, sourbread with cumin, and wheat bread.
She begins with a discussion on how to weigh flour.

One peck of rye or flour [sic] weighs 12 Lsp. [lispund=16 lbs.], but in the
country one can not determine the weight so accurately, since the millers
occasionally overcharge on the excise taxes, but in the cities, where weight
charges are paid, one can always demand to know the weight.[19]

She speaks of the difference between baking in the summer and
in the winter—one starts three hours later in the summer. She
includes the exact times that it takes for the bread to rise and

bake, discusses how to keep it fresh, and speaks of the difference between country areas, where bread is baked at home, and cities, where one takes the dough to the bakers for them to bake it, since private bake ovens are rare in city homes (see rye bread recipe, Third Intermezzo, page 76).[20]

There has obviously been a considerable change since earlier times when there was no mention of bread in cookbooks, but the change is not in the actual consumption of bread; that probably remained constant. Rather, the cookbooks evolve from ignoring it completely, as something too well known, through explaining why it should remain a part of the diet, finally, to how it should be prepared. Rosen assumes very little prior knowledge of how to bake bread or how to deal with millers and bakers. One suspects that she has felt cheated at times and wants to pass on this information to her readers.

Yet her recipe for wheat or white bread[21] is extremely rudimentary and would be difficult to follow if one were not familiar with baking bread. There is a presumption of knowledge about white bread that is missing from her recipes for rye bread. For instance, her white bread recipe presumes an understanding of how to work with yeast, of what the dough will be like, when it will have risen enough. Her recipe for rye bread goes into all this in much greater detail. This could be because white bread was more commonly baked at home and rye bread was more often bought or sent out to be baked; yet, we know that white bread was more expensive and hence less common and used mainly for special occasions. With her extensive discussion of rye bread, Rosen would seem to be encouraging her readers to bake it at home, which would be more economical than sending it out or buying it readymade. White bread was presumably already baked in most homes. In comparison, her recipe for rye bread is six times as long as that for white bread and much more detailed (see the Third Intermezzo, pages 76–80).

In 1901, Frøken Jensen asked the simple question, "Is there really an advantage to doing your own baking?" and answered it with a resounding "Yes," provided, of course, one has "a really good oven."[22] The very asking of the question, however, implies that this is an issue worth discussing. Either, there is less baking

going on in the home and Jensen feels that there should be more, or Jensen is trying to encourage the use of the new enclosed stoves for baking bread at home.

Unlike Rosen, Jensen has no recipe for rye bread. From at least the mid-nineteenth century, and perhaps for longer in urban areas, most Danes have bought rye bread at bakeries or supermarkets, a habit that continues today.[23] But her recipe for French bread (white or wheat bread) is not dissimilar to Rosen's in its presumption of prior expertise (see bread recipes on pages 78–80).

Jensen uses specific name brands, such as Pillsbury flour in her recipes. Whether or not she was paid for the advertising, it indicates product standardization and the existence of a mass market for individual products, if not yet for finished goods. This standardization can also be seen in the different amounts of milk one is advised to use; when using Pillsbury flour, there is an exact amount of milk to be used, while "regular" flour requires "a little less." Something may have been added to Pillsbury flour, or other flour may have been more variable and hence have required some adjustment on the part of the cook. Additionally, one no longer needed to get flour ground by the miller, with the attendant concern for waste and swindle that Rosen warned about. This certainly reflects a change in the world outside the kitchen, which is brought back into the kitchen.

While some foods, such as bread, begin to appear in cookbooks, others disappear. Two of the most obvious are the number of different spices and the extreme variety of wild fish and game. Modifications in seasoning probably reflect a change in cuisine from an older, sweeter kitchen to the newer, more savory French "haute cuisine," as well as the Danish loss of overseas trade and colonies; the disappearance of game definitely reflects a transition from the noble to a more middle-class table.

The medieval European kitchen commonly used spices such as cinnamon, cloves, allspice, and ginger, which we today think of as dessert spices, hence as sweeter. The new "French kitchen" relied more on herbs such as parsley, sage, rosemary, and thyme, and, hence, had a more savory taste. These cooking styles are obviously not exclusive but they do reflect tendencies.[24] The new

French kitchen may have originated in Italy but it was certainly prevalent in France by the mid-seventeenth century. It took a while longer to reach the Danish kitchens, and the decline in the use of spices in Danish cookbooks charts this change.

The loss of the Danish empire at this time may have helped to accentuate the changes already taking place in the kitchen. By the late eighteenth century, Denmark had acquired a small, but farflung empire encompassing three islands in the Caribbean (the U.S. Virgin Islands today), some holdings on the west coast of Africa, and Tranquebar on the Indian subcontinent. It held these tropical overseas territories in addition to Norway, Greenland, Iceland, and the Faroe Islands. The Danish king was also the duke of Schleswig and Holstein. Denmark had a flourishing merchant marine, the world's third largest, as well as a well developed smuggling culture—all of which meant that there was easy access to tropical spices. Denmark's disastrous experience in the Napoleonic Wars led to the loss not only of Norway but also of much of its shipping capabilities. The spices listed in cookbooks fall away in tandem with these losses.[25]

The following are examples of spices and herbs that appeared in cookbook recipes between 1616 and 1901:

1616, COOKBOOK[26]

cumin, anise, coriander, dill, fennel, lavender, sage, rosemary, mint, bay leaves, cloves, pepper, saffron, thyme, marjoram, nutmeg, cardamom, ginger, cinnamon, hyssop, wormwood, lemon balm, angelica-root

1785, NEW COOKBOOK FOR THE PROPER HOUSEWIFE[27]

cloves, basil, parsley, ginger, bay leaves, salt, pepper, nutmeg, thyme, cardamom, cinnamon, dill, horseradish, coriander

1837, COOKBOOK FOR SMALL HOUSEHOLDS[28]

vanilla, coriander, salt, nutmeg, curry, pepper, cinnamon, cloves, bay leaves, ginger, allspice

cayenne powder, curry, nutmeg, cloves, mustard, candied peel, vanilla

The issue here is not just that the use of tropical spices falls off, because curry, nutmeg, and cloves are still tropical, but rather that the use of seasonings in general slackens. Even the use of local herbs, such as parsley, thyme, and dill, dies out. Whereas the anonymous author of the 1616 *Cookbook* believed it was necessary to use seasonings to cover the loss of flavor due to "the Fall" (and subsequent expulsion from Eden),[30] Laura Adeler writes in 1893:

In my opinion, a mistake often made is the excessive use of spices which deprive a dish of its characteristic fundamental taste and at the same time make its preparation more expensive.[31]

There has, in other words, been a change in understandings of the use of spices, as much for religious, economic, and practical reasons as for reasons of availability.

Frøken Jensen's cookbook also begins to use meat extract and color in order to flavor, as well as color, her dishes. By 1901, commercially produced "cooking aides" have become available, so that the chef no longer has to boil down the meat extract from pan juices herself, but can now simply add some brown color to the gravy and make the sauce more attractive. Indeed, gravy can now be prepared without using pan juices at all. Once again, Jensen suggests brand names:

The gravy can be prepared with the help of Leibig's meat extract, tomatoes, spices, color and other additions. . . . It is most economical to prepare the gravy from butter, flour and gelatin or stock.[32]

An analysis of the suggested menus from cookbooks at the beginning of this chapter also reflects some of these changes. Although one can still find recipes for wild fish and game throughout the centuries, these items appear with less and less frequency in suggested menus from the mid-nineteenth century on. Snipe, partridge, pigeon, and hare all disappear from suggested daily

FOODS USED IN DAILY MENUS, AS LISTED IN COOKBOOKS

	MEAT	GAME	FISH	VEGETABLES	FRUIT	CARBOHYDRATES
1785 **CARL MÜLLER**	chicken	snipe	fish	spinach	apples	"patience bread"
	veal	wild pork	crayfish	cauliflower	jelly	Viennese tart
	turkey	ortolane	oysters	artichokes		
		hare	abalone			
		snails				
1796 **ANON.**	turkey	venison	crayfish	mushrooms	orange	noodles
	veal	hare	oysters	cabbage	compote	
	chicken	partridge	carp	spinach	fruit	
	ham	capon	pike	onions		
	beef		salmon	asparagus		
	lamb		herring	peas		
	poultry		bream	cauliflower		
			fish	greens		

FOODS USED IN DAILY MENUS, AS LISTED IN COOKBOOKS (CONTINUED)

	MEAT	GAME	FISH	VEGETABLES	FRUIT	CARBOHYDRATES
1857	chicken	venison	fish	potatoes	orange	dumplings
CONRADINE	pork			mushrooms	fruit	rice
HASBERG	beef			yellow peas	compote	buckwheat
	turkey			cabbage		barley
	veal			green beans		
	meat			kohlrabi		
	roast			carrots		
1864	turkey		salmon	green peas	gooseberry	dumplings
MARIA	veal			roots		
RASMUSSEN	chicken					
	meat					

FOODS USED IN DAILY MENUS, AS LISTED IN COOKBOOKS (CONTINUED)

	MEAT	GAME	FISH	VEGETABLES	FRUIT	CARBOHYDRATES
1885 NIELSINE NIELSEN	pork		fish	potatoes		rice
	veal			cabbage		barley
	meat			beets		dumplings
				yellow peas		
1910 MADAME MANGOR, 40TH EDITION	beef	venison	mussels	green beans	apples	white bread
	ham		oysters	brussel sprouts	fruit	rice
	chicken		herring	beans		rolls
	veal		fish	chestnuts		macaroni
	meat			potatoes		
				yellow peas		
				roots		
				vegetables		

dinners. Vegetables remain fairly consistent, heavily leaning towards cabbage, peas, and beans, all of which grow easily in the northerly Danish climate. Grains increase dramatically; the actual absence of bread from menus, though, probably has more to do with its presumed presence, than with its actual absence from the diet.

The suggested menus reflect several changes that are taking place in both eating habits and household maintenance. The first two menus, from 1785 and 1796, respectively, reflect *service á la française*. That is, each course, or remove, had several dishes placed on the table at the same time (see diagram of suggested serving placements on page 30). In a kind of buffet fashion, diners were thus able to pick and choose what they wished to eat. This service had its origins in presumed health requirements, allowing guests to choose what they needed for their own temperamental or humoral balance. As a recent author expressed it:

Taste was thought to be a matter of sympathy between the nature of the individual and the nature of certain foods; similarly, distaste was believed to be a consequence of physiological antipathy. . . . Since it was impossible to change a person's temperament, it was wrong to ignore the dictates of taste.[33]

Thus a good host needed to provide a wide variety to accommodate all sympathies and temperaments. Over time, this rationale was forgotten and meals with elaborate dishes became justifications in and of themselves.

Sometime in the mid-nineteenth century, middle-class patterns began to change to *service á la russe*. This involved a smaller number of dishes offered at each course, with one main protein dish and a couple of side dishes, each dish handed around separately by servants. Meals began to follow the pattern with which we are familiar today, starting with an appetizer, followed by one main protein dish, and ending with a sweet. This eliminated options to suit individual eaters' tastes, and although additional serving staff were now required, these meals would have cut down on the number of kitchen staff, since rather than having to

prepare dozens of separate dishes, hosts could make do with a mere handful, or fewer, depending on the level of the household. It must also have cut down immensely on waste, although it would have meant fewer leftovers for kitchen staff to eat and possibly sell. Felipe Fernández-Armesto also points out that "this allowed for the doubling of the mealtime spectacle: the festive board, vacated by food, could now house more magnificent tableware and flowers."[34]

The number of dishes served obviously varied with the households, and several of these cookbooks gave suggested menus for different economic levels. Hasberg even differentiates between what the family should be served and what would be appropriate for servants, who obviously ate separately. These are *suggested* menus and do not necessarily reflect what people were actually eating, and certainly not what was being eaten in peasant or lower-class households, where one simple dish of *søbemad* (spoon food) remained common.

Several cookbooks also give menus for special occasions or for entertaining guests. Although the menus here have been limited to those used in everyday service, it is nonetheless apparent that there is a change in the presumed audience of the cookbooks themselves, as the menus shift from the large-scale service of the earlier cookbooks to the smaller urban and rural households.

The tone of the cookbooks changes as their audience and purpose change; it becomes more didactic. As the titles change and as cookbooks begin to address themselves more specifically to women, the cookbooks become prescriptive. There is a greater emphasis on what the cook, or the reader, is supposed to do, besides just follow the recipes. The earliest Danish cookbooks mean only to help the cook prepare dishes she or he already knows and contain no such admonitions, but as the audience for cookbooks changes and the level of presumed expertise falls, the admonitions multiply. Thus Danish cookbooks become prescriptive literature sometime at the turn to the nineteenth century. There is a growing emphasis on cleanliness and orderliness; everything is to have a place and to be in its place, and everything, always and continually, is to be kept clean, cleaned up, and put away.

Slowly, cookbooks also begin to include prescriptive advice on how to run a kitchen and a household. By the early nineteenth century, Danish cookbooks have taken on the prescriptive quality evident in a modern American example from 1963, *McCall's Cook Book*:

Social customs radiate from the service of food in the home. So does the most fundamental kind of social status. Thus, the woman who can cook well and serve food graciously is a successful homemaker.[35]

This is neither strange nor, when one thinks about it, unexpected. Indeed, this change coincides with changes in middle-class women's roles, which pushed them back into the "private space" of the home, away from the "public space" of business. In other words, the literature of cookbooks mirrors the growth in the prescriptive domesticity of women. Starting in the late eighteenth century, the number of cookbook authors who feel compelled to lecture, if not actually talk down, to their audience strongly suggests that publishers did not believe that women knew how to carry out their housewifely duties without help, or, perhaps, that they thought housewifely duties were changing.

As cookbooks become prescriptive literature, they take their place together with the other "gift books" and manuals for women, such as those which circulated in the lending libraries mentioned earlier. A reading of this literature would lead one to believe that the ideal Victorian woman had indeed arrived in Denmark.[36] There is, of course, the problem with all such literature, that it is more reflective of the authors' sense of what is and ought to be going on than of reality itself. However, this can be read as an indicator of a society in transition. People only begin to write about how to behave when behavior patterns are changing; there is no need to explain what everyone already knows and accepts. So, prescriptive admonitions, in cookbooks and elsewhere, do not necessarily mean that the kitchens themselves were undergoing transformation or that the food was changing, but rather that something else was going on in these kitchens; in this case, what is going on is that there are new demands on the keepers of the kitchens.

As with all prescriptive literature, it is probably impossible to know which came first—did changes in society encourage authors to address new audiences or did this new literature encourage a change in familial roles? Possibly a little of each, although probably more of the former than the latter. That is, reading these new cookbooks would not have inspired women to change anything other than perhaps their style of cooking; rather, reading these cookbooks might have supported vaguely sensed changes that were already taking place around the women. However, there is no question that the cookbook authors firmly believed that women needed training and guidance in their roles as housewives and housekeepers.

second intermezzo

COOKBOOK INTRODUCTIONS

Anon., Cookbook, 1616

TO THE READER

....

Dear Reader. Do not be surprised that I, in our Danish language, now have distributed that material which previously among us never was published or by means of a press made available for everyone. This is not to reduce or diminish anyone's (be they [male] cook or [female] cook) honest craft in any way, but to be of particular benefit and advantage to each housekeeper in their housekeeping. Because it often happens that many complain that although they can afford and provide what is necessary for the table, they do not know how to create a good dish from it. Had it not been for the Fall, then the earth itself would have produced such well-tasting roots, herbs, fruit and plants that people would not have to cook them and the intentional seasoning with herbs would not be necessary. But due

to the Fall, the earth is cursed and damned, which damnation means that herbs and roots do not approach that level, strength and effect which they otherwise would have had if Mankind had not sinned. The Flood is a strong witness to this. On account of this, God's revealed and general punishment, herbs, roots, and growing trees are so violated and ruined that they do not have nearly the taste, strength and effect as before the Flood. For which, the Almighty God has with special favor given Man flesh of fish, fowl and animal to use and enjoy for their better survival. Read Luther, *Genesis*, chapter one, where he tells that a poor herb, which we now trample underfoot in common fields, was better and more delicious than our most common apothecary spices. Since the Fall caused God to damn the earth, and the produce of the earth has been weakened by this damnation, necessity has created the art, especially with fire, to prepare both food, roots, herbs, fruit, etc. that people will find acceptable and good-tasting and which will serve both the body's sustenance and health. This is especially so when fear of God is used with God's prayers and reading. According to St. Paul's wisdom, food is sanctified by means of the Word and the prayer. So I have this good hope of all right-minded individuals that no one will be blamed or complain of this little book which goes forth to every man's benefit and good. It is collected from well-standing and well-experienced housekeepers who have themselves tried and used what is found here. So it is held in high esteem. I would ask that if others who read and use the book and know more or better what is necessary for the kitchen and the cellar than is here briefly written, that they would, in Christian love for every man's use, be so kind as to inform me. So if this should be printed again, it would be an expanded and improved edition. In the meantime, every fine and God-fearing woman and capable journeyman will use this book in the kitchen with such good understanding as was informed by a good heart. May the favorable reader be in the protection of the Almighty.

COPENHAGEN, APRIL 21, 1616.[1]

Christiane Rosen, *The Thinking Housekeeper*, 1824

HOW A KITCHEN SHOULD BE ORDERED

....

For every woman, from all classes, it is of the utmost importance, from youth, to understand how a kitchen should be ordered. Keeping the pots

clean is the most important aspect of food preparation, either plain or fancy; this brings not only health, but other advantages.

A housewife should do her shopping the day before, even several days in advance, if it is the time of year during which food can be kept. Much will be won this way, as you will not have to accept whatever is available at the last minute. When the servant girl goes shopping, combine as many small errands as possible, so as not to waste time.

Before the food is put on, the fireplace must be swept, the ashes removed and the fire must burn well. When food begins to simmer, just before it boils, damp down the fire, cover the food . . . so that neither rain nor soot fall into it.

When the pots are taken from the fire, they must not be placed on a bare table, but on a trivet which is used for this. . . . When serving, take care that neither bowl nor dish is too full, and dry it with a clean cloth.

Frying pans must be dried with paper the instant they are used and then washed, but not scoured.

The sink must be washed inside every day with a cloth.

Dishcloths must be kept as clean as towels, and used to take pots from the fire, and not your apron.

It goes without saying that when you eat a late supper, you ought nonetheless to wash up the same evening.

The fireplaces must be swept clean every evening, and the fire banked carefully. See to the tinderbox with its equipment, and do not put it on the shelf over the chimney, but put it in the fireplace.

Once a week, wash the dining room, shelves, cupboards and kitchen goods inside and out, together with the floor; also, scour the fire tongs, drawers, ax, coffee and tea kettle.

It is a great advantage in all households to do your own baking; that way you can be sure of having good bread. Before you make the dough, be sure that your hands are clean and that there is no dust on you and that you do not have a bare head.

It is the housekeeper's job, every night, before she goes to bed, herself to check to make sure that everything is in order and in its prescribed place, also that the fire is either out or well banked. The tinderbox is on the chimney [sic; this would seem to contradict an earlier sentence]; the tea kettle is empty and rinsed out.[2]

Madame Mangor, *Cookbook for Small Households*, 1865

THREE DOMESTIC SPICES³

......

which are recommended to young housewives because they cost little, never lose their strength and have that quality that the plainer the food is the more they will improve its taste.

The first spice consists of *a fixed and firm eating time*, because husbands and others who eat together are commonly never more impatient than during the period between the fixed eating time and the time when the food is actually on the table.

The second spice is *a snow white tablecloth, a clean table setting*. Even the most simple food has an added good taste when the eye rests pleasingly on white linen, shining porcelain, and clear glass—thoughts of a capable housewife are instinctively connected to this.

The third spice is *the housewife's mild and friendly face*, which like the sun shines over everything and chases away the small bits of dissatisfaction or downheartedness, which might otherwise hover in the house's sky and eventually collect themselves into a rain cloud. [Emphasis in original]
(FROM A FATHER TO A DAUGHTER IN HER FIRST COOKBOOK)⁴

Kristine Marie Jensen, *Frk. Jensens Cookbook*, 1901

HOUSEKEEPING

......

How often one hears our housewives complain about how much work they have due to housekeeping and especially the daily chores. The reason for this must be the lack of the skills necessary for housework or, in many cases, lack of interest. Every task, no matter how ordinary, can always be made interesting or carried out perfectly; by this I do not mean that the housewife should only live for housekeeping, there are too many other, important demands on her. Her first duty must be to become acquainted with her husband's income in order to be able to establish a home in which the expenses match income, and first of all *to keep very accurate accounts*. Many small expenses, which might otherwise be overlooked, will thereby

become apparent and the account book will be a good guide for the next year's purchases, both in terms of quantity and price.

The housewife must then seek to organize her house and the remaining work in a manner so easy and practical that there is time to carry out all of the other work and housewifely duties which rest on her; not even the most inconsequential item should be without her knowledgeable oversight. A home is always characterized by the strength of its leader and as a consequence thereof the daily well-being of the several members of the household is a large part of her housewife's job.

To arrange for the food which is to be served at the daily meals is a difficult task for many and it often feels like a great relief when the dinner menu has been decided upon and the domestic tasks apparently finished for the day. To determine food one day at a time is both difficult and costly; a plan must absolutely be determined for several days at a time. This saves time both for the housewife and the servants. Maybe it can seem to be an easy matter to prepare the food when you have all the necessary requirements at hand, but a certain moderation is necessary here as well. The art, I find, is to achieve a good result with only small means available. What I have tried to do in this book, is to achieve a plentiful variety in daily living with a cheap and easy procedure—in other words, to seek to simplify our common dishes, which are largely based on French and English recipes, so that they may be available and practicable for more simple homes, where economy usually plays an important role. Everyone needs to understand that, everything can be used; nothing must go to waste; otherwise there is no true economy.

What actually gave rise to the creation of this book is thought of the many unfortunates in our society, particularly many of our servant girls; and here I am thinking also of both kitchen servants and maids of all work. Often much is required of them in terms of cooking knowledge, but the fewest are in possession of the means to acquire even the slightest training. For them, all that remains is long years of often difficult experience in order to acquire that fund of information which is necessary in order to be able, even somewhat, to fulfill the demands made of them.

Several considerations had been taken in connection with the publication of this book. For example, as much as possible recipes are presented concisely, but understandably, so that anyone without much prior knowledge might be tempted to try the preparation of different dishes, also to show that an attractive dish can easily be arranged without much work or

much ingenuity, despite the fact that expectations in this area have risen year for year.

I hope I will now be able to achieve, what my thought has been, namely to give a larger audience the benefit of my many years of experience in home economics, to be a true support and adviser, and to wake interest for domestic tasks so that they are not felt like a heavy burden, but rather as an important duty which rests with each housewife, and on whose successful achievement rests much of the comfort of a home.[5] [Emphasis in original]

third course

THE DEVELOPMENT OF A
BOURGEOIS CONSCIOUSNESS

*I*NTRODUCTIONS TO COOKBOOKS SERVE A PECULIAR
purpose. Who reads them? Most cookbook users go straight to
the recipe or section they are looking for; no one reads a cookbook from beginning to end. So why have introductions? Yet,
most of the cookbooks published in Denmark from the seventeenth to the mid-nineteenth century contain introductions.
These are useful for the historian, who can thus get a general
idea of both contemporary authors and audiences—who they
are, why the author thinks *yet another* Danish cookbook is important, and what the author expects of the reader—as well as how
these topics change over time; the preceding introductions are
cases in point. The first, from the 1616 *Cookbook*, is obviously
addressing a professional audience. The author addresses both
male and female cooks, referring to their "honest craft," and
hopes that "every fine and God-fearing woman and capable jour-

neyman will use this book in the kitchen." The author is hoping simply to help cooks provide "a good dish," and asks others to contribute to future editions. The frontispiece, depicting a well-dressed woman chef in a well-stocked kitchen, working over a sizeable stove, underlines the assumption that this book is addressed to upper and well-provisioned classes.

There is not only an assumption of literacy, as there must be for any book with text, but also an admonition to read Luther's version of the Bible; one hundred years after the Protestant Reformation, it is apparent that functional religious literacy has spread as well.

Had it not been for the Fall, then the earth itself would have produced such well-tasting roots, herbs, fruit and plants that people would not have to cook them and the intentional seasoning with herbs would not be necessary. . . . herbs, roots, growing trees are so violated and ruined that they do not have nearly the taste, strength and effect as before the Flood.[1]

Sinners all, religion has worked its way even into our kitchens, and so we now need cookbooks to help us overcome the corruption of the original, natural, organic produce of the earth.

A century and a half later, Carl Müller says in his *New Cookbook for the Respectable Housewife*:

The correct management of the kitchen is unquestionably one of housekeeping's most important tasks. Every sensible housewife therefore makes it a top priority, not just to see to its order and economy, but also to health, good taste and propriety. To supervise everything is to the honor of a good housewife, and using everything wisely is to her benefit and that of her family, while untimely economy not only opens her up to much unpleasantness, but also undermines her well-being and that of her family.[2]

While the 1616 *Cookbook* talks about the "honest trade" of its cooks (male and female), implying an artisanal profession, Müller addresses "good housewi[ves]"—women, whose main concern is or ought to be the well-being of their families. Additionally,

while the 1616 book aims to help with the preparation of a "good dish," Müller emphasizes "the correct management of the kitchen." There has been a definite shift from food in the kitchen to the management of the kitchen and the household.

In 1795, a few years after Müller's book, the publisher wrote in the foreword to the anonymous *Education for Young Women* that it was "not just for aristocratic kitchens, but especially for those of the middle class." The author claims, "it is an important duty for a young woman to be a good housekeeper; she will therefore be able to secure for herself and the man with whom she is joined together peaceful and pleasant days." It is also important for a housewife to be good to her servants, "to be as a mother to them." She should remember that servants must "perform hard work and often are father- and motherless, with no other support."[3]

The author was writing this book to help a young friend whose mother had died when she was young and who, therefore, had no one to train her in the arts of housekeeping. A parallel is drawn between the young friend's situation and that of servants, also helpless in the world. Thus the good housekeeper will not only take care of her husband, and, presumably, the rest of the family, but also include her servants within this network; it is the woman's role to create this family.

There is a paradox here—on the one hand, there is the expectation that women should learn housekeeping at home, from their mothers, and, on the other, the presence of the book itself suggests that this is not the case. Since the audience for such a book could hardly be limited to orphaned girls, the author apparently assumes that many girls are not learning the necessary skills at home. Or, perhaps, daughters are no longer willing to accept their mothers' knowledge and experience as relevant to their own needs, possibly because the expectations of womanly skills are changing. What is interesting about this change is not so much that it happens, but rather *how* it happens. Women have to be *taught* to be good housekeepers, for their husbands as well as for themselves, and cookbooks now offer to do this. Indeed, Carl Müller goes so far as to advertise in his cookbook that he will be in Copenhagen and available to give lessons, and readers

are advised to watch for his ads in *Adress-Contoirets Efterreninger* (a Copenhagen newspaper).[4]

"Three Domestic Spices" of Madame Mangor's *Cookbook for Small Households* follows the pattern set by *Education for Young Women*, which is representative of the change from the 1616 *Cookbook*. It, too, addresses small rather than large households, young housewives rather than professional chefs or experienced housekeepers, and only women rather than men and women. Literacy is, of course, still presumed, although not mentioned, and religion is absent altogether. Instead, Mangor's young women are to create a harmonious household, with fixed eating times, clean tables, and domestic sunshine. These young women have a responsibility for domestic, rather than religious, happiness, at least in the mind of the author.[5]

Mangor is somewhat ambivalent in her rationale for publishing a cookbook, although apparently determined to do so.

After I had collected [recipes] for several years, it occurred to me that they might be useful for others, so I organized it all as a cookbook. But everyone laughed at me and asked if I didn't believe that people could prepare their own food.[6]

Here again one can see the tension between the assumption that everyone knew how to cook and the apparent reality that many did not. The first publisher she approached, Reitzel, turned her down; so, she got paper and drew credit from her son-in-law's brother, and printed and sold 500 copies of her cookbook herself. Her cookbook was an immediate success and came out in thirty-nine editions through 1901. A *Continuation of Cookbooks for Small Households* was published in 1842 and it reached twenty-nine editions by 1901. In 1910, a combined volume containing both *Cookbook* and *Continuation* was published.

Despite Mangor's initial popularity, she had received an undeserved reputation for being overly fancy and upper class by the time Kristine Marie Jensen published a cookbook (*Frk. Jensen's Cookbook*, 1901). Jensen addressed herself to the growing numbers of lower-middle-class workers and small farmers, and her book was an immediate success.[7] The chimney pots on her fron-

tispiece address at least one group of her intended readers; in her tone, however, she seems less clear of her audience. She addresses housewives and their servants, both assumed to be literate enough to read a cookbook, although she does sometimes feel a need to talk down to her readers. The reason for her book, she says, is,

[the] thought of the many unfortunates in our society, particularly many of our servant girls; and here I am thinking also of both kitchen servants and maids of all work. Often much is required of them in terms of cooking knowledge, but the fewest are in possession of the means to acquire even the slightest training.[8]

Both Mangor and Jensen believe that a housewife's prime duty is to create a pleasant, attractive, and well-functioning home; she is to be "the angel in the house," to quote Coventry Patmore.[9] But, whereas Mangor's admonitions to this end are almost exclusively in terms of meals, food, and eating (even the word "spices" refers to food), Jensen has a broader vision.

In her text, Jensen highlights the following responsibilities for the housewife:

To keep very accurate accounts.

To achieve a plentiful variety in daily living with a cheap and easy procedure.

Everything can be used; nothing must go to waste; otherwise there is no true economy.[10] [Emphasis in original]

None of this advice derives exclusively from food, although all are certainly addressed to the housewife rather than to her servant. There is an emphasis here on thrift, economy, and accuracy, extending the housewife's province beyond the kitchen and its prime activity, the preparation of food. Quite obviously, Jensen is also presuming a level of arithmetic as well as verbal literacy.

This change reflects the development of a bourgeois consciousness and of the concept of domesticity, which I deal with in the fourth course, although the two concepts are obviously inter-

twined and one can certainly argue that domesticity is a function of the new middle class. The term "bourgeois" is used because it is a direct translation of the Danish *borgerlig*, although "middle class" would be an equally good term.

The term "bourgeois consciousness" is used to refer to several characteristics or traits that occurred at the same time as the transition to a modern capitalist economy. Without getting involved in the question of which came first—cultural or economic changes—suffice it to say that both start appearing in Denmark in the mid-eighteenth century. Here then, in no particular order, is a list of typical bourgeois traits:

Cleanliness
Thrift
Hard work
Self-control
Order
Time management
Moderation or temperance
Virtue
Construction of a private, gendered sphere[11]

There are several correspondences between this list and Madame Mangor's "spices." The first spice speaks of time management; the second deals with cleanliness and order, everything as it should be; and the last spice deals with moderation, virtue, and a gendered reality. Jensen, too, includes several of these bourgeois traits—thrift, order, moderation, and, finally, the construction of a gendered sphere by the housewife. In contrast, the 1616 introduction, "To the Reader," does not touch on a single trait on this list. Although the author does deal with cleanliness later in the book, it is not until chapter five, and then the reason given is that dirty food tastes bad. "Because if food is prepared and cooked in a dirty pot or pan, even were it only a spoon soup, it immediately takes on a dirty and bad taste."[12]

This is rather different from Mangor's and Jensen's connection between cleanliness and capability.

These changes in tone and audience begin to appear in cookbooks in the late eighteenth century, with Müller's *New Cookbook for the Respectable Housewife*, from 1785. Müller emphasizes management, order, thrift, virtue, and gendered space. He lays the responsibility for creating and maintaining the well-being of the family squarely on the housewife's shoulders.

From then on, in rapid succession, cookbooks preach bourgeois virtues to their readers. In a second cookbook, in 1793, *The Danish Housewife, with Attached New Cookbook for Town and Country People*, Müller, writes:

Cleanliness of the servants' rooms and beds, together with an orderly and clean table, will often remind servants to keep themselves clean and orderly.

No one can deny that one requires the strictest and most scrupulous economy in an urban household.

The housewife must manage her kitchen with appropriate thrift, cleanliness and propriety, and keep order in everything.[13]

Once again, it is the housewife who is responsible for the household, including the servants, who will follow her lead. Cleanliness, order, and thrift are the charge of the housewife.

The English authors Francis Collingwood and John Woollams follow suit in their book *New and Complete Housekeeping Book for Courageous Housewives, or Advice for the Preparation of all kinds of fine, good-tasting, but also solid Dishes*, which was written in 1792; its first Danish edition was published in 1796.

Cleanliness is the first duty for a cook or for anyone who understands the kitchen, not just for themselves, but also in connection with everything, such as inspection and treatment of the pots.[14]

In 1824, Christiane Rosen wrote a cookbook called *The Thinking Housekeeper*. This is an intriguing title; in assuming that housekeepers think, it implies a certain level of participation on the part of the reader/housekeeper. Someone who thinks does not follow prescriptions or recipes blindly, but considers and

decides what is to be done, and how. There is an implication here that the housewife is an active partner in the creation of the household.

Rosen was a professional chef who worked in several different households until she went blind. She had never been married and had never created her own household. After she stopped working, someone encouraged her to write a book with her recipes in order to support herself. In addition to *The Thinking Housekeeper*, she also wrote the four-volume, *The Economic Household Book*, whose individual volumes came out in two or three editions between 1818 and 1821. Evidently, she was popular enough for several editions of her work to sell.

In the introductory remarks to *The Thinking Housekeeper*, Rosen has a section called "How a Kitchen Should be Ordered" (see Second Intermezzo, pages 56–57). A reading of this section shows that Rosen, though writing somewhat earlier than Mangor, promotes similar principles. She speaks of cleanliness ("Once a week, wash the dining room, shelves, cupboards and kitchen goods inside and out, together with the floor"), health ("keeping the pots clean . . . brings . . . health"), care for material goods ("When the pots are taken from the fire, they must not be placed on a bare table"), time management ("When the servant girl goes shopping, combine as many small errands as possible, so as not to waste time"), and order ("it is of the utmost importance . . . to understand how a kitchen should be ordered"). All these qualities show up on the list of bourgeois traits. Thus in Rosen, we find an author who believes that the "thinking" reader of her book will be an active participant in the creation of a bourgeois household.

Shortly afterwards, in 1832, C. F. von Rumohr felt encouraged to publish a Danish edition of Joseph König's *Introduction to the Art of Cooking*. Here is König's rationale for yet another cookbook:

Even the simplest and seemingly most conventional among the large number of cookbooks we have are no more than small establishments for gluttony, which contain very little of what every good housewife or housekeeper really needs to know. . . . [von Rumohr continues in a footnote, that] it is far from [his] intention to say that this sort of book has no use.

An experienced chef, who can make independent judgments, and who is capable of separating the foolish from the sensible, will be able to learn something from most books.[15]

Von Rumohr joins Rosen in viewing (most) chefs and cooks as reasoning beings, capable of "independent judgments." However, König is much less sanguine about leaving housekeepers completely on their own, apparently feeling that they are basically incompetent and incapable of controlling their help.

Kitchen girls lack thorough training. . . . In vain have I tried to improve many hundred German kitchen girls. Cheating when shopping is unfortunately part of the order of the day, since housewives have become too lazy, too unknowing or too sentimental to supply their homes themselves.[16]

Later in the book, he advises strongly against reading novels.

Whoever decides to learn about the art of cooking must get used to order, cleanliness and punctuality. He [sic] must be forbidden from reading novels; if he wishes to train his spirit, he should learn natural science, history and mathematics. These will exercise his understanding, strengthen his memory and finally bring him knowledge which he will be able to use in cooking. Moreover, he may read my book, and nothing but my book.[17]

Note the attention to "order, cleanliness and punctuality." Novels, as is well known, weaken the spirit, and König is certainly not the only one who advised against them. However, note also the change in address. Whereas in the one paragraph König specifically speaks of house*wives* and kitchen *girls*, in the other he is consistent in his use of the masculine pronoun. One could assume that König is using the terms generically, for both men and women, but that would imply that men should not read novels either and, furthermore, elsewhere he is quite specific in his use of pronouns. In either case, all who would learn to cook should read *his* book.

At times, König openly addresses the husband rather than the housewife:

The husband should never bring his work troubles, or his discontent with his wife to the table. . . .

At this point, I must mention that even the best housewives, cooks and kitchen girls sometimes have accidents and dishes fail. . . . In such cases spouses and husbands must be able to control themselves, because by being irritable they will neither be able to improve the meal nor to win anything for the future.[18]

Underlying König's admonitions to the husband is his assumption that as the *pater familias*, the husband is ultimately responsible for the maintenance of the family. It is the wife's role to assure that the house is well kept, but the husband has the final authority and it is he who is ultimately responsible for his wife's well-being, and for pardoning her mistakes. This completes the circle of responsibility in bourgeois households.

By the mid-nineteenth century, however, these prescriptions begin to disappear from cookbooks. The 1864 *Cookbook for Smaller Households, containing 248 instructions for recipes in cooking, baking, roasting, preserving, etc.* starts with a table of contents and goes straight to the recipes.[19] There is no foreword, no introduction, no admonitions to the reader, and no explanations for yet another cookbook in Danish.

The following year, in 1865, Halvorsen wrote in the introduction to his or her *Cookbook*:

Housewives or housekeepers who understand and are used to housekeeping only need a cookbook because it is a very necessary . . . support for their memory. . . . For such housewives it is not necessary to set out rules for the handling of different implements, but this is necessary in regard to the many younger people. . . . A housewife must . . . strive to make her home comfortable and attractive for her husband. . . . A young housewife must also bear in mind that it is completely within her rights to know her husband's income and to be consulted in the use of it . . . in order to establish the housekeeping so that expenses are less than income.[20]

There is a slight shift of tone here; the housewife is still responsible for the maintenance of a proper home, but she now seems to

be more of an equal partner with a "right" to know and be consulted about her husband's income and its use. Cookbooks, Halvorsen seems to be implying, are not really necessary for the experienced except as memory aids; they are only important for the young. And, there is, for once, *nothing* about cleanliness, for experienced housekeepers understand the basic rules.

That all prescriptions did not disappear is evident in the introduction to *Frk. Jensens Cookbook* (see Second Intermezzo, pages 58–60) as well as in Petra Jacobsen's 1873 *Cookbook*:

The author of this book wants to help the young inexperienced housewife . . . to make a cozy home in order to win her husband's appreciation. . . . What a pleasure for a man, when he can hasten home after a full day's work and find domestic order and comfort. . . . The first order in a house is to have set mealtimes. . . . For businessmen, definite mealtimes are often impossible, but that ought not to keep the wife from being punctual and always greeting her husband with kindness. . . . A mild face spices up mealtimes.[21]

These late-nineteenth-century texts have shifted ever so slightly from the specifics of how to set up and maintain a good household, to general statements that this is to be done. Although the intended audience is apparently younger and less experienced, there is nonetheless a sense that new housewives will already understand that it is their responsibility to maintain the home; this fact is accepted and no longer has to be impressed upon young women. The further implication is that experienced housewives already have internalized this material. Jacobsen echoes Mangor's "Three Domestic Spices"; knowingly or not, the same virtues are being promoted. Mangor, of course, did not begin to include her "spices" until 1860, so the two are contemporaneous. Despite the common "cookbook" in their titles, there is a shift away from the kitchen to the home in general.

Carl Ginderup, in his book, *The Danish Kitchen*, from 1888, is a case in point. In his introduction, under a section entitled "The Housewife's Duties," he says,

... it is of course very important that the housewife, before she takes the important step of marriage, is prepared as much as possible for those tasks which will rest on her in order to make her home as comfortable as possible for her household and herself. It is therefore to be recommended that every mother will give her daughters a sensible preparation for their responsibilities when they get married.[22]

There is a presumption here—not only will daughters get married, it is the *mother's* responsibility to train them in household duties, not the task of the cookbook author—that does reflect a shift in tone. Compare this with Carl Müller's assertion in 1785 that many women are not familiar with housekeeping methods and therefore have to be taught. There is a shift from the presumption in the late-eighteenth-century *Education for Young Women* that daughters are not being taught by their mothers, to an expectation in the late nineteenth century that they are. Both begin with the premise that it is the mother's responsibility to teach her daughters; the difference is the degree to which the cookbook authors believe it is already happening and the degree to which they, as authors, feel the need to intervene.

It is the housewife's responsibility to see to it that the house or home space is appropriate for the creation of a good domestic unit. This space should be pleasant, stress free, and, above all, clean. Cleanliness shows up again and again in these prescriptions; it is a kind of cultural capital whose importance extends well beyond merely ensuring the good-tasting food of the 1616 *Cookbook*. Joseph König writes in 1832, "cleanliness is a major condition in a *cultured nation's kitchen*" (emphasis added).[23] And M. A. Weikard writes in 1799,

The most beautiful girls grow loathsome when all we find in them is a negligent lack of cleanliness; on the other hand, the face of another girl, who is not quite so beautiful, but who always keeps herself clean and neat more often wins our heart. . . . A bodily uncleanliness often reveals an equally unclean mind, an ignoble negligence and indifference, a sorrowful filth.[24]

In his discussion of "the civilizing process," Norbert Elias spends considerable time detailing the transition to what is today called "western civilization." This involved a privatization of social and bodily functions such as table manners, personal hygiene, and sleeping patterns; having privatized aspects of our lives thus, we identify our present-day culture as civilized, in turn labeling everything else barbaric. Elias is careful to point out, however, that these are not really opposites; yesterday's civility may be tomorrow's "barbarism." Rather, he sees it as an ongoing process, still in motion, though he acknowledges that we do tend to view everything prior to us as barbaric. Changes in habits and conventions, therefore, become infused with social values in such a western, progressivist view of history; as society's mores put more and more emphasis on bodily cleanliness, by extension, those who are considered to be unclean are also considered uncivilized, and vice versa.[25] Thus, König can identify cleanliness with "a cultured nation" and Weikard can connect an unclean body with a negligent mind.

"Dirt," says Mary Douglas, in *Purity and Danger*, her study of pollution and taboo, "is essentially disorder."

There is no such thing as absolute dirt; it exists in the eye of the beholder. ... Dirt offends against order. Eliminating it is not a negative movement, but a positive effort to organize the environment.[26]

Although Douglas mostly uses non-Western societies for her examples, she admits that "our [European] ideas of dirt also express symbolic systems."[27] Thus, the removal of dirt, with its consequent creation of order, represents an important element in the new bourgeois worldview. The fact that cookbooks locate this responsibility squarely with the housewife points toward the role of the housewife in the development of a bourgeois consciousness.

Jonas Frykman, in his study of the development of middle-class ideas among the Swedish peasantry during the nineteenth century, refers to cleanliness as cultural capital, a way for the middle classes to differentiate themselves from both the peasantry and the working classes. Cleanliness provided a way to

exercise and display discipline, one of the main ingredients of middle-class ideology, and people who stood outside society, such as gypsies, vagrants, and so-called immoral women, were always viewed as dirty. "The stamp of impurity functions here as a police force protecting the honest from the dishonest, the establishment from the outsiders."[28]

Frykman sees cleanliness as signifying new boundaries in a changing society. As the dimensions of the social and economic world changed, as peasants got title to land and moved into the middle class, or lost out in the new entitlements and remained propertyless, new rules were developed to help differentiate among these groups. In this process, the distinction between clean and dirty played an important role, and cleanliness became a measure of one's improved role or standing in society. When social boundaries are clear, physical boundaries are not as necessary; everyone understands where they lie, but as social boundaries start to slip and become porous, the physical boundaries of the body take on added significance. In such a context, this means the body must be kept clean and its excretions eliminated.[29]

As the independent farmer emerged in Sweden and Denmark during the nineteenth century, "[t]here arose a need to draw boundaries between people of different origins and from different economic backgrounds." Frykman details how multipurpose rooms disappeared; people ate from individual plates; servants and masters no longer ate together; and there was a redistribution of household roles.[30]

When country people came into contact with town life and the ways of the bourgeoisie, they began to display an interest in cleanliness. The dirt of the barn was consigned to the sphere of production and was therefore not to be brought indoors. Any animals kept in the house were there as pets, not as livestock. Dust and dirt were kept at bay through daily sweeping and weekly scrubbing. The boundaries between the individual and the people around him were marked by greater personal cleanliness.[31]

As the physical separation between the home and the place of work or production deepened, so too did a differentiation between the *clean* house and the *dirty* workplace. It was the

middle-class wife's responsibility to see that the home space—her space—was clean; this set her family household apart from lower, *dirtier* classes and established her household within the civilized bounds of Western culture.

As the peasant became an independent farmer and as the urban dweller needed to differentiate himself from the industrial worker, their wives helped to create obvious differences by providing clean spaces to display to the world, thus highlighting the distance between the owning middle classes and the propertyless peasants or workers. Cookbooks thus helped to create a middle-class space as well as a domestic and eventually also national, perhaps even "Western" space.

third intermezzo

BREAD RECIPES

Christiane Rosen, *Economic Housekeeping Book*, 1821

TO BAKE RYE BREAD

....

Flour which is meant for bread must not be sifted, because then one can not determine how much bread it will make; safest is to weigh it. One *tønde* rye or [wheat] flour weighs 12 Lpd., but in the country one can not determine the weight so accurately, since the millers occasionally overcharge the excise taxes, but in the cities, where weight charges are paid, one can always demand to know the weight. When one decides to bake a half *tønde*, or 6 Lpd. of flour, 20 pounds are first weighed and removed. The remaining flour is put into a kneading trough the day before it is to be baked. Add 2 pounds of sourdough, broken in small pieces, and a handful of salt. This is kneaded with warm water as hard as possible and until it slips from the hands. The dough is put in one end of the trough, but not so

high that it overflows, and is brushed with warm water. In the middle of the dough, make a deep hole with your hand, right to the bottom. Add as much as a half pot of warm water. Add some of the flour which was removed to the dough, but be careful that no flour comes into the hole. The dough should be covered with a sack or coarse tablecloth, on top of which is put a pillow. The evening before the morning of the baking, add firewood to the baking oven, half wet and half dry. The oven can be heated up with peat. If it's winter, put the dough in the day before, at 2 or 3 in the afternoon, but in summer, three hours later; the water should not be so warm then either. In the winter the dough should be in a warm room, but not too close to the stove. At 6 or 7 in the morning on the following day, when the bread is to be baked, cover the dough with the remaining flour, until it slips from your hands, but it should only be half as hard as the evening before. Then put it back in one end of the kneading trough and cover it as before. Now, finally, light the fire in the oven; let it burn for two hours. When the fire has fallen, then you begin to knead the bread. Meanwhile, spread the fire in the hearth, add kindling in order to keep the oven warm. After the bread has risen, it should stand for 15 to 20 minutes, but do not forget to remove some for sourdough [starter], which should be mixed and covered with salt and put away in the winter in a place where it will not freeze. The size of the loaves of bread is best at 10 to 12 pounds. Now the oven is swept, the bread is rubbed either with beer, sweet or sour milk, or egg mixed with water. The bread is pricked in 4 or 5 places with a sharp wooden stick about the width of a pipe stem. When the oven is ready, close it for 3 to 4 minutes, then put the bread in. Make sure that the first one to rise is put in first. After 15 minutes, open the oven and then a few minutes later, close it, and let it remain for 3 to 4 hours. Remove the bread and put it on a table with the top down, dry it off with a clean, well wrung out cloth and cover it with a towel, but leave the sides open.[1]

TO MAKE SIMPLE WHEAT [WHITE] BREAD

4 pounds of wheat flour of the medium kind is put into a tray; add about 1 1/2 pots of lukewarm sweet milk and 1/2 pound of melted butter. Knead the flour together with 1 spoonful or 1 1/2 lod thick yeast; when the dough no longer sticks to your hands, cover it, so that it can rise, for 2 to 3 hours. Knead it again and make it into 2 or 3 loaves; it may rise some more on the table, brush with egg or milk, put it in the oven and bake for 1 hour.[2]

Madame Mangor, *Cookbook for Small Households*, 1862

WHITE [WHEAT] BREAD

....

The yeast which is used for white bread must be fresh and good; if it is dry, it must not crumble, because then it has lost its strength. The yeast is dissolved in a little milk, which is put over heat, but without boiling; the butter is melted and the milk, which should be new-milked, and the dissolved yeast are added to be heated, but not too hot, which will prevent the yeast from rising. Stir in the flour, beat with a spoon and when the dough gets too hard to beat, knead it with your hands until it slips from them. In order to keep the dough from getting too cold, the whole thing must be done very quickly, but since different yeasts make it hard to give exact times, you can tell if the dough will rise by slicing it. If it has small air holes inside, it is ready to rise; otherwise it will need to be kneaded more, or, if this isn't sufficient, add more dissolved yeast. When the dough has been kneaded enough, the safest method is to leave it in the pot in which it has been kneaded together with the spices, and set it aside, covered, in the evening in a bowl with cold water which is deep enough that it comes up to the top of the pot. In the morning, that is, after 12 hours, it should have risen enough so that it can immediately be set up and baked. For this method, do not warm the milk and dissolve the dry yeast in the flour before it is kneaded together with the milk.

You can also let the dough rise by setting the pot, covered with a thick, folded and warm napkin or with a pillow, under which a cloth has been spread, in a bowl with warm water on a warm oven or next to a hot stove. Occasionally, it should be turned so that it will all be warm, but not hot, as that will prevent the dough from rising. It may well take a couple of hours before it has risen enough, and in order to see when it has, you can make a hole with your finger. If it closes quickly, the dough is ready.[3]

FRENCH BREAD

....

1 1/2 *lod* dry yeast is dissolved in 1 1/2 pails of warm milk; add 1 lb. flour together with a little salt and, if you want, 1 tablespoon salad oil; knead well and quickly, until the dough slips from your hands and there are small

air holes inside. When it has risen enough, put it aside without further kneading, on a baking sheet in whatever shape you want, brush with a little egg white or warm water and bake until the bread is light brown; first with a slow heat and then, after it has risen a little, with a stronger heat.[4]

Mangor's original 1837 *Cookbook for Small Households* had no recipes for bread. They show up first in the 1847 edition. these recipes come from the 14th edition, from 1865. Note the extensive description of how to work with yeast.

Kristine Marie Jensen, *Frk. Jensens Cookbook*, 1901

FRENCH BREAD BAKED IN A FORM

Pillsbury flour makes the nicest bread. 8 kvint yeast is mixed with 2 teaspoons salt, 2 ditto sugar. Add two lbs. Pillsbury flour and 3 pails half-skim milk to this, work well with a spoon until the dough slips from the bowl. 2 French bread forms are greased with butter before they are filled with the dough; let it rest 2 to 2 1/2 hours to rise. The bread is baked in a very warm oven for about 1 hour.

If you use regular white flour, use a little less milk.[5]

Ingeborg Suhr, *Food*, 1965

FRENCH BREAD (WARM RISING)

PREPARATION TIME: 2 HOURS   CALORIES: 1890

1/2 kg. Flour
1 tsp. Salt
1 tsp. Sugar
ca. 3 dl. Milk
25 g. Yeast

Put the flour, salt and sugar in a dish. Warm the milk to ca. 30° C., dissolve the yeast in a little milk. Mix everything together until the dough sticks

together; set it aside to rise. Cover with a lid or a cloth dampened with cold water. When the dough has doubled in size, form it into a bread shape, put it on a buttered cookie sheet or into a buttered form. Score the top of the dough with a sharp knife. Let it rise for 10–15 minutes. Brush with butter and bake until light brown, 30–40 minutes.[6]

fourth course

THE GROWTH OF DOMESTICITY

"Women were created by God to prepare food."[1]

CHARLES EMIL HAGDAHL,
ILLUSTRATED COOKBOOK, 1883

T HE VICTORIAN IDEAL OF "TRUE WOMANHOOD" dates from the late eighteenth and early nineteenth century. In 1966, Barbara Welter wrote a now classic article, "The Cult of True Womanhood," in which she defined the "four cardinal virtues" that characterized a "true woman"—piety, purity, domesticity, and submissiveness.[2] This chapter is concerned with the third of these virtues, domesticity. The assumption is that during the late eighteenth and early nineteenth centuries, cookbook authors responded to the changing expectations of women's roles in society and within the home. They presumed that housewives would now have a more hands-on experience in the kitchen, that they had not learned this previously and thus would need more specific instructions for running the kitchen as well as the household.

Women had always been in charge of food preparation and, by extension, the kitchen. That was not new; what was new was the

expectation that the domestic sphere was the only place for women and that women took their identity from their roles in this sphere. Earlier, pre-industrial middle-class women had been partners in their husbands' work, in the "family industry" and had been equal participants in the "household economy." The middle-class household had functioned as an economic unit, with specific and distinct roles for husbands and wives, both of whom were necessary. With the advent of a more modern, capitalist society from the eighteenth century on, the roles of husbands and wives and the relationship between them changed—the former took on an economic/productive function, the latter a social/reproductive function. With this change, women's function and identity became more closely identified with the household and, by extension, with domesticity and the kitchen.[3]

Recent research has challenged the degree of separation implied in the concept of gender specific separate spheres. There was probably a lot more overlap than historians have traditionally accepted. Indeed, one of the premises of this book is that nationalism—a characteristically political and thus male domain— can be found in the kitchen, a quintessential female space. However, none of this negates the fact that people at the time wrote as though female and male spheres were indeed, and should by rights be, separate and distinct. Thus, the growing discussion of domesticity in cookbooks can be seen as part of the discourse that was attempting to create separate spheres for men and women, rather than simply reflecting social reality.

When Hagdahl wrote that "women were created . . . to prepare food," he was not speaking of a new role for women; what was new is that this was how women's identity had come to be defined. He calls women "queens," and asks if they know where they still bear the scepter. "In the kitchen," he answers himself. Women have "the most worthy, the most influential position . . . marking a new cultural stage." He claims that this position is "new," that there has been a social change regarding women's role. And yet, there is really nothing "new" about women being in the kitchen. Rather, Hagdahl's emphasis on the kitchen as women's domain is part of the discourse that changed women's roles, identifying them now solely and exclusively with the domestic space.

It is the housewife's duty, continues Hagdahl, to "make the home comfortable with cleanliness, freshness and calm."[4]

If the lunch is well prepared, the food good and tasteful, it will have a marked influence on your humor for the rest of the day. On the other hand, a disorderly table, stale bread, bitter coffee or tea that is too thin, is more than enough to destroy both humor and stomach. . . . May our homes always be happy, comfortable and inviting![5]

And it is, of course, the housewife's responsibility to provide all this.

Eighteen eighty-three appears to be a little late to be writing in this way; much of such didacticism in Danish cookbooks had disappeared by the late nineteenth century. However, Hagdahl is one of only four identifiably male authors writing cookbooks in the second half of the nineteenth century. (There may have been others but if so, they were hiding behind initials or anonymity in their published works.) One senses a certain attempt to capture a bygone time that may be slipping away. The term "Lady," he says, using the English word, originally means one who gives out bread, "quite descriptive of women's domestic duties." But now it has come to mean "an excuse for laziness and pleasure-seeking, for a lack of knowledge of domestic responsibilities."[6]

There is an underlying assumption in the work of many late-eighteenth- and nineteenth-century cookbook authors that women do not know their responsibilities, that they have to be taught how to be good housewives. Women's tasks and duties, which may always have been implicit, are now being made explicit. Since this is a period of changing social and economic roles for women and men, it is not surprising to see a contemporaneous change in authors' expectations.

In Denmark, a large percentage of agricultural workers had become independent farmers and moved into a capitalist economy in the late eighteenth and early nineteenth century. The fact that Denmark remained a primarily agricultural country until the mid-twentieth century tends to hide the fact that Danish society had indeed "modernized." The agricultural sector was the first to industrialize in Denmark, a pattern that differed

from the well-known English experience, where the lead was taken by urban and heavy industry.

Industrialization in Denmark thus did not follow the dominant Western pattern in which urbanization can be used as a measure of industrial development first in textiles and then heavy industry. Instead, the late-eighteenth-century agricultural reforms in Denmark created a group of independent entrepreneurial farmers who had quite clearly moved into the capitalist system. Admittedly a minority of the peasants, they formed, nonetheless, the foundation for the next stage of development during the latter part of the nineteenth century, for it was during the late nineteenth century that Danish agriculture, due to a fortuitous combination of rural enlightenment (the *folkehøjskole* movement), the co-op movement, and new technology, was able to respond successfully to the agricultural crisis brought about by the availability of cheap grain from the United States. Danish agriculture converted from grain to animal farming and, in the process, modernized and industrialized. The majority, both of the general population and of this new agricultural entrepreneurial class, continued to live in rural areas.[7]

Cookbook authors responded to and capitalized on this shift as well. Early authors addressed their audiences as professionals; the author of the 1616 *Cookbook* talked about the "honest trade" of male and female cooks.[8] The introduction to Anna Weckerin's *A Good and Very Useful Cookbook*, from 1648, states that the first use of a cookbook "is in the daily use of ordinary living to maintain our life's necessities and health."[9] But this slowly changes as cookbooks emphasize a female audience and the importance of housewifery. In 1785, Müller addressed "every sensible housewife," one of whose "most important tasks" is "the correct management of the kitchen."[10] By 1821, Christiane Rosen, in the first chapter of her *Economic Housekeeping Book*, is simply addressing all women; she has "[n]ecessary information for every housewife and housekeeper."

No occupation brings the *female sex* such lasting happiness as starting early to care for the house; thus will be acquired the inclination for industry, capability and orderliness, which will train *young women to*

be clever and competent people. More and more perfection will be obtained in the distant future such that they will not need to learn from their inferiors, which will not bring them respect or advantage.[11] [Emphasis added]

Rosen's implication is that women have been learning household skills from servants, something of which she clearly disapproves. It is the housewife's responsibility to create an appropriate space. If she allows servants to take over the formation of this space, the housewife has abrogated her responsibility and allowed the servant, who is by definition "inferior," that is, less competent, to take control. This implies a severe loss of status for the housewife, her family, and her husband. Thus Rosen writes books so that women can learn from her instead and be competent to move into their new "occupation" as housekeepers. (The irony, of course, is that she had herself been a professional housekeeper, a servant, and never the mistress of her own home.) The tone of her books is light and chatty—she doesn't want to scare her audience away—and she includes some very basic information on how to care for and preserve food, as well as how to prepare it. But the ultimate goal remains to train women "to be clever and competent people."

This emphasis on basic information comes out clearly in several books. Indeed, one of the few extant reviews of a cookbook from the late eighteenth century specifically mentions the necessity for such books. The reviewer of the second edition of Louise Friedel's *New and Complete Confectionery Book*,[12] from 1795, laments that this is a very basic book but notes that, unfortunately, such basic books are necessary.

It is to be desired that such books were unnecessary, but as long as it is a requirement for, if not a majority, at least a large number of our women, in order that they not be unknowledgeable about the preparation of such sweets . . . [we will not] reject such good and purposeful instructions as this. The paper and print are far better than in the first edition.[13]

The Danish version of Collingwood and Woollams, *New and Complete Housekeeping Book*, from 1796, exemplifies the necessity

for basics with its use of descriptive language. About roasts, the authors say,

the heat must vary according to the size and weight of what is to be roasted. When it is a thin little piece, a strong fire is good, so that the roast is quickly done; but when you have a large piece, the fire must be moderated so that it doesn't just violently attack the outside without reaching the inside, and the outside dries out before the inside is done.[14]

This is one of the first references to types of heat. The fact that the authors feel the necessity for explaining such a very basic concept suggests that the people they are writing for (or for whom they *think* they are writing) are unfamiliar with basic concepts of cooking.

Christiane Rosen's very specific mandates for the kitchen in "how a kitchen should be ordered" from 1824 (see Second Intermezzo, page 55) also emphasize the basics. Sweeping the fireplace, using trivets so as not to burn the table, making sure dishes are not overfull, checking the fire before you got to bed at night[15]—all these are very basic and seemingly obvious recommendations. But they were new to cookbooks, and the instructive tone is new. Much of this advice, such as removing ashes and using hot pads, should have been obvious to experienced cooks, but these books are now addressing cooks who, the authors assume, have little or no previous experience in the kitchen.

Müller's 1793 *The Danish Housewife* begins by telling its readers that the housewife has to set a good example for her servants. "If servants see unclean handling of food, they will often shudder at the table." This will lead them to be "unfaithful in their positions" and leave her employ. In a perhaps unconscious role reversal, the author is implying here that servants have internalized the growing bourgeois emphasis on cleanliness, which it is the housewife's duty to maintain. "Cleanliness in rooms and beds, together with an orderly and clean table setting will remind servants to keep themselves orderly and clean."[16]

These warnings seem to reflect the growing change. The mistress of the house or farm had always been responsible for seeing to the servants; it had always been her responsibility to see

that they were hired and fed. Cleanliness is now brought into the equation; you can do your job well and keep good help, not only if you feed and treat them well, but *also* if you see to it that the home environment is clean and proper. Cleanliness and food are tied together in a new equation. This leads to the next element of the housewife's charge, that is, order. As we can already see in several of the previous examples, cleanliness is only part of the equation; keeping everything in its place is essential for ensuring order. It is not accidental that Rosen's first chapter is entitled, "How a Kitchen Should Be *Ordered*" (emphasis added). It is part of the housewife's responsibility to assure order in her part of the world—the domestic space. Good help is necessary for the effective running of the farm and the household, and order is necessary to keep good help.

C. F. von Rumohr, in his 1832 translation of Joseph König's *Introduction to the Art of Cooking*, claims that a lack of order in the kitchen will eventually lead to the destruction of the family. When "the housewife serves and arranges her meals foolishly," von Rumohr claims, this will lead to much domestic discontent. Mealtimes, which had previously been good times together, will grow more tiresome and soon it will be easy for the neighbor to lure the husband away "to cafés, restaurants and other similar poisoners." And from that follows, "with giant steps," the total downfall and destruction of the home. So, von Rumohr is hoping with this book "to wake interest for . . . the lost art of cooking."[17] This will keep the husband at home, the family together, and the world in order.

While von Rumohr writes of order in the home in an attempt to keep the family intact, Müller had written of order in the household economy and of the necessity of and ability to keep good help in 1793, almost forty years earlier. Paralleling this move to order toward the end of the eighteenth century, cookbook authors also started writing of order in the state. That is, part of the "job" of the housewife was to train good citizens for the state. She was to talk, explain, and set examples in order to train her help. "If this is successful, then the housewife has the opportunity to enjoy the fact that she has trained a capable member of the state."[18]

The line connecting order in the household to order in the state and the housewife's responsibility for both was not a phenomenon unique to Denmark. The new American republic during the same period witnessed discussions about educating women for "republican motherhood," so that they could train their sons to be good republican citizens. The idea was that new virtues would be needed in this new, American republic, virtues which would help to distinguish the United States from the old aristocracies in Europe. And women's role in this new order would be to be educated enough to train their sons for the new republic. Quoting Judith Sargent Murray writing in *The Gleaner* in 1798, Linda Kerber says that the "'felicity of families' is dependent on the presence of women who are 'properly methodical, and economical in their distributions and expenditures of time'." On the happiness of families rested the happiness of the nation.[19] As Kerber's other work also demonstrates, "Republican Mothers" were to be educated in order to "be better wives, rational household managers, and better mothers, for the next generation of virtuous republican citizens—especially sons."[20] And in France, there was talk of "maternal education," which was essentially the same idea. In all these cases, the concept of domesticity is extended outward from the family to the nation at large. Women are seen as having a definite and specific role to play in the creation of both, in the development of both the bourgeois household and the new nation state.

Yet, by the middle of the nineteenth century, the language in cookbooks changes yet again. The cookbooks start to drop most of their didacticism and concentrate almost exclusively on delivering recipes. Even when they continue to give advice, the tone has changed from Rosen's preachy sermonizing to that of a gentle reminder. For instance, in 1864, Maria Rasmussen writes in the introduction to her cookbook:

I hardly need mention here that cleanliness is the first, and that the various things which are used for cooking are of good quality is the second item in every household. One can never make good food from bad provisions, and a lack of cleanliness makes even good food bad.[21]

It is quite obvious here that the tone is less of admonition and more of mild prompting. This is probably because the cookbook authors, now incidentally almost all women, assume that women know all these kitchen protocols already; it does not hurt just to mention them, but such things need no longer be taught.

When prescriptions about behavior begin to appear in print, it is usually an indication that mores are changing. Authors write about how people ought to behave either to retain some supposed older form or to change to some new mode. When these prescriptions die out, one can assume that change has taken place and is no longer an issue. The job of historians is deciphering just what these *mentalités* are; societies do not often write about what is universally accepted.

fourth intermezzo

MAPS OF DENMARK

Opposite
PLATE 10. Map of Danish overseas possessions, ca. 1800. Adapted from Mountain High Maps®, copyright 1993, Digital Wisdom, Inc.

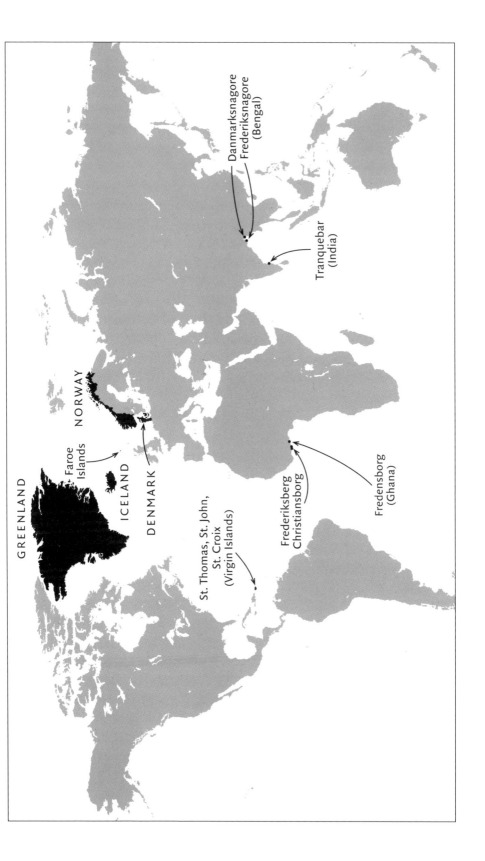

GREENLAND

Faroe
Islands

ICELAND

NORWAY

DENMARK

St. Thomas, St. John,
St. Croix
(Virgin Islands)

Frederiksberg
Christiansborg

Fredensborg
(Ghana)

Danmarksnagore
Frederiksnagore
(Bengal)

Tranquebar
(India)

PLATE 11. Map of Denmark showing Norway, 1814. Adapted from Mountain High Maps®, copyright 1993, Digital Wisdom, Inc.

PLATE 12. Map of Denmark showing Schleswig and Holstein. Adapted from Mountain High Maps®, copyright 1993, Digital Wisdom, Inc.

fifth course

THE DEVELOPMENT
OF NATIONALISM

C. F. VON RUMOHR'S 1832 TRANSLATION OF
Joseph König's *Introduction to the Art of Cooking* categorically
states that "it is confirmed in a thousand cases that people are
what they eat."[1] During the preceding three-quarters of a century, cookbook authors had been stressing more and more that
Danes should eat *Danish* food. From the mid-eighteenth century
on, there is a distinct growth in what can be called nationalism in
the prescriptive admonitions of Danish cookbooks, even when
they were translations from other languages, as Rumohr's was. In
1755, an anonymous author wrote that the *New Complete Cookbook*, published in Copenhagen, was "according to the latest
French manner . . . arranged in a manner useful for *our fatherland*" (emphasis added). The recipes could be used for "fancy
meals as well as common housekeeping."[2] As early as 1755 then,

one begins to see a differentiation between others, here, the French, and the Danish, who make up "our fatherland."

In 1762, Samuel Conrad Schwach, writing for *Monthly Papers on Household Improvements* published in Christiania (Oslo), Norway, addressed himself "to every patriot." He extolled the virtues of "*Norwegian vinegar* . . . vinegar made from our Norwegian currants is not only as good as foreign wine-vinegar, but even many times stronger, better and clearer" (emphasis in original).[3]

The following years witness a whole series of recommendations in cookbooks to use native, local, or Danish products. Carl Müller, for example, praised the virtues of Danish products in his cookbooks from 1785 and 1793. Müller was Danish; he had been a professional chef at the south Funen manor of Hvidkilde and had moved to Copenhagen in 1785. He ended his career as chef to Crown Prince Frederik.[4] Müller explains that he is writing a cookbook because there are so few books "in our Danish language" which deal with cooking.[5] In his *New Cookbook* of 1785, he says that will give,

advice to my countrywomen . . . on how to make healthy and good-tasting food, to be economical and easily to make use of *our country's own herbs and products* . . . in noble as well as middle class homes.[6] [Emphasis added]

And in 1793, in *The Danish Housewife*, Müller continues,

[a]ll sorts of cabbage, all sorts of beets, potatoes, strawberries, white and black 'viper's grass', the so-called asparagus, red onions and shallots, I have to praise as the *products of our own country*. Country people would rather run to the city to buy foreign spices with which to spice up their food, and thus waste their time and money. . . . Those who understand know better . . . and use the *products of our own noble country*.

Other countries' products and foods are not serviceable for us; we in our country have most of what we need and which is useful for our health; yes, many of *our own products are superior to foreign ones*. Still, one can not deny that many foreign products are better than ours, in terms of quality and taste.[7] [Emphasis added]

There appears to be a little defensiveness here. Müller claims that Danish products are more serviceable, but admits, contradictorily, that foreign products are sometimes superior. People run to the city to buy foreign products under the misguided assumption that they are better or more fashionable. But Müller insists that Danish products are nonetheless cheaper, contain everything that Danes need, and are preferable simply because they come from "our own noble country."

Even cookbooks translated from other languages manage to find a way to promote Danish virtues. The 1798 anonymous *Education for Young Women*, translated from German, is "enriched" for young Danish women with material added by a "Danish housekeeper."

This translation has not completely followed the original, because many pieces are not useful for our housekeeping. However, we have enriched the book with many new and useful pieces which have been added by a Danish housekeeper.[8]

The Danish housekeeper later adds what is certainly a nationalist and perhaps also mercantilist explanation to the housewife for not using foreign coffee—it is a way to keep Danish money within the country.

It would be an extremely great advantage to the country if one could find a substitute whereby the use of expensive coffee would be reduced, so that many thousand *rigsdaler* would annually remain in the country which are now lost for good.[9]

Tode's 1799 translation of *The Core of the Diet for Housewives and Husbands* from the original Russian propounds a more general nationalism, one that would probably work for any country and is not directed exclusively at Denmark. However, although he extols generic virtues such as simple food and hard work, he nevertheless does it in anti-foreign terms—stay at home and use homegrown products.

The finest chefs, who are in a position to give even the most simple dishes the best taste, are hunger and work. One would need many fewer spices and *foreign dishes* and take better care of one's health, if one welcomed these chefs more positively.

We have many herbs which contain positive values instead of the *foreign spices*, for example, elderberry flowers, basil, marjoram, sage, cumin, juniper, chervil, thyme, fennel, anise, etc. These grow in our gardens and could easily be used instead of *foreign spices*.[10] [Emphasis added]

Svendsen, in his 1800 *Economic Health Cookbook*, goes one step further—not only are domestic goods better, foreign ones are positively harmful. Svendsen is willing to include all of Europe within the domestic; presumably, the "foreign, fiery" spices come from tropical areas.

Spices, especially the *foreign, fiery* ones, should only be used as medicines, and at best in small quantities and sparingly, and only be used in cooking when they can make certain dishes more digestible . . . [Svendsen advises against frequent use of] nutmeg . . . cardamom, ginger, cloves. More acceptable are pepper, coriander, allspice and cinnamon. Even less harmful, yes, even to be recommended, are the *domestic or European* products, garlic, onions, leeks, juniper, cumin, anise, parsley, dill, sage, marjoram, thyme, etc.[11] [Emphasis added]

Svendsen is the Danish translator of this cookbook. There is no indication of the original language, though it is presumably European, which might account for the inclusion of the general category of Europe as an acceptable source for products.

And finally, in this selection of examples of a growth in self-aware national preferences, the 1801 anonymous *Danish House-wife's Kitchen Catechism*, which admits that there are already many cookbooks written in or translated into the Danish language but does not believe that they really *are* Danish. Danish tastes and Danish dishes are distinct and unique and not to be found anywhere but in genuine Danish cookbooks.

Despite the fact that there is no lack of Danish cookbooks . . . it must be admitted that the best follow foreign rather than Danish tastes . . . [and] that many good Danish dishes are omitted.[12]

The pattern here seems to be that it is best to use domestic products and Danish recipes or preparation methods. The strongest opprobrium is reserved for the use of "foreign" spices, which are viewed as unhealthy because they agitate or excite the blood. Foreign preparation methods range from distasteful to destructive. Homegrown or domestic (sometimes expanded to include European) herbs, as distinguished from spices, are viewed as acceptable. (However, one might question the assumption that fennel or anise are somehow less "excitable" than nutmeg or cloves.) The common denominator seems to be, "keep it at home." Whether this is a holdover of mercantilist traditions (as in "keep the money in the country") or the precursor of new nationalist traditions, the end result is the same.

After Denmark's disastrous experience in the Napoleonic Wars, the new Danish National Liberal Party agitated both for a written constitution based on some form of manhood suffrage and for the creation of "Denmark to the Ejder [River]," as the Party's slogan went. That is, for the creation of a *national* Danish state which would include the traditional kingdom of Denmark and the Duchy of Schleswig (at the base of the Jutlandic Peninsula and north of the Ejder River), and the exclusion of the German-speaking Duchy of Holstein. Questions of what constituted Denmark and Danishness (*danskhed*) were hotly debated in the print media and in the new advisory assemblies at the time.

Until 1848, Denmark was an absolute monarchy, ruled under the provisions of the Royal Law of 1665, which gave the monarch complete and absolute power. There were only very pale echoes in Denmark of the late-eighteenth-century revolution in France. The single radical event was the singing of the *Marseillaise* in Copenhagen's Tivoli Gardens one evening in the 1790s. Copenhagen was home to a flourishing club life that affected revolutionary ideals until one of its members, P. A. Heiberg, was actually exiled from the country for writing a song that was charged with *lèse majesté*.[13]

Although Denmark withdrew from the League of Armed Neutrality in 1801, after its defeat by Nelson in the Battle of Copenhagen, the Danish monarchy maintained a neutral stance in the wars that were ravaging Europe. But in 1807, after the English bombarded Copenhagen for three days and sailed off with the Danish fleet, the Danish king, Frederik VI, openly allied with Napoleon and stuck with him until the bitter end in 1814. Denmark was thus never occupied by French troops; it was, however, quickly defeated by Sweden after the Battle of Leipzig in 1813, and in the ensuing peace Denmark ceded Norway to Sweden.

In defining its nationalism, then, unlike Germany, Denmark did not describe itself in terms of opposition to an outsider. Rather, it began to identify itself in terms of a loss, the loss of Norway; that which was left over was Denmark. This process of self-definition through loss accelerated after Denmark also lost the duchies of Schleswig and Holstein to Prussia and Austria in 1864 (see map, page 93). At that time, Denmark lost considerable territory, population, and economic resources; out of a total population of 2.15 million in 1840, 850,000 had lived in the duchies of Schleswig and Holstein. Upon losing the duchies, the Danish kingdom lost two-fifths of its work force, with a corresponding loss in production and consumption.[14]

On the occasion of the Great Nordic Art and Industry Exhibition held in Copenhagen in 1872, H. P. Holst, poet, author, and newspaper editor, wrote an inscription for tokens used at the exhibit: "For every loss a replacement will be found!/What was outwardly lost, shall be inwardly gained."[15] This phrase soon became part of Danish culture and symbolic of the Danes' need to compensate for territorial losses.

The Danish National Liberal Party also demanded a representative government, and successive Danish kings eventually felt constrained to curtail and finally dismantle their own absolute powers. First, they endorsed the establishment of four advisory provincial assemblies in 1834, and then, in 1848, they agreed to a constitutional government based on universal manhood suffrage.

The increasing popular investment in a Danish government is reflected in the literature of cookbooks, both through the refer-

ences to consuming things Danish, as noted above, and through an emphasis on the development of a Danish citizenry. Carl Müller explains in *The Danish Housewife* from 1793 that housewives need to set examples for their children and their servants. In so doing they will have the pleasure of knowing that they have "trained a smart member of the state."[16]

To be a citizen or member of a state presupposes the existence of that state. And yet, the very process of becoming a citizen helps in turn to create the new nation state. A dialectic interaction takes place between the concepts of citizen and state; each is dependent on the other. Each supports the other and, in doing so, helps to create the other. A citizen cannot exist without a state, nor can a state have no citizens. Thus, when Müller tells a housewife that she is training "a smart member of the state," he is, in fact, encouraging the development of the state. Danish cookbooks thus become a part of state creation in Denmark.

Although this rationale may help explain the existence of Danish nationalism in cookbooks printed after the loss of Norway in 1814, how do we explain its existence as early as 1755, that is, *before* Norway's loss? In an article in the volume *In Search of Danish Identity*, Ole Feldbæk discusses the growth of a Danish "bourgeois consciousness,"[17] which he dates to the mid-1700s. He clearly sees signs of this consciousness in a periodical called *Danish Magazine* (*Dansk Magazin*), which started appearing in 1745 and in which expressions such as "our language," "our fatherland," "our history," and "our countrymen" were quite commonly used. Cookbooks parallel this development, as can be seen in the 1755 *New Complete Cookbook*, which was "useful for our fatherland."[18]

Then in 1789 in Denmark, there was an outpouring of anti-German sentiment in a series of written works that has since become known as "The German Quarrel." Feldbæk believes that the specifically anti-German nature of this event was due to the perception on the part of the urban middle classes that the multicultural Danish monarchy favored the German upper class over the growing Danish bourgeoisie. "It was regarded as national treachery that Danes were put in a client relationship to the German upper class," in other words, that resident German speakers

were given preference for high government positions over native born Danish speakers. It is important to note that this "quarrel," although perhaps economic or political in origin, was nonetheless couched in antagonistic "national" terms. Indeed, Feldbæk comments that what was "new in 1789, was what could be called a demand of Denmark for the Danes."[19] He links this sentiment to the introduction of a Citizenship Law in 1772, which stated that "admission to government positions in His Majesty's realm is limited to those subjects who were born there." This law overturned the perceived practice of favoring Germans, and place of birth won out over residency. Danes, however, demanded its implementation in national terms, excluding even those German speakers who were born within the Danish realm.[20] Similar sentiments are reflected in cookbooks that call for the use of Danish products, "products of our own noble country" and "good Danish dishes."[21]

Of course, there is another side to this issue: What were nationalist sentiments doing in the kitchen? As mentioned above, part of the responsibilities of the new bourgeois mother was to train members of the state. Whereas wives and mothers were no longer considered active participants in the household economy, they were now given a role in the new national economy. There is a growing body of literature on the gendering of the state in this period,[22] and an examination of Danish cookbooks of the time would seem to support this thesis.

One way of signaling one's identity is through the use of names and titles. Indicating that you are Danish and that someone else is not is one way of underlining who belongs in the nation and who does not, who is in and who is out. When we give people or food dishes foreign names, we are labeling them as the "other," as not of or from us; it distinguishes "us" from "them."[23]

In the foreword to his *New Cookbook*, written in 1815, C. Jacobsen, chef at Tranekjær Castle, stated that he would "not use so many foreign and strange names, which are found in other cookbooks, since I believe that these names are neither necessary nor understandable for most of those who will use these recipes."[24] Jacobsen was probably talking about cooking processes in which

foreign terms were used, for instance, *coulis, fines-herbes, gratinée, quenelles,* and *sautere.* Several cookbooks of the time contained glossaries of such foreign terms. Jacobsen's implication is that the average Danish cook is experienced neither with accepted culinary terminology nor with much of the foreign world outside, and that, equally importantly, this knowledge is not necessary.

Seemingly contradicting Jacobsen's Danophilia, the Danish editor and translator of Francis Collingwood and John Woollams's *The Universal Cook, and City and Country Housekeeper* believed that "our countrymen would profit from having available in Danish the most important contents of Principal Cooks Collingwood and Woollams' universal London cookbook." This is because, "Englishmen are known for being fond of real and tasty dishes," and Danish cooks neglect to include information on "the art of cooking."[25] But even this explanation is couched in nationalist terms—Englishmen have what Danes lack.

Moreover, more recipes in Collingwood and Woollams's cookbook had names referring to foreign places than did most of the other cookbooks published in Danish. This feature of the original English text is carried over into the Danish text and even extended as "English" is now added in the title of some of the dishes. Whatever the explanation for the proliferation of foreign names in the English text, its carryover into Danish helps to support and extend the application of the concept of otherness to those outside Denmark's cultural boundaries.

A list of recipe titles with foreign names from the Danish translation of Collingwood and Woollams's cookbook:

French "Bullioi" ["bouillie" in English]
Portuguese beef
Veal shoulder á la Piedmontôise
Florentine veal
"Scotch collops" in the French mode
Goat in the Turkish mode
Roast pork in the French mode
Cheshire pork paté
Chicken á la St. Menehoult
"Chiringrate," an English chicken dish

French duck
Florentine rabbit [no spinach; in English "to Florentine"]
Portuguese rabbit
Plovers á la Perigord
Lark á la Françoise
West Indian turtle
Sicilian sauce
Italian noodle soup or vermicelli soup
English goose gizzard soup
English green pea soup
English crab soup
English chicken soup

The "English" in the titles of these four recipes was added by the Danish translator.

Spanish cream
Pecadillo or Indian marinade
"HodgePodge of Mutton"
"Mutton cutlets Lovers Fashion"

The last two appeared in English in the Danish version as well.

There is no way that the average kitchen could have prepared even a tenth of these dishes. They fall into the category of exotic recipes that may have been used in some large or noble homes, or may have been included in cookbooks simply to allow people to dream of foreign places. The late years of the eighteenth century were the "palmy days" of Danish history, a period when Danish shipping spanned the globe and goods were sent home from colonies both Danish and foreign. In this, of course, it paralleled the British Empire, already spreading over the globe and with a similar access to "exotic" ingredients. But whether or not one actually used or even had access to these ingredients, the detail of these listings of foreign dishes or places underlined the fact that they were not one's own, in this case, Danish, which in turn made obvious the reality of separate identities.

There is a subtle albeit significant shift in cookbooks around the middle of the nineteenth century when much of this overt nationalism dies out. The word "Danish" disappears from cookbook titles; foreign names are noticeably though not completely absent from dishes. Simultaneously, as admonitions to "use Danish" begin to fade, the recipes, too, change, becoming much less "foreign" and relying on fewer exotic ingredients.

The term "Danish" disappeared from cookbook titles for thirty years—from 1841, when C. Hansen titled her book *The Danish Kitchen Girl*, to 1871, when A. V. Madsen wrote *Cookbook for the Danish Housewife*. Even when the term "Danish" appeared in the text, its meaning had changed from "Danishness" to a simple statement of place. In 1842, the anonymous author of *The Housewife*, wrote:

The contents of this book are based on many years of her [the author's] own experience; she has also compared this with many other good works which we have in the Danish language in this field, and of these she has used what she thinks is worth using; a similar comparison of her own experiences has been made with foreign authors, especially French and German . . . and from them she has taken some good advice which she feels is superior to that which she had previously followed.[26]

Although there is a reference to material already available in the Danish language, this time foreign cookbooks are admitted as being superior and Danish national or product identity is not evident. Gone is Müller's defensiveness in trying to prove that that which is Danish must, by definition, be better.

In 1855–1856, the author Bishop edited the two-volume *Illustrated Cookbook*, a work revised by "a Danish housewife" and based on several foreign cookbooks—seven English, two French, and two German, to be precise. The Danish editor felt that although there were numerous cookbooks in the Danish language, none of them were really complete or took account of the latest culinary methods.

Certainly, many Danish housekeeping and cookbooks have been published—from Christiane Rosen's several volume work in the previous

century to Miss Eibe's latest comprehensive cookbook . . . but none of them, yes, all of them together, would not make superfluous a work of larger magnitude which would take advantage of the latest developments and advancements in the art of cooking. There is only one Danish cookbook which has recently gained extensive distribution and with its practical usefulness has deserved it—we mean, of course, Madame Mangor's . . . but even this work stands well behind the newer and best foreign books of this sort.

It is our intention with this book to give the Danish public a larger practical work on the art of cooking based on the newest developments and advancements . . . to make our home economists and especially the Danish housewife acquainted with the results of the recent important reforms in the previously simple English art of cooking, which has now been combined and fused with the French gastronomes' richness of composition.[27]

The references here are to Danes as people, not to Danish products. Both the previously quoted anonymous author as well as Bishop make favorable reference to foreigners, from whom it may actually be possible to learn something useful. Compare this with the earlier exhortations to refrain from all things not Danish.

Nor were there as many foreign dish names after the mid-nineteenth century. They did not (and probably never will) die out completely but there were not nearly so many as there had previously been. Instead, there were more local references, such as to "Tivoli cakes" and "Mrs. Heiberg's cookies." Johanne Luise Heiberg was a well-known actress of the mid-nineteenth century who probably had several servants baking her cookies, but the use of Mrs. Heiberg's name was a way of bringing the cookies home through the known and the familiar.

Discussions of "our country" and "our land's products," evident in the earlier cookbooks falls off at about this time as well; one cookbook in 1849 does refer to "our country" but in connection with "remedies for colds," and the reference has nothing to do with the nationalist sentiments of earlier cookbooks. *The Latest Cookbook for Middle Class Households* says, "[d]ue to the changing and damp climate of *our country*, colds, especially in the

spring and fall, are one of the most important enemies of health" (emphasis added).[28]

This change needs some explaining. Why, during a period when Denmark was fighting both foreign and civil wars (1848–1852, in Schleswig-Holstein), establishing a new form of government, writing a new constitution, trying to establish itself on the international scene, negotiating to sell the Virgin Islands, all issues which might well appeal to and foster nationalism, why during this period do nationalism and overt references to citizenship disappear from the cookbooks where they had previously been present?

The answer probably lies in the fact that society and, by extension, cookbooks have by now become more Danish in their essence; they no longer need to talk so much about being Danish—they *are* Danish. Translations of cookbooks from other countries and in other languages begin to disappear, and the use of foreign products is determined by what is good for Danish culture. In other words, a Danish cuisine has developed with simple recipes that use Danish products, reflecting, in turn, a greater acceptance of what it means to be Danish. Early cookbooks, through the first two periods, contain a wealth of "exotic" recipes. They not only recommend dishes that require the standard meat from domesticated animals—beef, pork, chicken, and fish—but also those that call for an eclectic variety of game (of the walking, swimming, and flying varieties). Recall the list of dishes with foreign names from Collingwood and Woollams's cookbook.

The list of spices used in these recipes is endless (hence the admonitions at the end of the eighteenth century to keep to Danish spices). But by the mid-nineteenth century, the use of exotic foods and spices has toned down considerably. In 1864, Madame Mangor put out a small cookbook for soldiers titled *Soldiers in the Field*. Soldiers in the Danish army were issued raw rations and this was her attempt to help them cope with cooking on their own. Salt and pepper are regularly used in these recipes, mustard for fish, "if you have it." And the recipe for peas says, "if you have herbs, a little parsley, a little stalk of thyme and a couple of onions, will make the peas taste good."[29] Of course, it is hardly

to be expected that soldiers in the field will have access to any particularly large store of spices, but this is an example of what Madame Mangor apparently thought was adequate for cooking—salt and pepper, maybe also parsley and thyme.

Partly, this change has to do with a shift in cookbook audiences—from the early cookbooks addressed to an upper-class elite clientele, through the middle period, when cookbooks are addressed to the middle classes, to the extension of cookbooks to newer audiences, such as Mangor addressing small households. But this change also has to do with the fact that Denmark's loss of Norway and subsequent bankruptcy ended much of its overseas trade and Danes were, of necessity, forced back into eating what was locally available; what was Danish, with the inclusion of a limited number of "colonial products" such as coffee, tea, and chocolate, was now incorporated into a *Danish cuisine*.

It is also probable that by the mid-nineteenth century, this cuisine had come to be accepted as authentic Danish cuisine. One of the most obvious changes in the cookbook recipes is the growth in the use of potatoes over the course of the century. Earlier in the eighteenth century, cookbook authors could not even decide what to call these new vegetables, and *kartofler*, *patater*, *jordæbler*, all show up in recipe titles. By the late eighteenth century, "*kartofler*" emerged as the accepted name. Madame Mangor's original 1837 cookbook says to serve roast beef on a platter garnished with strips of horseradish. By 1865, Mangor's cookbook is suggesting that the dish be served with peeled potatoes.[30] The 1865 edition also contains several more recipes for potatoes than the 1837 version does, including one for plain boiled potatoes, which was to become a Danish national dish.[31]

Other changes parallel this reliance on domestic food; for instance, Mangor has an entire section on roasts in 1865, which was absent from the 1837 edition—roast beef, veal, ham, pork, lamb, goat, venison, rabbit, turkey, chicken, goose, duck, and poultry. By contrast, the anonymous female author of the 1796 *The New and Complete Cookbook* listed recipes for veal, beef, pork, rabbit, ham, lamb, wild boar, venison, partridge, capon, snipe, pheasant, quail, duck, chicken, goose, and pigeons,[32] a somewhat

more "gamey" collection. The inclusion of roasting certainly parallels the development of new enclosed stoves, making roasting a feasible option for housewives, but the new stoves do not, in and of themselves, explain the shift in *what* is to be roasted.

Of course, just the fact that a cookbook has a recipe for a dish does not mean that people actually ate the dish, nor, conversely, that people did not eat that for which there were no recipes in cookbooks. Peanut butter and jelly sandwiches, for instance, probably the most common lunch for American schoolchildren, never appear as such in American cookbooks.[33] Everyone knows how to make them, so why waste space on the details of their preparation?

However, quite apart from the question of the difference between recipes in cookbooks and the food that people actually ate, there is a change in the sorts of dishes for which the Danish cookbooks *did contain* recipes (see First Intermezzo, pages 26–35). The later cookbooks suggest menus with fairly straightforward dishes. Rasmussen's menus from 1864 include fried turkey, roast veal, veal cutlets, and roast chicken.[34] Mangor did not include menus in the early editions of her *Cookbook for Small Households*; however, the editor of the later editions did. The 1910 edition suggests winter menus that include roast veal, veal meatballs, macaroni pudding, reheated veal leftovers, yellow pea soup, calf's liver, and boiled beef.[35] There is nothing especially elaborate about either of these suggested menus; indeed, many of these dishes would be quite acceptable in cookbooks today.

A 1999 article in the Copenhagen daily newspaper *Politiken* discussed the results of a report on Danish eating habits published by the Commission on Veterinary and Feed Products. The author of the original report was quoted as saying, "[f]or years we have heard these predictions . . . that fast food has drowned our fatherland. . . . Now we can prove that this is not true."[36]

The article went on to list the top ten Danish meals according to the report:

1. hamburgers/meatballs (*hakkebøf/frikadeller*)
2. open sandwiches (*smørrebrød*)

3. stew (gryderet)
4. pork cutlets (svinekotelet/nakkekotelet/hamburgerryg)
5. chicken (kylling)
6. beef/veal, for example, roast beef (okse-kalvekød, f. eks. roastbeef)
7. roast pork (flæskesteg/ribbbensteg/stegt flæsk, m.m.)
8. lean fish, for example, cod (mager fisk, f. eks. tørsk)
9. beef/veal with fat layer (okse-kalvekød m. fedtkant)
10. soup (suppe)

Even if this is not what Danes actually eat, it is either what they *think* they eat or what they want others to think they eat. It represents what Danes think are appropriate dishes for Danish consumption. Note also that the journalist couches the survey in nationalist tones, talking about dishes that have, or have not, "drowned our fatherland." The main point, of course, is that these dishes are not all that different from those suggested by Maria Rasmussen and Madame Mangor's new editor.

So, if it is true that you are what you eat, and if by the mid-nineteenth century Danes were eating Danish products, then they *were* Danish.

fifth intermezzo

DANNEBROG

PLATE 13. *Dannebrog*, the Danish national flag. Courtesy of Kolonihaveforbundet for Danmark.

PLATE 14. Painting by C. A. Lorentzen, 1809. *Dannebrog falls from the sky during the Volmers Battle, at Lyndanis [Estonia], June 15, 1219.* Statens Museum for Kunst, Copenhagen.

PLATE 15. Danish parliament flying *Dannebrog* in honor of Prince Consort Henrik's birthday, June 11, 2006. Photograph by André Layral, Fairbanks, Alaska.

PLATE 16. *Dannebrog* flying in a summer garden plot. Courtesy of
Kolonihaveforbundet for Danmark.

sixth course

POTATOES AND DANISH
NATIONAL IDENTITY

"What would be left of Denmark without potatoes?"

AALBORG AKVAVIT WEB SITE, JUNE 29, 2005[1]

T HE DANISH POTATO COUNCIL ISSUED A PRESS release on June 7, 2000, in which it suggested that June 15 of every year, Valdemar's Day, be designated Danish National Potato Day. Valdemar's Day commemorates the day in 1219 on which the Danish national flag, *Dannebrog*, fluttered down from heaven during a battle in Estonia (see page 112) and it is, as such, an official "flag day," a day on which the Danish flag is supposed to be flown. It is also *genforeningsdag*, or "reunification day," in memory of the day in 1920 on which northern Schleswig was reunited with Denmark after its loss to Prussia and Austria in 1864.[2] A recent work titled *National Symbols in the Danish Realm* states that "[t]he most used symbol of Danishness is *Dannebrog*," and concludes that "no other object has played as important an ideological role for the Danes as *Dannebrog*."[3]

Choosing a day with such heavy national overtones to celebrate potatoes was not merely a coincidence. Indeed, the Danish Potato Council stated that "Valdemar's Day is thus on its way to being a memorial day both for *Dannebrog* and for our last, true national seasonal food." Afraid that pasta was edging potatoes out of the Danish diet, the Council continued,

the serious background for this initiative is that new eating habits have recently driven out the potato as the *Danish national dish*. Especially young people have turned their backs on potatoes.[4] [Emphasis added]

The year before, the Copenhagen daily newspaper *Berlingske Tidende* carried an article on June 6, the day after *grundlovsdagen* (Danish Constitution Day) about new potatoes, which "lay there like jewels and shone in the dark earth."[5] Constitution Day celebrates the day in 1849 when the formerly absolute Danish monarch promulgated a constitution granting universal manhood suffrage and a two-house legislature. Since 1849, with one exception in 1863, all Danish constitutions have been promulgated on June 5. This day, therefore, also has very heavy national political overtones. So, here are new potatoes, "jewels," shining on one of the most national of Danish holidays. Most Danish holidays are indeed holy days connected with the Christian calendar. Other than New Year's Day, Constitution Day is the only secular holiday in Denmark—a day that workers have off and on which shops and businesses close—as distinguished from "flag days," when the flag is flown in commemoration or celebration but work continues as normal.

Else-Marie Boyhus, the author of the newspaper article and a food historian, writes lovingly of harvesting new potatoes and preparing them for a special outdoors Constitution Day lunch.

First an open sandwich with freshly peeled fjord shrimps, next open potato sandwiches: pieces of dark rye bread, buttered with first class butter, covered with slices of [cold] boiled potatoes, sprinkled with a little salt and decorated with chives. With this, a cold beer and, in honor of the day, a cold aquavit. Lastly, a slice of bread with cheese and red & white radishes. *Beautiful and Danish.*[6] [Emphasis added]

An analysis of what the author obviously thinks of as a quintessentially Danish meal raises some interesting issues. It is June 5, Constitution Day; the lunch is outside, in the open, with any luck the sun is shining; it is close to the summer solstice and the days are long and light and lazy. The food is all Danish. The shrimps come from Limfjorden, in the north of Jutland. Rye is the staple grain. The cheese and butter are local products; Denmark is, after all, a dairy country. Beer and aquavit are also produced in Denmark; even the red and white radishes show off the Danish national colors. But potatoes? Potatoes are a relatively new import into Denmark and were initially rejected by Danish peasants. Yet somehow these "new world" products have come to be so symbolic of Denmark that the decline in their consumption can be seen as a threat to Danish identity.

Not surprisingly, Aalborg Akvavit, the best known producer of aquavit (snaps) in Denmark, also endorses the importance of potatoes on its web site.

Danes are raised on potatoes. Without potatoes our hardworking forefathers would not have had a healthy vegetable to live on here in the cold north. There probably also would not have been anything called AALBORG AKVAVIT, since potatoes have been one of the most important ingredients in the Danish production of aquavit. And, most important of all, you would not have had the pleasure of greeting the year's new potatoes with a cool glass of your favorite aquavit under the Danish summer sky . . . yes, what would be left of Denmark without potatoes? Cheers![7]

Since potatoes are the principal ingredient in Danish aquavit, it is hardly surprising that Aalborg Akvavit should support their continued production in Denmark. But there is also a nationalist tone to their text. Potatoes are connected to the past through "your hardworking forefathers" and to Denmark itself. And here again the reader is imagined as being outside, in the Danish summer, bringing one back to a Danish belief in a rural agricultural past. There is a strong nationalist component on this web page, tying Denmark together with potatoes and an agricultural past.

Further, a 1955 Danish cookbook, written in English for a foreign audience, discusses potato sandwiches. Explaining that

the sandwiches are so common that they can not even be ordered in restaurants, the author nonetheless fails to describe how to make them; after all, everyone knows how to make potato sandwiches. Even the title, "An Easy Sandwich," fails to disclose the ingredients.

There is an open sandwich which, probably, cannot be found on any printed [restaurant] menu. Perhaps it is too plain for that. Nevertheless, it is very highly prized. It is called *lard with potatoes*, and all it needs is a bit of coarse salt. If the potatoes are new, the sandwich naturally becomes still more attractive and one might honor it with a sprinkling of minced chives or parsley. But even a lone, old potato, left over from dinner, gains a certain charm when it rests in slices on an open sandwich. If there is no lard in the house one can "do" with butter.[8]

Potatoes are hardly native to Denmark; they are a product of the Americas, introduced in Denmark in the late eighteenth century and only accepted after great difficulty. Eighteenth-century Danish peasants wanted nothing to do with this strange new food, a member of the deadly nightshade family. Indeed, Laurits Minis, a pastor and civil servant, wrote in 1772 that he thought it would be easier to establish a new religion in Denmark than to introduce "*popatos*."[9]

As potatoes came to be accepted by Danish farmers as human food, they gradually became the staple carbohydrate, almost displacing the customary rye bread, though not quite. Historian Søren Mørch estimates that by the beginning of the twentieth century, "potato use was greatest in the countryside—by weight, almost as great as the use of rye bread, 1/2 kilo per day/per adult man." Potatoes were the staple warm food around which meals were prepared.[10] According to Ole Hyldtoft, in 1897, carbohydrates made up from 54 percent of the diet of Danish workers (in Copenhagen) to 61 percent (in the rural districts in Jutland). They ate "bread, porridge and potatoes, but only a little meat."[11]

This happened over the course of the nineteenth century. During this same time period, the political structure in Denmark was changing, expanding slowly to include the newly independent peasant-farmers within the political system. As these

farmers moved into political power they brought their food culture, including potatoes, with them, and as the Danish political system expanded, farmers' cultural identification with Denmark caused a parallel identification of potatoes with Denmark. Potatoes became part of the popular (*folkelig*) culture, so that eventually the new-world origin of these tubers was forgotten and potatoes became as Danish as the *Dannebrog* and Constitution Day. So, today, the decline in potato consumption can be a matter of some concern.

Eugen Weber, in *Peasants into Frenchmen*, describes the process of creating a French national identity that moved from the cities to the rural areas.

We are talking about the process of acculturation: the civilization of the French by urban France, the disintegration of local cultures by modernity and their absorption into the dominant civilization of Paris and the schools.[12]

An analogous acculturation process took place in Denmark but it went the other way, starting in the countryside, with the rural culture, and spreading throughout the country, to be absorbed by the cities. This process was helped by the widespread development of the *folkehøjskole* movement. *Folkehøjskoler*, literally "people's high schools" but more closely akin to America's community colleges, were private, live-in schools in rural areas. Not part of the official public school system, they nonetheless attracted large numbers of rural youth, who thus were able to continue their education in a more informal manner. The networks that developed among Danes who had attended the *folkehøjskoler*, participated in the cooperative movement, and been active in the various new political parties helped immensely in the dissemination of a rural, *folkelig* culture.

Potatoes were possibly first brought to Denmark in the seventeenth century by French Huguenots who settled in Fredericia, on the Jutland peninsula, but they had definitely arrived by the middle of the eighteenth century, along with *kartoffeltyskerne* ("potato Germans"), who were brought to Denmark to cultivate the Jutland moors. The Germans left; the potatoes remained. It

took a while (a century or so) before potato cultivation spread outside kitchen gardens, but by the late nineteenth century, potatoes were ubiquitous. They grew well in the sandy Danish soil, flourished in the rainy Danish climate, and were easily grown in the small plots and ditches available to the poorer farmers.[13] Additionally, they turned out to be an excellent nutritional source, supplying most vital nutrients. According to Zuckerman, one acre of potatoes can provide the annual energy and protein needs of ten people.[14]

The first mention of potatoes in a Danish cookbook was in a 1766 work by Marcus Looft, *The Royal Danish . . . Cook, Baking and Preserving Book . . . for Noble and Aristocratic Families*. The recipe calls for boiling them first, then braising them with butter, cream, bread crumbs, and nutmeg.[15] But Looft is addressing noble and aristocratic families, not peasants or common people, and it is unlikely that potatoes had yet made it into many kitchens.

First in 1785 and again in 1793, cookbook author Carl Müller addresses the Danish housewife with several recipes for potatoes—boiled, creamed, fried, with celery, and for dessert.[16] In fact, by 1793, Müller expresses approval of "potatoes . . . as products of our own country."[17] And from then through the nineteenth century, virtually every Danish cookbook contains some mention of or recipe for potatoes. A 1798 cookbook, *Education for Young Women*, includes a "way to cook potatoes so that they taste very good." Basically, the recipe calls for steaming rather than boiling potatoes, with a result "much more tasty than with *the usual method*" (emphasis added).[18] By the turn to the nineteenth century, then, cookbook authors feel that although cooks may not understand the best preparation methods, potatoes are both national and common.

Others, however, were not so sure that potatoes were already part of Danish national cuisine. In a 1788 speech to the peasants on his family property, on the occasion of issuing them hereditary land contracts, Count Christian Reventlow, privy councillor and one of the crown prince's chief advisors, said,

I see a time ahead in which the outlying fields will resemble the well-fertilized villages, the sour meadows and marshes will be changed into

productive fields . . . a time in which the cultivation of clover, *potatoes* and other useful roots *will no longer be a rarity.*[19] [Emphasis added]

Almost fifteen years earlier, Torkel Baden, manager of the Bernstorff estates during a period of agricultural reforms, wrote that when strip farming was eliminated and peasant plots consolidated, it would be possible for individual peasants to choose what to plant. Instead of the usual barley and oats, peasants would be free to experiment with such crops as potatoes, cabbage, beans, peas, tobacco, and hemp.[20] A. P. Bernstorff was to be the prime minister in the government set up by the young crown prince in 1784.[21] He was one of the leaders behind the series of agricultural and social reforms that allowed peasants to purchase title to their own land,[22] and this would indeed make it possible for individual peasant landowners to experiment with new crops, including potatoes.

What is apparent here is the hope, or intention, of expanding the cultivation of potatoes and including them in the ordinary diet of Danes. Whether or not potatoes actually were a common everyday food, by the turn to the nineteenth century they had become a part of the discussion on both agriculture and diet. The assumption underlying the attitudes of noblemen such as Reventlow and Bernstorff is that peasant farms will provide subsistence for peasant families, that they will eat what they grow. There will, perhaps, be some extra produce for sale, but most of the food will be eaten by the farmers who grow it. Discussion of "new crops" then is also a discussion of a change in diet.

From 1803 to 1808, Agronomy Professor Gr. Begtrup wrote a series of books on the condition of agriculture in Denmark. He meticulously surveyed the country, area by area, and included information on local eating habits. About peasants in Sjælland and Møn, in eastern Denmark, he wrote:

It is well-known that the Danish peasant demands much solid food; his usual food is: porridge, gruel, peas, cabbage and meat soup; in the evening he eats beef and pork; he eats a lot of bread, but no vegetables, except potatoes, which have recently started to be used.[23]

On Lolland, in southeast Denmark, Begtrup noted that the peasants ate potatoes but said, "they are good once, but are not used to save or stretch meat."[24]

Dr. Henrich Callisen, general director of the Surgical Academy in Copenhagen, also addressed Danish eating habits in 1807. About Copenhageners he wrote that their most common food was meat. He felt that both for "moral, physical and economic reasons, it would be preferable if our meat consumption could be reduced and the use of plant products increased." Among these,

there is none in Copenhagen so commonly accepted and popular as potatoes. This fruit can be found on the sybarite tables of the rich and at the beggars' poor meals. A taste for potatoes is also spreading everywhere among the country people, so that we can expect that the culture of this useful fruit will soon be common.[25]

It seems obvious from these accounts that although potatoes were beginning to spread through the country in the early nineteenth century, they were not yet as common as the "experts" hoped they would be, or as they later would become.

It was, nevertheless, during this same period that cookbook authors' assumptions expanded to include potatoes as an integral, albeit new, part of the household economy. In 1821, Christiane Rosen wrote a section on storing potatoes.

It is most common to put potatoes in a tight cellar, where they will keep without a cover. If you have no cellar, they can also be kept in the house . . . but they must be well covered. . . . The method which I think is best is to put these roots in a barrel or in boxes.[26]

In discussing methods for storing potatoes, Rosen is addressing issues of household economy as well as of food preparation. Her *Economic Housekeeping Book* assumes that potatoes are now an ordinary commodity in most homes. She presumes that there is a "common" way of keeping potatoes, although she is not certain that everyone knows the *best* way.

Writing in 1855, cookbook editor Bishop said of potatoes that "they are the most important of all vegetables used in cooking."

Despite the English-sounding name, Bishop claims to be writing for "the Danish audience" in order to provide "Danish homemakers" with new, simpler methods of cooking; moreover, the cookbook has also been vetted by "a Danish housewife." It contains seven pages on potatoes—on buying and cooking potatoes; good, bad, old, and new potatoes; large and small potatoes—and includes recipes for boiling, baking, and stuffing potatoes.[27] Devoting seven pages to potatoes indicates both their importance in the editor's mind and the editor's assumption that people need information about potatoes.

A few years later, in 1866, E. A. Scharling, a professor of chemistry, wrote, "in this country there is no longer anyone who doubts the benefits and advantages of eating good and well-cooked potatoes." He continued, "potatoes have become an everyday dish for the rich and the poor, so that it is missed when it is not served."[28]

A generation later, in 1883, Dr. Charles Emil Hagdahl connects potatoes with a housewife's moral qualities:

An excellent connoisseur maintains in full seriousness, that he can determine a housewife's moral character according to the quality of the potatoes which she serves.[29]

Although Hagdahl tries to distance himself somewhat from this sentiment, attributing it to "an excellent connoisseur," he obviously agrees enough with it to include it positively in his text. He follows this comment with a story about "another unchallenged authority" whose first question to potential chefs is, "Can you cook potatoes?"[30]

Potatoes even show up in a delightful cookbook for children from 1889, *The Best Gift for Young Girls*, with the statement that they are "to be peeled and boiled in water with a little salt until they are tender." Ulla and her sister, who are listed as the authors of the book, say that these recipes are ones that they "have tried in their play and found good." The book "is not written by an experienced housewife," but rather presumes to be by the two playmates. There is no general discussion of cooking methods or techniques, and the book contains individual recipes for the girls'

favorite foods. With little to go on, one assumes that the young readers are familiar enough with potatoes to know when they are cooked and that potatoes are common enough in the diet to be an appropriate dish for children's play.[31]

Hans Kyrre, a potato historian, quotes an unnamed source who wrote in 1887 that in order to get some "variety" into their diet, peasants "ate *Kartofler* in the morning, *Jordæbler* at noon, and *Poteter* in the evening."[32] These are, of course, three different words that all mean "potato"—*kartofler*, from German; *jordæbler* is a translation of the French *pommes de terre*, "apples of the earth;" and *poteter*, from the English potato. So, peasants "ate potatoes [German] in the morning, potatoes [French] at noon, and potatoes [English] in the evening." Kyrre's source is being ironic, of course; the reference is not to different varieties of potatoes or different methods of preparing them but rather to the pervasive use of the vegetable. The significant point is that, whatever the name, potatoes were now a staple of the ordinary Danish diet, a food one missed if it were not present daily. Potatoes had moved from being an exotic, upper-class dish to common food for ordinary people, at least in the minds of cookbook authors.

In 1901, Kristine Marie Jensen echoed Bishop, saying that,

potatoes, which are our most important root vegetable, have so many varieties, that you need to experiment in order to figure out which ones should be cooked with the skin on and which without.[33] [Emphasis added]

Quite obviously, the assumption is not only that potatoes have been completely accepted as an important element in the Danish diet, but also that cooks will be able to figure out how best to prepare different varieties of potatoes. They will have enough familiarity with the finished dish that they will understand what potatoes are supposed to taste like and when they taste best.

So, were cookbooks ahead of popular culture with their assumptions that cooks had a "usual method" for preparing potatoes? Understanding that cookbooks should be viewed as prescriptive literature, this question rests on the issue of whether prescriptive literature leads or follows. It probably does both,[34]

but in this case an understanding of cookbook audience helps to clarify the matter. Up until the mid-eighteenth century, Danish cookbooks addressed themselves to an upper class who may have had access to and been willing to experiment with these new vegetables. It was a group of upper-class reform-minded noblemen who were the earliest in advocating the use of potatoes as a way to increase peasant self-sufficiency.

Not until the late eighteenth century do cookbooks address themselves to middle-class housewives who might well have begun to use this new food in their kitchens. Some of the cookbooks are translations from other countries, which may have had an earlier potato culture. *Education for Young Women*, for instance, was translated from German, where, by the late eighteenth century, potatoes were probably more common than in Denmark.

It is first in 1837, with the publication of Mangor's *Cookbook for Small Households*, that Danish-authored cookbooks begin to address families in the lower social classes as well, who were possibly still resistant to the use of potatoes. Mangor's earliest cookbooks contain, as we have seen, many fewer potato recipes and suggestions for the use of potatoes than do later editions of her book. By the end of the nineteenth century, this resistance has faded and potatoes are now common enough to include in cookbooks for children. Their acceptance was undoubtedly helped along by the new groups of home economics teachers who promoted the use of potatoes as cheap and nutritious vegetables. That potatoes show up with increasing frequency in Danish cookbooks, attests not only to an increasing familiarity with the vegetable but also to the success of the nobles' experiment with dietary change.

The important point is that by the end of the nineteenth century potatoes have become an accepted part of the Danish diet. The question then is not so much how the change occurred, but rather how it grew to be so closely connected with the Danish national image. Appadurai, in discussing how cookbooks help in "constructing conceptions of a national cuisine," says that one device is "to inflate and reify an historically special tradition and make it serve, metonymously, for the whole."[35] Did Danes use potatoes as shorthand for their peasant traditions? In order to

explore this question, we need a discussion of nationalism and of how, when, and why national images are created, as well as a discussion of political and social changes in Denmark and the development of the Danish national state.

For those who grew up in the shadow of World War II, the standard definition of nationalism had to do with some intangible essence. People just *were* Americans, Germans, or Danes. How, therefore, could people who were born in a place called Germany, albeit in north Schleswig or *Sønderjylland* (south Jutland), still consider themselves to be Danes, as they did? Nationalism, for better or worse, was considered to be something essential to a person; we learned about "the awakening" of peoples—Germans and Italians lurking under the surface of Prussia or Savoy, just waiting to come out. Massimo d'Azeglio's 1861 comment, "we have made Italy; now we must make Italians," was treated as an amusing anecdote, certainly not seriously or literally.[36]

However, starting in the 1980s, there has been a reconsideration of the question of nationalism, which is proving d'Azeglio to have been more accurate than he perhaps knew. Benedict Anderson's highly influential book *Imagined Communities: Reflections on the Origin and Spread of Nationalism* transformed our understanding of the phenomenon. He "proposes the following definition of the nation: it is an imagined political community"[37] and refers us to Ernest Gellner's 1964 *Thought and Change*:

The central mistake committed by both the friends and the enemies of nationalism is the supposition that it is somehow *natural*. A man has a "nationality" just as he has a height, weight, sex, name, blood-group, etc. . . . Nationalism is not the awakening of nations to self-consciousness; it *invents* nations where they do not exist."[38]

Gellner and Anderson both directly attack the idea that nation states and nationalism are somehow universal and eternal. Rather, they maintain that these ideas have been constructed by human societies at specific times and for very specific reasons.

"Nationality," according to Anderson, is a "cultural artefact of a particular kind." It arose in Europe in the late eighteenth

century, due to "the spontaneous distillation of a complex 'crossing' of discrete historical forces." When "the impact of economic change, discoveries (social and scientific), and the development of increasingly rapid communications" made it historically possible for "rapidly growing numbers of people to think about themselves, and to relate themselves to others, in profoundly new ways," it became possible for groups of people—communities—to organize themselves in new ways, as nation states. Still, one of the best parts of Anderson's book is his title because it so succinctly counters the earlier image of essentialist nationalisms.[39]

Also in 1983, Eric Hobsbawm and Terence Ranger edited a collection of essays published as *The Invention of Tradition*.[40] Here again is a stunning juxtaposition. How can traditions be invented? Traditions simply *are*. They have always existed; that is what makes them *traditions*. And yet the authors in this volume convincingly argue that various "traditions" were deliberately and consciously created "to inculcate certain values and norms."[41] Hobsbawm notes that traditions are invented to establish social cohesion, legitimacy, and the indoctrination of beliefs. New traditions support the consolidation of power structures, often new, but not necessarily.[42] One need only think of the designing of national flags, national anthems, and national holidays, all of which are deliberately created by independent political units to symbolize an *essential* identity.[43] Consider the conscious creation of a European flag in 1986 for the then very new European Union.[44]

Eric Hobsbawm's 1990 work, *Nations and Nationalism since 1780*, provides the concept of nationalism with a history. Also starting where Anderson began, in the mid-eighteenth century, Hobsbawm discusses how nationalism as an ideology evolved and altered over the following centuries.[45] Whereas Anderson discusses the genesis of nationalism at a particular moment in time and place, Hobsbawm addresses the evolution of the concept over time. Early nineteenth-century romantic nationalism, for instance, was not the same as mid-twentieth-century expansionist nationalism.

Saying that the concept of nationalism changes over time

appears to be stating the obvious, because, of course, no concept or phenomenon remains static. However, the idea that nationalism is neither natural nor static does directly contradict the belief that nationalism has an essential and eternal nature that is, or was, just waiting to be awakened. Instead, we must now view nationalism as a construct, an ideology rooted in the specifics of time and place. And, by extension, this means not only that the idea of nationalism is a construct that changes over time but that specific nationalisms themselves also change over time. Thus, Danish nationalism may have meant one thing in 1864 and something quite different in 2004. It is a two-way process, in which the creation of a state helps to develop a nationalism which in turn helps to solidify the state.

In today's era of the European Union, the issue of "national identity" has become a topic of intense soul searching. As the European Union expands its authority and seeks to create a European identity, Danes are trying to understand what it means to be Danish, before and even as they relinquish their Danishness for a wider Europeanism. Recent years have seen the publication of books such as the four-volume academic *History of Danish Identity* and a more popular version, *In Search of Danish Identity*.[46] In 1999, on the occasion of the 150th anniversary of the promulgation of the first Danish constitution, several retrospective conferences were held on what it means to be Danish, and Danes continue the process of refining or redefining their identity in the current period of cultural and political flux.

If national symbols, national songs, and even national dress[47] can be invented, why not a national cuisine?[48] In *Acquired Taste*, Sarah Peterson cogently argues that French haute cuisine is largely a creation sponsored by Louis XIV in his attempt to divorce himself from the English regicides who favored the "sweet" alchemic cuisine of the middle ages.[49]

Sidney Mintz, taking a slightly different perspective, argues that it was the coming into being of centralized states that created national cuisines.

It is no secret that nations were not made in heaven, but by political and military activity. The food of the monarch's court and the court language

may be created by different processes; but the political reality of the central state is what brought them both into being, in their national manifestations.[50]

And Michael Symons, in *A History of Cooks and Cooking*, maintains that "[c]ooks are not mere victims of social forces, but intimately involved in creating them. . . . cooks maintain culture."[51]

For a tradition to function, it can not be completely artificial; it has to have some basis in known and accepted reality.[52] Danish folk costumes, for instance, had some basis in the Sunday attire of well-to-do peasants. Flags and songs often came out of a known or generally accepted past historical experience. So, Danes did, and do still, eat potatoes. Cookbooks only support and reinforce other available evidence.

In her newspaper article on "New Potatoes" Boyhus comments: "The history of the potato in Denmark is just about as old as that of the constitution."[53] Actually, the original June constitution (of which Constitution Day is a celebration) was promulgated in 1849 and potatoes, as we have seen, are somewhat older, but Boyhus's conflation of the two is telling. She sees a connection between the founding of the nation state (distinct from the old dynastic state) and the entry of potatoes into the Danish cuisine; suggesting that the two happened at the same time and are somehow intertwined.

A connection can indeed be made between the development of the Danish nation state and the use of potatoes. As peasants became independent farmers and moved into the political sphere, got elected to parliament as members of *Venstre* (the Liberal or Agrarian Party), and helped to form and create the new nation state, they brought their eating habits with them. Somewhat in the same way that the trousers, or *sans-culottes*, of the middle classes become standard dress for men in the nineteenth century, so rural eating habits in Denmark become entwined in a pattern of Danish nationalism. This theory is based on the assumption that cultural patterns and changes, be they in dress or eating habits, follow those of the groups that are either already powerful or moving into power. So, as entrepreneurial non-aristocrats in England become part of the establishment, the long pants or

trousers of these men's clothing become standard clothing for all; as independent, middle-class farmers gain economic and, eventually, political power in Denmark, they bring their food culture with them.

The other side of the argument is that since peasants were considered to be somehow closer to nature and to some "original state" of being, they were seen as the true representatives of the people (the *folk*).[54] These two views are not contradictory. Peasants, as farmers, could be members of a successful middle class, while still viewing themselves as representatives of the "original" or "natural" Danish *folk*. This has to do with self-image and with the image one wishes to portray of one's self. Danes still view themselves as somehow only a generation or so removed from "the soil."

Urban Danes still invest in small plots of land on which they can garden and grow things. That there is a connection between these summer garden plots (*kolonihaver*) and Danish nationalism was recently articulated by a professor of marketing at the Copenhagen Business School, when she spoke of a "nationalist *kolonihave* thinking" in Denmark. She meant the phrase to "as a metaphor for the celebration of national values."[55] This association can also be seen in the periodical *Havebladet* (*The Garden Paper*), which is issued by the Danish *Kolonihave* Association. A recent edition had a short article, "Remember to raise the flag," suggesting to readers that it would be a good idea to fly the *Dannebrog* "against a hopefully blue, sunshiny sky." And each issue of *Havebladet* lists upcoming flag days, as a gentle reminder.[56]

The connection between having a summer garden and growing living things in it should be obvious. Each edition of *Havebladet* includes articles about planting food and flowers, and timetables of when to plant what. Several include articles on potatoes, such as the recent "Advice on buying and planting potatoes in 2006,"[57] and one on the Danish Potato Council's competition for the most number of potatoes grown outdoors. The *Kolonihave* Association encouraged its members to compete so that "as *kolonihave* people, we can contribute to spreading knowledge about potatoes."[58] There is an interweaving here between the outdoors, farming, potatoes, and Danish nationalism. It is not specifically

articulated but it is nonetheless apparent behind the scenes and in the way in which these issues are discussed.

Myths can become very potent representations of people's beliefs about themselves. The American myth of the frontier is one such example. In this context the reality (How violent *was* the frontier? To what degree *did* it influence future American history?) is not as significant as people's perceptions of or beliefs in some mythic past. Similarly, Danes still see themselves as members of a small country, their identity tied to "the soil." They are still fighting to gain "inwardly," that which was "outwardly lost." And this, in turn, is based on their belief in their agricultural, peasant past.

Palle Ove Christiansen feels that these independent peasant-farmers were so successful in transforming their own self-image, that "other classes in Danish rural society also had to adapt to the revised cultural expectations of the farmers." Their conscious revival of "their old regional dress, folk dances, and other similar rituals for festive occasions . . . was a demonstration of class identity." The farmers' new "self-image" was based on a "haphazard mixture" of several of these elements, including the use of "mundane food."[59] This new self-image not only served to delineate farmers from peasants but also came with them into the political process as they started to assert demands for political power. By the time that the farmers were ultimately politically successful in the introduction of responsible parliamentary democracy with the so-called change of system in 1901,[60] their own self-image had become part of Danish popular culture, coterminous with a Danish self-image.

In the historical development of the modern nation state, citizens' continued acceptance of symbols and traditions plays a crucial role in the creation of the new nation. This helps people to identify with a specific area, to see themselves as part of "Denmark" or "Germany," rather than of any other unit. So one must understand the use of national flags,[61] national anthems, and even of images such as Uncle Sam in the United States or Marianne in France; these were largely "invented," but have retained immeasurable importance in defining national groups.

The Danes have a national flag, *Dannebrog*, with its national colors of red and white but, interestingly, they have never been able to agree on a single national song; thus, there are two, one from 1779 and the other from 1819.[62] There are few recognizable symbols, other than red and white, which unmistakably and universally say "Denmark" to the Danes. *Denmark: An Official Handbook*, published by the Danish Ministry of Foreign Affairs for use by foreigners, speaks only of the monarchy, *Dannebrog*, and coats of arms in the section titled "symbols."[63] Nor is there a Danish revolution to go back to, with all its possible related incidents and symbols. The Danes can and do, however, celebrate "Constitution Day."

The day after a popular demonstration in 1848 and the demand for a new form of government, the Danish monarch dissolved his absolute powers and declared that henceforth he was to be regarded as a "constitutional monarch," thus averting a possible revolution.[64] The promised constitution was promulgated a year later, on June 5, 1849, which marked the introduction of universal manhood suffrage in Denmark. All men aged 30 years or over who lived on their own, had not been convicted of a crime, and had not received economic help were now allowed to vote for *Folketinget*, the "people's" lower house of parliament. Eighty percent of the population of Denmark lived in rural areas, and the voters, were, therefore, overwhelmingly men from rural agricultural areas, accustomed to consuming their own produce, including potatoes.

But it was more than just voters who counted in this context. The important people in this situation were those who were perceived to have power and those who were moving into power; *that* was the group whose habits were emulated by others. There is a dramatic disjunct in Danish history between the class with political power and the groups with burgeoning economic power. Although there are similar disconnections elsewhere in European history, traditional Danish history often omits this phenomenon. In France, these tensions erupted in violent revolution in 1789 and in England, they took the form of a more prolonged urban industrialization process. Since Denmark experienced neither a violent revolution nor the urban industrialization of

heavy industry, the fact of agricultural industrialization with the attendant increase in the economic power in the hands of independent farmers is often overlooked. Until 1957 (*after* World War II) the majority of Danish exports continued to be agricultural products. This has tended to hide the fact that the economy had nonetheless modernized and industrialized. The majority, both of the general population and of the new entrepreneurial class, continued to live in rural areas.[65]

In the revolutionary year of 1848, the absolute Danish monarch agreed, without barricades, violent demonstrations, or blood in the streets, to relinquish power to a popularly elected assembly—thus, we have the liberal 1849 constitution, celebrated on June 5 every year. However, if one takes a step back from this nonviolent, almost anticlimactic event, it turns out that actual political power remained in the hands of the same group of propertied agricultural aristocrats and civil servants who had wielded power prior to the 1849 constitution. Indeed for almost twenty years, from 1873 to 1890, the country was run by the conservative prime minister, J. B. S. Estrup, through a series of "provisional laws" passed without reference to *Folketinget* (the lower house of parliament) but with the approval of the king and his cabinet.[66]

By 1890, *Venstre*, the Agrarian or farmers' party, had elected 74 members of the *Folketinget* out of a total of 102; together with the three Social Democratic members of parliament, they held 75 percent of the seats. Viewed somewhat differently, thirty-eight M.P.'s identified themselves as farmers of some sort (not including the six owners of manor lands). The largest group of these were independent farmers (*gårdejer*) who owned their own lands; there were twenty-nine of them. Additionally, there were six smallholders (*husmænd*), two copyholders (*fæstegård-mænd*) and one "farmer," who probably rented rather than owned his land.[67] Rural residents, therefore, were amply represented in parliament.

Estrup was finally removed in 1894 but real power did not shift to the *Folketinget* until the change of system in 1901. Thus, throughout the latter part of the nineteenth century, independent farmers, the motive economic force in the country and the majority represented in parliament, were kept out of effective

political power. By the time independent farmers were allowed into political power, they had already created a well-developed political and cultural identity, based on their political parties, rural education, the cooperative movement, and half a century of political struggle.

And potatoes had a role to play in that identity—easy to grow, nutritious, and available, they had become the standard food in rural agricultural areas. They cost little and did not have to be imported into a country that had survived the Napoleonic Wars only to lose its overseas possessions and declare bankruptcy. As independent farmers carved out their own identity, demanded and got political power, they became emblematic of the country. They brought with them many of their customs, including their food. Potatoes had by then gone from being the exotic upper-class food of the early eighteenth century to the ubiquitous peasant meal of the nineteenth century; as peasants moved up in the social and political structure, so, too, do potatoes.

By the mid-twentieth century, potatoes comprised, along with roast pork and red cabbage, *the* Danish cuisine. The official Danish government web site has a section titled "Traditions and Food," which describes "what is considered traditional Danish cuisine with dishes based on minced meat, gravy and potatoes."[68] However, by the end of the twentieth century, Danes had begun experimenting with other foods, thereby jeopardizing the importance of potatoes.

Not until things begin to change and there is fear that the known may slip away, do people consciously begin to talk about it. In the shadow of the European Union, it is not surprising that Danes are talking about their national identity. In the fear of losing their Danishness, they need first to find out what it is. So, too, as potato eating seems to be falling off, Danes identify a "potato day" to save this national dish from the inroads of pasta. Connecting potatoes with the introduction of the Danish constitution, the return of *Sønderjylland*, and the advent of *Dannebrog* is just another way of underlining how *Danish* potatoes are.

sixth intermezzo

CHRISTIANE ROSEN

COOKBOOK AUTHOR 1767–1847

WHEN SHE WAS SIXTY-NINE AND BLIND, Christiane Rosen published her autobiography. In addition to an autobiographer's desire to leave material for posterity, Rosen desperately needed the money. She had been blind for twenty-six years and thus unable to work at her previous profession of housekeeper. Instead she had supported herself by writing cookbooks. By 1836, when her autobiography appeared, she had written the four-volume *Economic Housekeeping Book*, which came out in several editions, *The Thinking Housekeeper, The Competent Housewife*, and two volumes on spring–summer and autumn preserving. She had thus been, more or less, earning her living as an author.

Rosen was born in 1767, in Køge; her father was a dyer and her mother's father had been a grocer. She was thus a member of the middle class, or the petty bourgeoisie. She says she started

school at age three and a half years and that by the age of five, she could read, knit, and darn. This is quite plausible, as there were schools that provided this kind of early training at the time.[1] She had a close relationship with her father, who taught her to read and reckon, and supervised her education. By the age of twelve, she was sewing clothes for sale and contributing to the household.

In 1781, an uncle from Norway visited and suggested taking one of Dyer Rosen's daughters back to Norway with him to help in the house. Christiane, the oldest, begged her parents to be allowed to go. She had always wanted to travel, she tells us. And so, at fourteen, she set off for Norway, alone (her uncle having apparently returned earlier). The situation in Norway did not live up to her expectations. Her uncle had married for money and the match was not an ideal one, and Christiane missed the close relationship she had had with her parents, particularly her father.

At fifteen or sixteen, she secretly got engaged to Customs Inspector Jerrild but her aunt and uncle disapproved strongly and nothing ever came of the match. Soon after, her father died and she returned to her family in Denmark. For the next twenty-six years, from 1784 until she went blind in 1810, Christiane Rosen supported herself by working as a housekeeper in several different noble households. She lists seven different places by name but never seems to have stayed more than four years at any one place, and worked for only a year or two at most places. In between positions, she lived with her mother or grandparents. In her autobiography she also mentions one six-month period in which she did private catering, being between "situations."

When she was no longer able to work as a housekeeper, she decided that she wanted to write. But this was not easy, as she could not see to write anything down and would have to hire someone to take dictation, an assistant to proofread and edit, and to deal with a printer. But all this cost money and Christiane had none. She was, however, incredibly successful in raising money in various ways and, after eight years, the first volume of her cookbook was published.

As she continued to write and publish her cookbooks over the

years, she was rarely completely healthy and in and out of public hospitals (some through others' charity, and some for which she paid), moving constantly (during the last ten years of her life, she moved every year).[2] She seems to have had an eye for publicity and arranged for regular—and free—announcements of her books in the Copenhagen daily papers.

It is rare that we get any insight into the life of women like Christiane Rosen—not noble, not well-known, lower-middle-class women who worked to support themselves. They were protected to some degree by the concept of domesticity that had emerged in the early nineteenth century, but not supported by it. Even making allowance for the fact that any autobiography comprises what the author wants us to know about herself, Rosen seems to have been an unusually strong, determined, and successful woman. She did it; blind, she survived and supported herself until she died, at the age of eighty-one.[3]

Selections from Miss Christiane Rosen's Life Story

My sight now grew weaker and weaker. I also had rheumatism in my head, but I assumed that was due to a cold, since I had no pain in my eyes. It seemed to me sometimes, when I saw some light, that there was a ring around it in all the colors of the rainbow. When close, the ring seemed to be the size of a saucer, but it grew until it was the size of a wheel when I was farther away from the light.

After a couple of months, I had to go to Friderik's Hospital, where my cousin, Johannes Rosen, was an intern. That was a great comfort to me; I remained there for a half year and suffered very much. My sight was not completely gone, but so dim that I could only distinguish objects when I lay in bed. As soon as I stood up, I was almost blind. Shortly after I left the hospital, I could walk around without a companion, but if I met someone, I couldn't tell if it was a man or a woman.

A year later, I applied for admission to Abel-Catrine's Foundation. I was granted this, but my situation did not improve much. I had a free residence and 1 rigsdaler a week, which was not very much at that time and my expenses, in comparison with others, were much greater.

My sister, Else Catrine Bauer, from Svogersløv Inn, invited me for a visit and transported me, without charge, there and back. I stayed there for 3

weeks. It was a great delight for me to listen to the peasants talk. There is just as much genius to be found under their straw hats as between golden walls. My sister took care of me with everything I could want and when I left she sent so much food along that for a long time I didn't need anything. In my hour of need, she stretched out a sisterly hand to me. It is often common that the rich sister does not recognize the poor one.

Count P. Schack gave me 10 *rigsdaler* yearly—but—to my great loss, he died in 1815.

Justice Klingberg gave me 10 to 12 *rigsdaler* yearly, until he died in May 1835. His passing was a great sorrow for me, and cost me many bitter tears.

My comfort is that God's promises do not fail, even if everything in the world goes.

In this, my hour of need, friends advised me to speak with Miss Reiersen, who received me in a most friendly manner and offered me 2 *rigsdaler* a month. I was able to draw this money uninterruptedly until her death, in 1820.

Goldsmith Ekstrøm came to the Foundation one day to hear the minister; he spoke with me and offered me, unasked, 2 *rigsdaler* monthly. This I received from him, in addition to often eating at his home, until he died.

There were 6 dyers, who also gave me something quarterly, but—when I published my books they stopped—as the proverb says, in the time of temptation—just when I needed it the most, because my expenses far outweighed my income, since I expected to publish more books. But they thought that I no longer needed it, partly because I moved out of the Foundation, and partly because I received an offer through the Poor Board of an additional 4 *marks* a week more than I needed, from the Classenske Fidei-Commis. Nonetheless, among the latter were some who were faithful and truly magnanimous, who continued voluntarily, because I was blind, to contribute to me quarterly until they died.

Dyer Holst is still alive and continues to contribute quarterly to my support. He was taught by my father.

May Providence grant you, and all of my benefactors, long life. Our Lord, who in secret sees what is granted the blind, will return it a thousand-fold, and the rich blessing of God will be your payment and you will—God willing! reap the reward for your generosity towards the blind.

Shortly thereafter, I was affected by several illnesses, a spotted fever, nerve fever and lay for 12 hours speechless; no one came or helped me in the slightest. —I had my senses, but could not move a muscle.

Coincidentally, an acquaintance, Madame Falck came to see me. I was aware of her talking and immediately got my speech back. But I was both hungry and thirsty and I didn't have a single shilling—just bread.

At my request, she got me some herring and a bottle of beer; this tasted as good as the most delicious dish.

My most important and almost only support was my cousin, Engraver Nicolai Rosen. He supported me as much as he could and was a faithful friend to me in every respect. "Poor cousin," he said, when I came to him, "You have been like a mother to me, and it is my duty to help you." If I visited him when he had no money, he asked me to send a message. Every time he gave me 3 or 4 *rigsdaler*. He died in 1812, in the fall.

. . .

Immediately afterwards, I applied to the Chancellory for a portion of the [Classenske] grant which my cousin, deceased Engraver Nicolai Rosen, had received, as I believed that none of our other relatives were more needy than I.

In April, 1813, I was told by Inspector Bauman of the Common Hospital, that there was an answer to my application, but I wasn't told how much I was to be given, just that I would receive 4 *marks* more weekly than I had.

I rejected this and requested that I be paid my grant quarterly, as were others who received grants. When that was denied, I said that I would leave the Foundation, in hopes that I would thereby receive what I was entitled to.

I was called in several times by the Director of the Poor Board and asked what I would live on if I left the Foundation, since what I had been granted was completely insufficient. My answer was, "God, who has taken care of me until now, will not let me, since I am blind, remain in want." Shortly thereafter, I received orders to move. I didn't know what I would do, as I was sick and without money, so I went to the Common Hospital where I was put into a room for which one had to pay. Here I used the money I had with difficulty saved. I was often asked why I would not take the offered grant. My answer remained the same—that I wanted to dispose freely over what I was granted, as did other grant recipients.

My first decision was to publish a cookbook, which I had been thinking about since I was 11. But I couldn't do that here, and if I had mentioned it, everyone would think I had lost my senses, because all would have believed it to be impossible for me, as blind.

By so consistently rejecting the money, the Directors believed that I was not fully competent—but—before they would attest to that, I was, in the presence of a second Director and other officials, asked several questions in order to determine if I had the full use of my mind. These questions I answered so well, that it was determined that I was completely competent in the use of my mind. It was a priceless blessing that I was under the protection of the Poor Board at that time. They worked hard for me, strived manfully both for and with me; they were my secret friends. Therefore, I wish to give the Board my most sincere and respectful thanks.

Due to my sickness, I remained there for two years.

. . .

After a time, I got better and had so much strength that I could begin to go out on my own.

A young sailor met me and offered me 5 *rigsdaler*, but—even though I owned nothing—I didn't want to accept his gift, unless he told me who he was. He gave my companion the 5 *rigsdaler* and asked her to give them to me, which she did. Shortly thereafter, I met someone with whom I had worked at Count Bille Brahe's. He started to talk with me and gave me 5 *rigsdaler*.

The next day he brought me 10 *rigsdaler* from his master. Now I thought about leaving the hospital. So I went out and met an elderly lady who gave me some cash. With God's gracious help, I was now able to carry out my plan and contacted an acquaintance who agreed to receive me after I left the hospital and, to be sure of a room, I paid a half year's rent in advance.

The day before I was to move, the people I was to live with still hadn't moved, so my money was returned, but now I was homeless. This was terrible for me, blind as I was.

I remembered a woman where I had once roomed when I was unemployed, so I went there. She received me in a very friendly manner and the next day, I moved in. But it was very uncomfortable as there was no stove, so I didn't have any heat. Still, I stayed there for a half year. Now I approached a friend and we agreed with a widow to rent me a room. I paid her a quarter year's rent, 15 *rigsdaler*.

Now I was calm and even happy, so I could begin to work, which is my greatest joy. In May 1818, I published a subscription plan for my first volume. I went up to the offices of *Berlingske Statstidende* with my plan and was not only fortunate to have my plan printed for free, but also every

time I have published something and several times a year for all the time I have been publishing. I can truthfully say that was the strongest marketing incentive and therefore I would like to extend my most sincere and warmest thanks to all concerned.

A message came from the offices of *Dagen* that they would print my plan and since then everything which I published has often been included in *Dagen*, as long as Justice Didericksen was editor. Thus my publications were well known and as a consequence, sold better. After his death, the inclusions were less often—and—now only a single time.

I needed a copyist. I advertised in *Adresseavisen*, but no one responded. After a long time, a man was recommended to me who didn't have the time to write it out for me himself, but offered to read it, for pay, and to convey it to the publishers. I hired a boy, to whom I dictated, and it went very well, since for several years I had been thinking this over. In my blind condition, I was fortunate to have an excellent memory, which stood me in such good stead, that with the sales I continue to have, I must consider myself fortunate, as a publisher. But in order to carry this out, I needed money, in addition to which I had large debts.

About this time I met Brewer Schou, who was generous and unselfish, and he lent me 70 *rigsdaler* without contract, guarantee or collateral. This was a noble act, which deserves public notice. Now I was able to publish the first volume; it came out in 1818, and since I had over 100 subscribers I was able, with its publication, not only to pay the printer, who had the list of subscribers as surety, but even Schou was paid, although it was left to those who were in charge, to pass out the books and collect the money. I gave 100 *rigsdaler* to my assistant (although he had to pay the person who had copied it himself). Now I thought of the second volume—but—how much more a blind person uses than a sighted person. I needed money, if I should accomplish anything. I was now so fortunate that wood dealer Jørgensen lent me 100 *rigsdaler*. In order to accomplish this as quickly as possible, I had to, at the advice of my assistant, hire a student as copyist, in order to lighten his work, since, due to his own business, he could not write out the clean copy. But he continued to read it over and deal with the printer. This went so quickly that the second volume came out the same year—but—my debts were now so large and I was not as fortunate with subscriptions, that I had no money. So, no matter how much I wanted to, I could only pay the printer. I fought as well as I could against adversity and would like to thank those generous people who took care of me, as

blind. Without them it would not have been possible for me to get what was necessary to maintain life. Sales were indifferent.

I published a subscription plan for a third volume, but the few who signed up gave me little hope for sales and I had so many debts. I couldn't remain unemployed, so I considered publishing a book on preserving, but since it was late summer in 1819, it was necessary to publish one on fall preserves first. The next spring, therefore, I published one on spring and summer preserves. These had good sales, but as an honest and well-informed man, Jørgensen was patient and accepted repayment gradually when I had the money.

Sales of the first volume went so well that it was almost sold out.

My copyist died.

The Lord provided for me and my assistant found me another student who, without payment, at my dictation, got not only the third and fourth volumes, but also the first volume, expanded and improved ready for the printer. Since there weren't enough subscribers to pay the printer, both the student and my assistant stood as guarantors and all three parts came out in 1821. Now I believed, that since the work was complete, I would have many sales—nonetheless—the sales were slow and the large expenses I had incurred gave me much concern. My gracious supporters helped me and I never neglect to include in my prayers the generous charity which they gave me.

Sales began to pick up and since I now had four volumes, the income was larger, so I was able, little by little, to pay off the large expenses which the publication of the third volume had occasioned, and I have since been fortunate.

Since there was no prospect to publish a second edition of the second volume, I send out a subscription plan for The Thinking Housekeeper, which came out in 1824.

. . .

On account of sickness and falling sales, I was so anxious that I felt I had to repeat my application for a [Classenske] grant; I received 60 rigs-daler in one sum, in 1827, and have since then received the grant. Time passed, and with the guarantee of my assistant, the second edition of the second volume was printed that same year. After several requests for an alphabetic index of all four volumes, I decided to publish one, even though it would not make money. I owed it to the many who had bought the whole work. It was published in 1828; but I paid for it myself.

Now sales went well, but the result was that the first volume's second edition was soon sold out. Now I had to think about a new edition. I had no money and through the papers tried unsuccessfully to borrow some. I decided, therefore, to go to Popp's Office, where the first volume's third edition had been printed in 1832, and to ask Mrs. Popp to keep the inventory until it had been fully paid for.

At my application, the Directors for *Adresse Comptoirets Efterretninger*, agreed in 1832, to give me free advertising three times quarterly. Not only is this a large savings, but also a distribution of everything I've published, so I would like to tender my most dutiful and humble thanks.

Most people believe, because they see how frequently I advertise what I publish, that I must be putting away money, but they don't realize that my expenses are greater than others and often outweigh my income. Yes! if I could have just one quarter in which my expenses were no greater than what I needed for my daily living, then I wouldn't worry when I publish something.

In 1833 the third edition of *Spring and Summer Preserves* was published.

In 1834, I published *The Competent Housewife*.

. . .

1836–February 20, I am 69 years old. It gladdens me that I can still serve my fatherland.

From the writing of a certain woman from ancient times, I repeat a couple of words: I walk only poorly in the world, but decorated and ornamented enough, if only my heavenly and earthly judge is satisfied.

RESPECTFULLY,

CHRISTIANE ROSEN,

DAUGHTER OF DECEASED DYER ROSEN, IN KØGE

COPENHAGEN IN FEBRUARY, 1836

PLATE 17. Marinated herring for a cold sandwich (smørrebrød) with boiled egg. Courtesy of Danish Lutheran Churches in British Columbia.

PLATE 18. Frikadeller with red cabbage. Courtesy of Danish Lutheran Churches in British Columbia.

PLATE 19. Cold potato sandwich. Courtesy of Aalborg Akvavit.

PLATE 20. Roast pork with red cabbage, caramel potatoes, and a side dish of boiled potatoes. Courtesy of Danish Lutheran Churches in British Columbia.

seventh course

HOW RECIPES CHANGE

EVERAL DISHES HAVE CONTINUED AS PART OF THE
Danish kitchen over the centuries. In some cases, although the
names remain the same, the ingredients or method of preparation changes. In others, there is little change at all and elements of the medieval kitchen continue to the present day.
Marinated herring and beef à la mode are good examples of the
latter, non-changing type of recipe. *Frikadeller*, a kind of Danish meatball, and *rød grød*, literally, "red pudding," are examples of how dishes can change over time, yet keep the same
name. Other recipes come and go, such as those for bread,
although the consumption probably remains fairly static. New
ingredients, such as potatoes or chocolate, show up in recipes
or menus. Availability of kitchen help could change menus and
affect recipes. Prior to the advent of mechanical cooking equip-

ment, labor-intensive dishes, such as those involving extensive cutting or chopping, would probably be limited to those households that had kitchen help.

This chapter is mostly a chronological listing of recipes, showing how some standard Danish dishes have either changed or remained static over the course of the past few centuries. The focus is on herring, *frikadeller*, beef à la mode, potatoes, and *rød grød*, all still standards in today's Danish kitchen.

HERRING

Anon., *Cookbook*, 1616

TO COOK HERRING

....

I. Salted herring is soaked overnight.
II. When it is soft, hang it to dry, fill it with onions, prick it with a knife and then roast it on a grill.
III. Put barley or oats to soak overnight in milk, blend it with pepper or coriander or small raisins, so that it is mixed together as a porridge. Cut the herring along its side and fill it with the porridge, tie it with string. It has a distinctive taste.[1]

Weckerin, 1648, has the same recipe.[2]

Anna Elisabeth Wigant, *An Aristocratic Lady's Cookbook*, 1703

FRESH HERRING

....

Clean and dry the herring / hang them up / let them dry; fry them on a grill / remove the skin / put on a platter / add a spoonful of butter / and the juice of a lemon / cook it well / add grated nutmeg / and put it on another platter.[3]

Carl Müller, *New Cookbook*, 1785

MARINADE FOR FRIED EEL, HERRING . . . TO BE SERVED COLD

For this you need to parboil the following: half wine vinegar and half water, some whole peppercorns, a little dill, some bay leaves, some whole onions, a little chopped or sliced horseradish; and when this is, as said, parboiled, then pour it on the fried fish.[4]

Christiane Rosen, *Economic Housekeeping Book*, vol. 1, 2nd ed., 1821

TO MARINATE FRIED FISH

In wine vinegar and water, equal parts of each, cook bay leaves, some whole onions, horseradish cut in slices, and a little whole pepper, and when this is cooked and cold, it is used with some dill to pickle the cold fish.[5]

Madame Anne Marie Mangor, *Cookbook for Small Households*, 1837

HERRING

[Herring] are best in the spring and after harvest; they should not still be alive, but when they are fresh, the palates should be red, clear and stiff. Scrape off the skin. Boiled, they are eaten with cold horseradish in cream or with vinegar and butter. They can be fried like eel, just with a little more butter, and eaten with vinegar to which has been added a little butter and pepper. They can be cooked for soup or jelly, which can be seen from the accompanying directions. [No directions given.] If you will smoke herring, then treat it like eel, but hang it for a shorter period in the smoke. It is not eaten with vinegar, but with vegetables, such as beans or potatoes.[6]

The same recipe also appears in the 14th edition, from 1865.

Sørine Thaarup, *Cookbook for Town and Country Households*, 1868

COOKED HERRING, WHICH IS EATEN COLD

....

Vinegar, Salt,
Bay leaves

When the herring are washed and cleaned, take a pan, add water and salt, bay leaves, some vinegar, put it over a fire and when it boils, add the herring. Take a deep platter and put the herring in it as they are cooked, and continue this way until you are finished. You must always make sure that the herring lie flat on top of each other on the platter, so that they don't fall apart. When they are all cooked, pour the soup in which they have been cooked, over the herring in the platter, remove it to a cold place. Eat with vinegar and pepper.[7]

Laura Adeler, *Illustrated Cookbook for City and Country*, 1893

HERRING

....

[Herring] are used mostly salted, smoked or in jelly, but can also be boiled or fried. They are cleaned as usual and served boiled with peeled potatoes and sour butter sauce. If they are to be fried, after they are cleaned, make some slices across the fish, sprinkle with salt, after which they should sit for 2–4 hours. Then they are dried, dipped in beaten egg, turned in breadcrumbs mixed with flour and fried in shortening. They are served on a platter with vinegar.[8]

Kristine Marie Jensen, *Frk. Jensens Cookbook*, 1901

MARINATED HERRING

....

Salted or pickled herring are equally useable. The latter doesn't usually have to be soaked, whereas salted herring should be soaked overnight in milk. When they are skinned and cleaned, cut off the head and tail; the herring is split down the back and the bones and guts removed. The half herring is cut across in small pieces which are laid together again and

placed with the skin side up when they are served. The herring is sprinkled with a little sugar and ground white pepper, and covered with thin slices of onion. Vinegar is poured over them some hours before they are served.[9]

Asta Bang, *Open Sandwiches and Cold Lunches*, 1955

In cities only very few housewives pickle their own herrings. They buy them at the delicatessen store, or perhaps from a grocer, because space conditions in an apartment rarely permit keeping large stores on hand.

But if one does have a cellar it is pleasant having one's own tub of herrings. And the trouble of pickling them is negligible in contrast to the many uses to which you can put them.[10]

COMMON MARINATED HERRINGS

Steep kippered herrings. In olden days they were usually soaked in milk but now water is used most frequently, and if they are good, fat herrings water is just as good. Many housewives make the mistake of soaking them too long but a watery herring is disappointing; of course, salt may be added to the marinade later on, but that does not make the herrings any the more delectable. If the kippered herring is very salty it, nevertheless, should be sufficiently soaked after about 8 hours in a good, roomy bowl of water. A couple of hours before they are to be used skin and clean them, cut them in fillets and lay them in a marinade of vinegar, sugar, pepper and plenty of onions. Just before serving them take them out of the marinade and place them, overlapping each other, on a platter; garnish with onion rings.[11]

Although these recipes do change over the course of the three centuries covered, there are continuities to be traced as well. Starting in 1785, the recipes tend to use vinegar, horseradish, pepper, bay leaves, dill, and, often, onions. They frequently call for frying or boiling the fish first, and then salting or pickling it. By and large, though, the tastes have not varied.

FRIKADELLER

In connection with an exhibition put on by the National Museum in Copenhagen in 1984, Mette Skougaard wrote that *frikadeller*, a kind of Danish meatball, were not served until the late nineteenth century with the advent of mechanical meat grinders.[12] Actually, *frickedeller* show up as early as 1703, in Anna Elisabeth Wigant's *An Aristocratic Lady's Cookbook*. She uses lamb rather than the pork, which became common later, but calls for "cutting it into pieces and chopping them very small."[13] Of course, the "aristocratic lady" probably had servants to do her chopping for her. The anonymous author of *Education for Young Women*, from 1796, actually has two recipes for *frikandeller*, both of which require the cook to "chop lean veal."[14] Rosen's recipe for *fricadeller* says, "one may use various kinds of fresh meat, either separately or mixed together, such as beef, veal, lamb or poultry, just do not mix wild and domesticated meat together." Meat should be "chopped very fine."[15] All of these predate mechanical meat grinders. Although there is a change in the spelling of the dish's name and the meat used, the basic recipe for a chopped meat dish remains constant.[16]

Anna Elisabeth Wigant, *An Aristocratic Lady's Cookbook*, 1703

MEATBALLS (FRIKANDELLER)

....

Take fresh lamb thigh / cooked or raw/ cut it in pieces and chop them very small / add coriander / four eggs, crumbled Dutch rusk / finely chopped parsley / pepper and salt / some well melted butter / a little finely chopped suet / ground cardamom / mix this together with your hands / take some cheesecloth / make small sections the size of half a hand / put a little chopped meat in each section / pull the cloth over it / so it is the length of a finger / when it is cooked, pour the soup over it / or use browned butter / as you wish.[17]

Anon, *Education for Young Women*, 1796

MEATBALLS (FRIKANDELLER)

....

Finely chop lean veal with beef marrow, or the fat of veal kidney, spice with salt, pepper and ground nutmeg; mix this all well together and make small oval balls, wrap it in net and grill or bake them until brown in butter. Then pour some good wine and bouillon over, spice with fine herbs and lemon peel and let them cook some more. They are served as a side dish with a ragout, a sauce, or with seafood.[18]

MEATBALLS ANOTHER WAY

....

To the mixture above, add wheat [bread] crumbs, which have soaked in cream, 3 whole eggs and 3 egg yolks. Make oval balls of this, dip in egg white and cook in boiling water. Remove and fry in butter. For gravy, take a little butter, some bouillon and wine, let it come to a boil, and when they are served, pour this gravy over them.[19]

C. Jacobsen, *New Cookbook*, 1815

MEATBALLS (FRECADELLER)

....

Take the minced mixture of beef or veal, from chapter 8, roll it into suitable sized balls, press them flat, score them lightly with a knife, and fry them in browned butter. Serve with a brown gravy or vegetables.[20]

MINCED BEEF MIXTURE

....

Take tender meat, scrap the gristle off, chop it together with onions and suet; pound a little nutmeg and cloves in a mortar, add the meat, pound it for a while, add some wheat [white] bread, which has soaked in milk, together with a little butter; pound it again; add 3 or 4 eggs, depending on how much there is, salt and some cream. If your mortar isn't big enough, just pound the meat, put it on a platter and work the remaining ingredients into it. To make the mixture really nice, as for roulettes, add fewer egg whites than egg yolks.[21]

Christiane Rosen, *Economic Housekeeping Book*, vol. 1,
2nd ed., 1821

MEATBALLS (FRICADELLER) OF ROAST OR BOILED MEAT

....

For this one can use different kinds of fresh meat, either separately or mixed
together as, for instance, beef, veal or lamb together with poultry, just do
not mix wild and domestic meat together. The meat is best when there is little fat; it is chopped as finely as possible and mixed together with some
peeled wheat germ, which has soaked in cold water, dried and baked in butter as if for rolls; 2, 3 or 4 eggs, some ground cloves, finely chopped onions,
a little ground nutmeg and possibly a little stock. When the mixture has
been blended well together, it is made into either round, long or heart-
shaped figures and baked in butter, either in a tart pan or a covered casserole with heat both above and underneath. When the meatballs are light
brown, they are served either with cherry sauce or a sharp gelatin sauce.

If the meat is lean, the wheat germ can be baked in more butter than if
it is fatty.[22]

Madame Anne Marie Mangor, *Cookbook for Small
Households*, 1837

MEATBALLS (FRICADELLER)

....

[Meatballs] are made of minced meat and fish—the mixture should be
thicker than for dumplings—taken with a spoon dipped each time in cold
water and laid on the pan in simmering shortening, on which they are
fried with a steady heat, not too fast to be brown without being cooked
through.[23]

Anon., *Latest Cookbook for Middle Class Households*,
1849

MEATBALLS (FRICADELLER) OF MEAT

....

5–6 PORTIONS

2 Lb. of meat is scrapped and finely chopped. Into this is mixed 4 spoonsful of white flour, 2–3 eggs, and whole milk or cream, as much as the mix-

ture can hold so that it doesn't become too thin. Onions, pepper and salt are added to taste. With this mixture one can fill a cabbage head, which is hollowed out, filled, covered, bound with string and either cooked or roasted in a pot with enough butter and water.[24]

Kristine Marie Jensen, *Frk. Jensens Cookbook*, 1901

MEATBALLS (FRIKADELLER) OF BOILED OR ROASTED MEAT

....

FOR 10 TO 12 PEOPLE

A quarter pound fatty, smoked pork is finely chopped with 1 lb. boiled or roasted meat and 1 onion. When the mixture holds together, it is further worked with a chopping knife, 10 øre white bread, cut in slices, which had been dipped in milk and soaked, covered, for one hour. Finally, salt, pepper and 4 to 5 eggs are chopped and added, so that the mixture holds together. Make balls with a spoon, which is dipped in egg and bread crumbs and form them round or long, but flat, because otherwise they will take too long to be cooked through. They are fried in shortening over a slow fire and served with a sharp, brown gravy and boiled macaroni or other vegetables.[25]

Ingeborg Suhr, *Food*, 1965

MEATBALLS (FRIKADELLER)

....

PREPARATION TIME: 1 HOUR. FOR 6 PEOPLE

Chopped meat from 1/2 kg meat
Fat

Preparation of the chopped meat, see page 171.

The fat is warmed in a pan or pot. The mixture, which must not be too loose, is shaped into large balls with a spoon. It is fried for ca. 5 min. on each side until they are *light brown and cooked through*. If you make a larger portion, put the meatballs, after they are browned, in a baking pan in a warm oven for ca. 20 min. at a low temperature.[26]

CHOPPED MEAT MIXTURE I

....

PREPARATION TIME: 1 HOUR. FOR 6 PEOPLE

CALORIES: 1451   1 PERSON: 242 CAL.

1/2 kg tender meat
1–2 eggs or egg whites
ca. 5 dl. milk
ca. 100 gr. flour
pepper, chopped onion

Remove the gristle and membranes from the meat and cut it into strips, then put it through the meat chopper 2–6 times, together with salt. Add egg, milk and flour and mix until it thickens; add the meat little by little. Finally, add, if necessary, more salt, a knife end of pepper, together, if you wish, with just a little onion juice or chopped onion. A test meatball is cooked to see if the mixture has the right taste and consistency.

You can add 1 part boiled, mashed potatoes or rolled oats to 2 parts meat.[27]

Although the ingredients used in *frikadeller* change over the centuries, the dish remains basically the same. Although the meat changes from lamb to veal to beef to the generic "meat," it is always chopped, bound with a mixture of eggs, milk, and bread, shaped into balls, and cooked. The choice of spicing varies over time; by Madame Mangor's time, spices other than onions and pepper seem to have died out, reflecting the general falloff of spices in the Danish kitchen. But since *frikadeller* is a dish that can be stretched whether it has more fillings or less, the specifics of meat and other additives should probably not be taken too literally.

BEEF À LA MODE

Anon., *Cookbook*, 1616

BEEF WITH SAUCE
....

Take good beef / press it / until it is beautifully soft and tender / peel some
white onions / as many as you think / chop them finely / put them through
a sieve / with wine or vinegar. When the meat is cooked / serve it / but don't
forget the salt.[28]

Anna Elisabeth Wigant, *An Aristocratic Lady's Cookbook*, 1703

BEUFF À LA ROYALE
....

Take a piece of beef / as for game, pound well with a wooden hammer /
lard with a finger-thick piece of lard / which has soaked in salt and ground
pepper / let it sit for 24 hours in vinegar / prick holes in the meat and put
whole cloves in each hole / let it dry in a Halland stone pan / and let it cook
slowly from the morning to the evening over a slow fire / turn it occasionally / so that it does not burn / and let it keep cooking under a closed lid /
so that the sauce remains / when it has cooked enough / pour a glass of
spirits over it / this makes the meat tender.[29]

Marcus Looft, *Cook, Bake and Preserving Book*, 1766

BEUF A LA MODE
....

For this one uses a piece cut from the inside thigh, as big or small as you
need it, pound it well until it is tender. Lard it well with pieces of lard cut
long and thick, which have first been rubbed with salt and pepper; then
put some butter in a pan and let it brown. Brown the meat well on both
sides, put it in a pot or pan and add enough water to cover the meat. Then
take some whole onions, stuck with cloves, bay leaves, a little pepper and
a piece of ginger, all added at once. Cover it and let it cook slowly until it
is done. Finally, when it is completely tender, add some brown flour and if
the gravy is still too thin, let it cook over a slow fire as much as it needs.

Add some salt. When it is served, put the gravy through a strainer, so it is smooth. Whoever can tolerate it, can add lemon, wine vinegar and a little sugar, which is good for a change, but *au naturelle* is the best.[30]

J. C. Pelt, *Cookbook*, 1799

BOEUF À LA MODE

....

You usually use the inside thigh of the beef, pound it well. Put the meat in a ceramic pot, in which there is a half pot of water, some wine vinegar, a couple of pieces of whole ginger, salt, bay leaves. After that, cover it well and set it over the fire. When it begins to boil, take it from the fire, and put it over a steady coal fire, so that it just simmers. After three hours, check if it is tender enough, then put it over a hotter fire. The sauce must be so short [boiled down], that it will begin to fry. Then add water, soy sauce, lemon juice. Cook it together with some crumbled rusks and serve.[31]

Christiane Rosen, *Economic Housekeeping Book*, vol. 2, 1818

TO MAKE BOILED BEUF À LA MODE

....

Remove the fat, put the Beuf à la Mode, with bouillon which hasn't been diluted, in an appropriately sized casserole or bouillon kettle; put it over a hot fire and skim it well. Before it starts to boil, add a bouquet of pot-herbs, a piece of ginger and some whole peppercorns. Let it boil for 16 to 20 minutes. Remove it to another casserole with a piece of butter and a little gelatin, or bouillon if there's no gelatin. Let it cook slowly and turn it often until it is tender. Then it is ready to serve.[32]

Madame Anne Marie Mangor, *Cookbook for Small Households*, 1837

BOEUF À LA MODE

....

A piece of inside thigh, about 5 pounds (it is good if it has hung for several days after being slaughtered), is pounded well on all sides and covered with cut up pieces of shallots, preserved fat smoked pork, which has been

cut into rather thick pieces and rolled in ground pepper, allspice, cloves, ginger and salt. A piece of butter is browned in a casserole or pot, not too big, so that the gravy will not boil away. The meat is seared, having first been rubbed with the same spices in which the pork is rolled, until it is brown, then hot water is poured over it, little by little, until it covers the meat. Cook with a little bay leaf, whole pepper, some cloves and an onion, covered, for 4 to 5 hours. Then a couple of spoonsful of flour in water and a little soy sauce is added. When the meat is served, sieve the gravy into a gravy boat.[33]

Laura Adeler, *Illustrated Cookbook for City and Country*, 1893

BOEUF Á LA MODE

A tender, boneless piece of inner thigh is well pounded on all sides, the gristle is cut away. Then it is larded with strips of smoked, half lean and half fatty pork, the size of a little finger, with peeled, cut shallots. Ground ginger, pepper, cloves, allspice, finely minced onion and salt have been well mixed together and the meat is rubbed with this. The pork is also rubbed with these spices before it is used on the meat. The meat is larded on all sides. A not too large pot is put over the fire with butter, which is browned, and when it begins to turn brown, the meat is put in and browned slowly on both sides. Then add water to the pot, so that it just covers the meat, add a few bay leaves, some peppercorns, a couple of onions and a beer glass filled with red or port wine. It is cooked for about 4 hours, until the meat is tender. The liquid is poured off; the fat is skimmed off and the remainder is cooked down over a strong fire to about half. Add salt to taste. It can also be thickened with butter and flour.[34]

Kristine Marie Jensen, *Frk. Jensens Cookbook*, 1901

BØF À LA MODE

6 LB. TOPSIDE. FOR 12 PEOPLE

Inside thigh, which should not be freshly slaughtered, is pounded on all sides and pricked with a sharp knife and covered with preserved shallots and very thick pieces of lard, which have been rolled in a mixture of salt,

ground pepper, allspice and cloves. The meat is rubbed with the spices. It is browned in butter or shortening in a pan and thereafter covered with water with coloring sauce. It is cooked, covered, for 3 hours and turned during the cooking. The gravy is made as usual with butter, flour and gelatin. When served, a little of the gravy is poured over the meat. The rest is served in a gravy boat. Boiled or mashed potatoes and either cucumbers or pickles can be served as an accompaniment.[35]

Of the several varieties of beef recipes in these books, Beef à la Mode was chosen because it is a constant, showing up in almost every cookbook over the course of the centuries. It is a fairly simple recipe, and changes little with time. One lards the beef with some form of fatty pork or bacon, then boils it for several hours until tender, together with onions or shallots and a fairly constant bouquet of spices—cloves, allspice, bay leaves, ginger, and, of course, salt and pepper. A gravy is then made from the liquid in which the beef has cooked. What distinguishes this dish from a stew is the lack of any vegetables other than onions, and those are added probably more for flavor then to stretch the meat or create a one-pot meal.

Although pork is a staple of the current Danish diet, beef has a long history in Denmark. Indeed, there was a period in early modern Danish history when the country was a chief exporter of cattle and cattle products. According to Else-Marie Boyhus, "pig's meat was not a basic food in [early modern] noble kitchens, but an aid for larding and in braising."[36] The emphasis on pork is relatively new, dating from the nineteenth century, when a combination of small farms and cooperative slaughterhouses turned pig raising into a profitable venture. Pork dishes, although they have a long history behind them, do not appear in suggested menus until the mid-nineteenth century.

POTATOES

Marcus Looft, *Cook, Bake and Preserving Book*, 1766

"EARTH APPLES" OR POTATOES

First wash the potatoes and peel them clean, then boil them with a little water and salt. But be careful, as they get tender quickly. Pour the water off and put the potatoes in a broad pan or in a deep dish with a piece of butter, a little sweet cream, crushed rusk, a little salt and nutmeg. Let it simmer until they are good and as they should be.[37]

Carl Müller, *New Cookbook*, 1785

SUGAR POTATOES TO STEW AND BOIL

When they have been well thawed in water, boil a little in water. When the skin is removed, cook them in cream, flour, butter and a little salt. When they have boiled a little, a large piece of clear butter is stirred in. Then they can be served.

SUGAR POTATOES WITH CELERY

They are treated as described. After they have been peeled, they are cut in pieces, with an equal number of pieces of celery. The potatoes and celery are cooked together with some strong bouillon or stock, flour, butter and a little salt. After they've been cooked, thicken with cream, butter and a couple of egg yolks and then serve.

FRIED POTATOES

After the potatoes have been treated as above, they are fried in brown butter and grated sugar, until they are light brown, and then served.

TO MAKE DESSERT POTATOES

Well thawed potatoes are put in a tart pan, which has first been sprinkled with salt, covered with salt and baked until they are soft. They are then served in a napkin for dessert.[38]

Anon., *Education for Young Women*, 1796

POTATO TART

For this you need 3 pounds of potatoes, 2 pounds of sugar, 24 eggs and the grated peel of 2 lemons. The potatoes are cooked, but not too soft; when they are cold and peeled, they are grated with a grater. Put the egg yolks in a big pot and stir well together with grated sugar and lemon peel; add the potatoes, stirring constantly. Whip the egg whites, add them last, just before the form is put in the oven. The form should be well buttered, add the batter and bake in the oven or a tart pan. But the pan should not be opened until the tart is tender, otherwise it will fall. Bake for a good hour with slow heat.[39]

Christian Olufsen, *Economic Annals*, 1797

THE BEST WAY TO COOK POTATOES

When potatoes are boiled in water, they fall apart and the water removes the sugar which they contain, so they are deprived of much of their good taste. Potatoes should therefore be cooked in the steam of boiling water, which will suffice to penetrate them without destroying the sugar substance. For this, the easiest equipment is a cyclindrical tin kettle with a tight-fitting lid, which is closed with a couple of hooks. In a colander which reaches halfway down the kettle and hangs from three hooks from the top of the kettle, put the potatoes. The kettle is filled with water which reaches the bottom of the colander, and put over the fire. The lid is closed tightly. The steam which comes up from the water will in the enclosed space soon cook the potatoes sufficiently.

This method of cooking is common in England and the described equipment is used especially in Lancashire. In other parts of the country, there are other cooking machines, which are more complicated without being better.[40]

Anon., *Education for Young Women*, 1798

A WAY TO BOIL POTATOES, SO THAT THEY ARE VERY GOOD-TASTING

Put a kettle or a casserole over the fire, make sure it has a lid that fits tightly. Into this put water; put in a sieve or the bottom of a basket, about three or four inches above the bottom of the kettle, and put the potatoes on top.

The steam from the boiling water makes the potatoes tender and this method uses much less hot water, less fuel and the potatoes are, within a short time, tender and much more tasty than cooked in the usual way.[41]

J. C. Pelt, *Cookbook*, 1799

STEWED POTATOES

Potatoes are cooked in water with some salt; after they have cooked enough, peel and then cut in pieces; add a little cream, ground pepper, a piece of butter and some salt to a pan; then cook them a little until they are done. You can also prepare them with celery, in a meat soup put pieces of cut-up celery buds and some nutmeg. The celery buds are cooked until soft, add the potatoes to this celery sauce; add a piece of butter and bring to a boil.

POTATOES ANOTHER WAY

Take some fat pork, cut it in cubes, a handful of onions, cut in strips. Fry the pork until light brown, add the onions and fry with the pork; then add peeled potatoes, some water, a little mustard and salt, vinegar. Let it boil for five minutes and serve.

ANOTHER WAY

Potatoes, which are to be fried in butter, should be the smallest ones. After they are thawed, boil and peel them, put a pan with butter over the fire. After the butter is well browned, add the potatoes and shake the pan while frying. As soon as they are light brown, add a little grated sugar; fry and shake.

POTATOES WITHOUT BUTTER

Add a finger of salt to a tartpan, add the potatoes and then cover with a layer of salt. This way you can roast them in a tartpan with heat over and under them; test often to see if they are done. Serve on a platter covered with a napkin.[42]

Christiane Rosen, *Economic Housekeeping Book*, 1818, 1821

Christiane Rosen included one potato recipe in each of her four volumes; the first three are variations on boiling different-sized potatoes; the last includes a glazing process as well.

TO BOIL POTATOES

Large potatoes are washed, peeled, cut in pieces and should sit in cold water for 1 hour before they are cooked. The water is poured off and the potatoes are put in a pot or a casserole together with some finely chopped onions and their own water or a salty soup to cover. They are boiled over a hot fire, stirred a couple of times while boiling and, when they are tender, add some butter, if the season is right, a little parsley.[43]

BOILED POTATOES

One takes potatoes the size of walnuts, rinses and boils them with a little salt. Peel them and put them in a casserole, add some bouillon; when it comes to a boil, add a piece of butter, cover with a lid and cook slowly for 10 minutes. Shortly before serving, stir the potatoes until the sauce is smooth, salt to taste and serve. Some enjoy adding finely chopped onions or parsley, or some grated nutmeg; it depends on one's taste.[44]

TO BOIL "EARTH APPLES"

When the apples [sic] are washed clean, put them over the fire with cold water and salt, boil them tender, then remove the skin. Now add a spoon-ful of butter, an equal amount of flour, a little grated nutmeg, pepper, 1/2 pail of good wine vinegar and a little sugar; then add a 1/2 pot of cold

water. Put this over the fire and stir until it begins to boil; if it is too thick, thin with boiling water. The potatoes stew for some minutes.

They could also just be cooked in salt and water, wrapped in a napkin and eaten with melted butter and pepper.[45]

TO MAKE BROWNED POTATOES

For this one uses small potatoes, which after having been partly boiled are peeled; cook a piece of butter until light brown in a casserole and shake the potatoes in this. When they are almost brown, sprinkle with some grated sugar, after which they are shaken again. Add stock or bouillon and cook, but while cooking, shake or stir often, until they are tender and the sauce even. They are served with some ground pepper.[46]

Madame Anne Marie Mangor, *Cookbook for Small Households*, 1837

BOILED POTATOES

Melt butter, add flour, milk or bouillon; after it has cooked until it is smooth, let the peeled potatoes boil, together with nutmeg and finally salt. You can also peel the raw potatoes, boil them in half bouillon, half water, until they thicken the sauce; then stir in a good piece of butter, salt and some ground pepper or curry powder.[47]

POTATO CAKES

A dozen medium-sized raw potatoes are peeled and boiled in enough water to cover; when they begin to break up, pour off the water and mash them with a wooden spoon together with 4–5 *lod* butter, a good pail of cream or milk, a little nutmeg; boil a little, finally add salt.[48]

FRIED POTATO CAKES

The cooked and peeled potatoes are pressed to pieces with a spoon while they are warm, together with a little butter and salt. A little butter or shortening is melted in the pan. The potato cakes are added and fried until light brown with a steady heat, so that they don't burn. They are

turned and fried with new butter on the other side. They are eaten with roasts, cutlets, carbonade, etc.[49]

BROWNED POTATOES

....

After the powdered sugar is browned, as for caramel pudding, add a piece of butter together with the boiled, peeled and cut up potatoes. Cook with a steady heat until they are brown.[50]

Wilhelmine Christensen, *Latest Cook and Cake Book*, 1849

POTATOES

....

When the potatoes are large enough to peel raw, they are most well-tasting if they are treated and cooked in the following way: the potatoes are peeled raw and put in cold water, where they remain until the next day. Remove from the water, which often looks dark, put over the fire with lots of cold water with salt, cook covered until they are completely cooked through. Pour off the water and put over the coals, uncovered, where they should remain for 15 minutes in order to cool and dry off.[51]

Bishop, *Illustrated Cookbook*, 1855

Mrs. Mangor recommends that if you will cook large potatoes, then you should peel them the day before and soak them in cold water. Remove them, put over the heat with sufficient cold water and salt, cook until tender, covered; remove the water and let them sit for 15 minutes, uncovered, over the coals, to dry off. When they are cooked with the skin on, put them as they are peeled in hot water with sufficient salt, cover, put in the oven or by the heat and shake in a colander before they are served. You can also keep them warm by putting them in a colander over a boiling kettle. Another way is to pour off the water before they are cooked through and then steam them under a tightly closed lid until they are tender.[52]

POTATO RAGOUT

....

Potatoes sprinkled with flour and mashed and made into balls with egg yolks. The balls are rolled in flour, and fried in fat. Then pour

off the fat and serve them in brown sauce which covers them completely.[53]

Nicoline Schmidt, *Cookbook for Small as well as Large Households*, 1865

POTATOES

....

If you want good, well-tasting potatoes, you need to be aware of the differences in potatoes. Some need to be cooked quickly, others slowly, some in a lot of water, others with little water; some are best when they are cooked before peeling, others should be peeled first. There are no rules; if you don't get good potatoes cooked one way, then try a different way. Trying different ways is not difficult. You need to salt them, and as soon as they are cooked and begin to crack pour off the water, otherwise they will lose their taste. If the potatoes are watery, they should be cooked quickly in boiling water; if they are very watery and will not stay firm when they are cooked, put them in a pot with the skin on, pour water over them and add a piece of chalk, as big as a nut; then they will stay firm. Towards spring, potatoes are best if you put them in water overnight before they are cooked.[54]

Carl Ginderup, *The Danish Kitchen*, 1888

POTATOES

....

Summer potatoes should, before they are cooked, be peeled, sprinkled with salt, and covered with a wet cloth, so that the large amount of water which summer potatoes have, is removed. After washing, boil them without salt. Winter potatoes are best when they are peeled and left overnight in cold water. It is easier to remove the eyes and much of the pungent smell is removed. For both summer and winter potatoes, it is best to throw away the first water after they have boiled and then finish cooking them. The water should cover the potatoes while they are cooking; when they are tender, pour off the water and cover with a cloth until ready to serve. When new potatoes are served separately, they are served with cold butter or a butter sauce.[55]

Kristine Marie Jensen, *Frk. Jensens Cookbook*, 1901

BOILED POTATOES

....

Of potatoes, which are our most important root vegetable, there are so many kinds that one needs to experiment in order to discover which ones should be cooked with the skin and which without. When you buy them, choose the smoothest. The very early, new potatoes should be washed well, dried with a coarse cloth and are best when cooked over a fire in hot, but not boiling water, with salt. They need very little cooking. Towards winter, on the other hand, potatoes are best when they are peeled and sit in cold water for several hours before they are cooked. Put them in an enamel pot with cold water, salt and one teaspoon vinegar for every half dozen potatoes, which will then stay white and look good. After they are cooked, pour off the water and put them over a low fire and shake dry, until the water has completely evaporated. If the potatoes are cooked long before they are served, pour off the water and cover immediately with a cloth. This is the best way to keep them warm. We do not recommend potatoes cooked in hay.[56]

Ingeborg Suhr, *Food*, 1965

HOW TO COOK POTATOES

....

When cooking potatoes one should choose potatoes of the same size, so that they finish cooking at the same time. They are scrubbed clean with a stiff brush and rinsed several times in cold water. When cooking potatoes, there are several methods to choose from.

METHOD 1. UNPEELED. 1 KG. POTATOES—1 L. WATER—20 G. SALT.

The scrubbed and rinsed potatoes are put on the stove in salted water. They are cooked with a steady heat, until they are tender, 20–30 minutes, or 5–10 minutes and then in a haybox. The water is poured off and the potatoes are peeled with a little knife. While peeling, cover with a lid or a cloth, as they should be served as warm as possible. If a large portion is to be served, the potatoes can be treated as discussed, but also heat them quickly in salt water just before serving; the water is poured off and the potatoes steamed for a few seconds over the stove.

The cleaned potatoes are peeled as thinly as possible (with a potato peeler) and put immediately into cold water. Rinse them and put them on the stove in salted water. They are cooked until they are tender (20–30 minutes) or in a haybox. Pour off the water *which can be used for soup, sauce, etc.* The potatoes are steamed for a few seconds, after which they are served steaming hot.[57]

There are admittedly many more recipes for potatoes included here than for any of the other dishes. This is partly because potatoes were a new food—they do not show up in cookbooks before 1766—and Danes spent some time trying to figure out how best to cook them, not to mention what to call them. It is also because of the importance of potatoes in modern Danish cuisine. By the mid-twentieth century, the standard way to cook potatoes was to boil them. Occasionally they were served as a dish known as "burning love" (*brændende kærlighed*). This is a huge mound of mashed potatoes with beets (the red of the beets was the reference to "love") and occasionally bits of bacon sprinkled over it. French fries were already known and potato chips were just coming in, but neither of these substituted for boiled potatoes, which were always to be found on the table. A typical meal at a country inn might consist of a platter of roast pork and red cabbage, accompanied by French fries and potato chips, and edged with mashed potatoes. A bowl of boiled potatoes would also be served as an accompaniment.[58]

Early Danish recipes for potatoes experiment with browning and frying, but they all seem to start with boiling. There is obviously also some experimentation going on about when the potatoes should be served—with the main course or courses, or as dessert? But the ingredients remain the same—butter, salt, pepper, nutmeg, onions—there is not much variety here.

One of the other intriguing elements of the potato recipes is the constant need to explain to cooks that there are different kinds of potatoes and they require different cooking methods. There is not any one standard way to cook potatoes, according to the cookbook authors. One gets the sense that they are arguing

against the grain, trying to counter a standard potato preparation method. *Education for Young Women* suggests that steamed potatoes are "more tasty than [those] cooked in the usual way,"[59] and Nicoline Schmidt reminds her readers that "there are no rules . . . trying different ways is not difficult."[60]

The other interesting element is the explicit nature of the discussion of steaming potatoes. Here, too, the authors are obviously trying to introduce a new, healthier cooking technique. However, they fail; steaming, of potatoes or any vegetables for that matter, although it may have gained some ground in institutional cooking, never became really popular in Danish homes.

Finally, a large number of the recipes refer to thawing the potatoes before cooking because potatoes were generally stored outside or in root cellars over the winter, where they might well have frozen. So it was obviously important to remind the cook that the potatoes should be well thawed before they were cooked. The subtext of many of these potato recipes is that since the new vegetables were not native to Denmark, Danish cooks, housekeepers, and housewives did not really understand them very well. They needed to be reminded of how to buy and store potatoes, as well as of the many varying ways to cook them.

RØD GRØD
(RED PUDDING)

Anon., *Cookbook*, 1616

A PORRIDGE OF SOUR CHERRIES

Soak them in wine / and take white bread and put it under / so that it gets a good soaking / press it through a cloth / that is not too thick or too thin / add ginger / pepper / cinnamon / sugar or honey.[61]

Anna Weckerin has the same recipe in her 1648 book.[62]

Anna Elisabeth Wigant, *An Aristocratic Lady's Cookbook*, 1703

RED PUDDING

....

Take a half pound of rice flour / and a pot and a half of red wine / add sugar, cardamom / cinnamon and small pieces of sugar / let it cook until it is thick / take 4 shillings of almonds / chop them finely and sprinkle them in / and let it cook / if you will, you can put it in stoneware forms / or you can put it in a plate / add wine / sugar / grated lemon peel / or sprinkle with small pieces/ of sugar/ as you wish.[63]

Anon., *A Small Tested Cook- and Preserving Book*, 1740

RED PUDDING

....

Take a half pound of grain and 2 pots of cherry wine, cook a pudding of this; add sugar, cinnamon, cardamom and a little lemon peel.[64]

Anon., *New Complete Cookbook*, 1755

RED PUDDING

....

Take a half pound arrowroot to two pots of young French wine; add cinnamon, sugar, cardamom and lemon peel, and let it cook to a pudding; then add cherry and currant juice. If you don't have this, then add half red wine and half white wine to a pail of water. When it has cooked, serve it on a platter, or in teacups. Serve it cold with sweet cream.[65]

Anon., *Education for Young Women*, 1796

RED PUDDING

....

Take two pots of currant juice, put it over the fire, when it comes to a boil, add sugar to taste, together with the peel of a lemon, finely grated, and ground cinnamon. Take a half or three-quarters of a pound of arrowroot, rinse in cold water and add; stir constantly while it cooks. Now put a little

on a plate and when it is stiff enough, pour it in forms or teacups which have first soaked in cold water. Let it cool off before you remove it, add sweet cream and sugar. If you don't have currant juice, you can use cherry wine and rice flour instead of arrowroot.[66]

Christiane Rosen, *Economic Housekeeping Book*, vol. 4, 1821

RED PUDDING WITH RICE FLOUR

About 2 pots of juice from fresh currants or raspberries is cooked in a tin casserole together with 3/4 lb. sugar. After it is skimmed, add 1/2 lb. rice flour, mixed with a little juice, a piece of cinnamon and the peel of 1/2 lemon; stir while boiling, 10 minutes. Serve the pudding as the previous recipe.[67]

RED PUDDING WITH ARROWROOT

As soon as . . . the pudding has the right consistency, it is put into teacups or on a deep salad plate, which is first dipped in cold water, and when it has settled, it is sprinkled with grated sugar.

It is eaten with cream or wine.[68]

Madame Anne Marie Mangor, *Cookbook for Small Households*, 1837

RED PUDDING

3 pails of pressed juice and 1 pail of water are put over the fire with sugar, cinnamon or vanilla. 4 lod of a thickening agent are mixed in with enough cold juice to make it liquid. When the juice boils, it is thinned even more and poured back and forth, and constantly stirred; continue this while it boils, about 15 minutes. After the pudding is poured into the form, pour water over it, spread it out with a silver spoon, which will keep the pudding from forming a thick skin. Slivered almonds are added after it thickens. It is eaten with cream.[69]

Maria Rasmussen, *Cookbook for City and Country Households*, 1864

RED PUDDING

2 lb. cherries and 2 lb. currants are peeled, crushed and set over heat with 3 pots of water; when it has boiled for one hour, strain it and for each pot of juice use 4 lod thickener or 5 lod arrowroot flour, which has been stirred into a little of the cold juice. The strained juice is put back over the heat to cook together with sugar to taste and a little vanilla; when it boils, add the stirred thickener and cook, stirring constantly, for about 15 minutes. Add 1/4 lb. coarsely chopped sweet almonds and pour into a form which has been dipped in cold water. Pour a little sugar water over the pudding, so that it doesn't form a skin. It is eaten with thin cream. One can also use 1 lb. raspberries and 3 lb. currants, as raspberries have a nice taste.[70]

Laura Adeler, *Illustrated Cookbook for City and Country*, 1893

RED PUDDING (10 PORTIONS)

This dish, which is characteristic of Denmark, is made for the above portions, with 4 pots juice, 1–1 1/4 lb. sugar and a thickening agent, for which one usually uses 1/2 lb. arrowroot flour, but can also use 3/4 lb. rice flour or 1 lb. arrowroot meal. One gets the best red pudding from 3 pots of currant juice and 1 pot of raspberry juice, which is boiled. When it starts to boil, add the thickening agent, which has been stirred into a little of the cold juice, to the pot, and boil stirring constantly for 5 to 8 minutes; it takes least time with arrowroot flour. Before you pour the pudding into large flat bowls, check to make sure it is stiff enough by putting a teaspoonful in a saucer that's placed in cold water. If the pudding is too thin, add more thickener; if it's too thick, thin it with boiling water. It is served with cold sweet cream, and sprinkled with finely chopped almonds, including some bitter almonds. For the juice, you can also use only currants (from 3 lb. of berries) or 2 lb. of cherries and 1 lb. currants. When boiling the fruit, figure 1 pot of water to every pound of fruit; after straining there will be 4 pots of juice from 3 lb. of berries.[71]

Kristine Marie Jensen, *Frk. Jensens Cookbook*, 1901

RED PUDDING

....

3 LB. BERRIES. FOR 12 PEOPLE

Red pudding is best made from different kinds of fruit, such as equal parts of currants and raspberries, red and black currants or currants and cherries.

3 lb. of berries are stemmed, rinsed and cooked in 2 pots of water; then they are strained, the juice sweetened, add vanilla and thicken with 12 kvint flour to each pot of juice, half arrowroot and half potato flour. If you use cherries, these should be crushed in a mortar. Chopped almonds may be added to the strained juice, before it is thickened, or they can be sprinkled over the pudding.[72]

Ingeborg Suhr, *Food*, 1965

RED PUDDING I

....

PREPARATION TIME: 1 1/2 HOUR. FOR 6 PEOPLE

CALORIES: 1463   1 PERSON: 244 CAL

250 g currants
250 g raspberries
250 g rhubarb stalks
1 liter water
possibly 1 tsp 40% calcium chloride
ca. 200 g sugar
potato flour

The rhubarb stalks are rinsed, cut in pieces and boiled in water together with the rinsed currants and raspberries. The juice is strained and one can add calcium chloride. Sugar and thickener are added as described (p. 47). For 3 dl of juice, use 20 g of potato flour.[73]

Of the recipes here, *rød grød* is probably the one that changes the most, yet, it too remains basically a red fruit pudding, "charac-

teristic of Denmark," to quote Laura Adeler.[74] It starts off as a wine-based pudding, and the recipe from 1703 has no fruit at all; by mid-century, juice starts appearing to complement the wine, and by 1821 the wine has disappeared altogether, replaced by a variety of red berries. The berries themselves remain fairly constant—cherries, currants, and raspberries. Here, too, the spices change and eventually disappear, replaced occasionally by vanilla. And the thickening agent varies, to include rice flour, arrowroot, and even potato flour. But the process of cooking down wine, juice, or fruit, thickening it with some sort of starch, and serving it cold with cream remains constant over the centuries. Today one can buy *rød grød* in boxes at the supermarket, and one need only add water to have the dish.

Else-Marie Boyhus claims that *rød grød* was a "new creation" from the same time as the enclosed stove (mid- to late- nineteenth century), made possible with the development of larger and better strawberries.[75] Yet the name, at least, goes back to the early eighteenth century, when it had nothing to do with strawberries.

Niels Kayser Nielsen suggests that "it is not because of the difficulty of pronouncing the soft Danish 'd' that foreigners are taught to say *rød grød med fløde* [red pudding with cream]; the reason is also that we regard the dish as typically Danish."[76] He goes on to point out that the red and white colors of the pudding with cream are, of course, also the Danish national colors.[77]

In this one dish alone, one can trace a course of Danish history, from alcohol to fruit, from colonial spices to a reduced empire, and from home-made dishes to the convenience of supermarkets—all topped with national colors and a particularly Danish pronunciation.

ᕍessert

AFTERWORD

OME YEARS AGO, WHEN I STARTED THIS PROJECT and would tell people that I was working with old cookbooks, the most frequent response I got was a laugh or a snicker. Cookbooks! What kind of subject was that for serious academic study? After all, history deals with "important" issues—politics, wars, disasters, economics—not food! And so I developed a "cocktail party response." The human race, I would say, needs two things to survive—sex and food. Without sex, we can survive for one generation; without food, for maybe three days, or three months, if one has water. How long could we survive without politicians, or generals, or economists?

Anthropologists and sociologists have long appreciated the need for understanding how food fits into society, for understanding differences in the kinds of foods eaten, in preparation methods, in the presentation and serving of food. Historians are

beginning to understand the importance of food as well, and this book is an addition to such historical studies.

Cookbooks tell stories, as do all books. Perhaps the stories are not linear; they do not have a beginning, a middle, and an end, but they are stories nonetheless. Reading old Danish cookbooks, one can learn about changes in the economy, in the social make-up of the society, in women's roles, and in what it means to be a nation state and to be a member of that nation state. I have tried to tease some of these stories out of the cookbooks printed over several centuries in Denmark. And so, in a sense, I have come full circle in answer to my early critics, for my study does deal with politics and economics and social groups. By asking different questions of one's sources, or old questions of new sources, one can discern new patterns and supplement old ones.

The story I have told is partly an old one and partly a new one. The development of a new middle-class society with a concomitant change in women's roles in the nineteenth century is a well-known story. Others have charted the growth in domesticity for women and prescriptive changes aimed at creating separate spheres for women and men. Cookbooks add a further dimension to a well-known story.

The new story that emerges suggests that the so-called separate spheres of the private (home, kitchen) and the public (politics, nation) were indeed not so very separate after all. I am certainly not the first to explore this idea but the existence of nationalism in the kitchen is, I believe, a new story. I certainly did not expect to find such clear statements of nationalism and debate over nationalist issues in cookbooks as I did. It is quite apparent that politics intruded into women's spheres, or, put differently, that there were no clear lines between women's and men's spheres, that prescriptions were just that, they were hopes and ideals, not necessarily reality. Even the emergence of nationalism in Denmark differed somewhat from what we might expect to find. It built gradually and changed meaning over the course of the late eighteenth and the nineteenth centuries. Not just a response to the territorial losses of the nineteenth century, the development of a new nation state based on Danishness reached back temporally to the eighteenth century, as well as spatially

across the Danish countryside and into individual families. The changing nature of the family structure paralleled a changing nationalism and women had a role in this development as much as men, even if "only" as wives and mothers.

Cookbooks also tell stories of literacy and numeracy, of a society which believed in educating all its members, girls as well as boys, to a fairly high level of functional literacy. The ability to use a cookbook, in and of itself, may not seem very important. Does it matter whether one can follow a recipe to create a tasty dish? But the ability to follow what may be a sophisticated set of directions is also indicative of an ability to understand and follow other directions, and that is surely important in the development of a civil society.

Cookbooks open up the worlds in which the people who wrote them actually lived. Through changes in cookbooks we can chart changes in the societies which produced them. With Danish cookbooks, it is possible to follow changes that resulted from the development of new social and economic forms in the eighteenth and nineteenth centuries, namely, the development of a new capitalist economy and the contemporaneous development of new domestic roles for women. It is possible to watch the impact of the loss of empire through the availability of certain tropical spices and the change in the balance of the society through the disappearance of game in recipes. Cookbooks also chart the growth in the development of a new nationalist nation state, in the meaning of what is Denmark and what it means to be a Dane.

Cookbooks can open up worlds. They can allow our imagination to wander freely across the globe. They can also, over time, allow us to trace the course of empires, of social roles, of new nations. It is time, not only for cookbooks to come out of kitchens, but also for kitchens to move from the back of the house and to take their rightful places as centers of home, hearth, nation, and history.

coffee or tea

NOTES

FIRST COURSE

1. Nicola Humble, "A Touch of *Bohème*: Cookery Books as Documents of Desires, Fears and Hopes," *Times Literary Supplement*, June 14, 1996, 15.
2. Arjun Appadurai, "How to Make a National Cuisine: Cookbooks in Contemporary India," *Comparative Studies in Society and History* 30, no. 1 (1988): 4, 6.
3. Jack Goody, *Cooking, Cuisine and Class: A Study in Comparative Sociology* (Cambridge: Cambridge University Press, 1982), 152.
4. C. F. von Rumohr, ed., *Joseph Königs Veiledning til Kogekunsten* (Copenhagen: Gyldendal, 1832), 59. All translations of Danish into English are mine.
5. Anna Elisabeth Wigant, *En Høy-Fornemme Madames Kaagebog* (Copenhagen: Christian Geertzen, 1703). See also Else-Marie Boyhus, "Kogekunst og Kogebøger: Fem Eksempler 1581–1793," *Bol og By*, no. 2 (2002): 12.

6. Fannie Farmer's book was first published in 1896 and appeared in six revised editions from Little, Brown and Company until 1965. Still published, several editions can now be found as *The Fannie Farmer Cookbook* by Marion Cunningham.

7. First published privately by Rombauer in 1931, the book was commercially published by The Bobbs-Merrill Company in 1936.

8. Anna Weckerin, *En artig oc meget nyttelig Kogebog* (Copenhagen: Peter Hake, 1648).

9. Anon., *Nye fuldstændig Kaage-Bog* (Copenhagen: Friderik Christian Pelt, 1755).

10. Charlotte Appel, *Læsning og bogmarked i 1600–tallets Danmark* (Copenhagen: Det Kongelige Bibliotek, Museum Tusculanums Forlag, 2001).

11. Ingrid Markussen, *Til Skaberens Ære: Statens Tjeneste og Vor Egen Nytte* (Copenhagen: Institut for dansk Skolehistorie, Danmarks Lærerhøjskole, 1991), 109–10.

12. School Law of 1814 as quoted in, Carol Gold, "The Danish Reform Era, 1784–1800" (PhD diss., University of Wisconsin-Madison, 1975), 243.

13. Markussen, *Til Skaberens Ære*, 529.

14. Carol Gold, *Educating Middle Class Daughters: Private Girls Schools in Copenhagen, 1790–1820* (Copenhagen: The Royal Library and Museum Tusculanum Press, 1996).

15. Christiane Rosen, *Jfr. Christiane Rosens Levnets-Historie* (Copenhagen: Forlagt af Udgiverinden, 1836), 4–5.

16. The records of *Den københavnske Skolekommission*, 1809–1815, and its successor, *Direktionen for Almue-og Borgerskolevæsenet*, can be found in the Copenhagen City Archives (*Stadsarkivet*).

17. Anon., *Underviisning for unge Fruentimmere, som selv ville besørge deres Huusholdning, indeholdende adskillige udvalgte Kunst-Stykker eller Oekomoniske Haandgreb ved Krydderiernes og andre i Huushold-ningen brugende Tings Indkjøb*, vol. 3 (Copenhagen: P. M. Liunges, 1798–1799), 16.

18. Christiane Rosen, *Oeconomisk Huusholdnings-Bog*, vol. 1, 2nd ed. (Copenhagen: C.A. Bording, 1821), 1–2.

19. See Appel, *Læsning og bogmarked*, vol. 1, 75–80, for a discussion of the seventeenth-century teaching order in Denmark.

20. Wigant, *En Høy-Fornemme Madames Kaagebog*, 1703, 165.

21. Marcus Looft, *Den Kongelige Danske og i Henseende til alle slags Maader fuldstændige Koge Bage og Sylte-Bog, eller Syv Hundrede og Ti Anviisnings-Regler indrettet for Herskaber og fornemme Familier saavelsom for Alle og Enhver*, 1st ed. (Copenhagen: Johann Gottlob Rothe, 1766), 366.
The complete recipe reads as follows:

Take 24 to 30 eggs; beat them well, and add one and a half pails of whole milk; beat it well with a whisk; put it in a tin bowl, put the bowl into a kettle with cold water so that the water comes to the top of the bowl. Then put it over the fire, uncovered, until it begins to get hard. Take it off; it will run together and become a true egg-cheese. Ladle it into a colander, so that it can run clean. Next put it into a container and beat well. Add a pound of clear butter, a half pound of finely granulated sugar, a half pound of finely chopped almonds, 24 egg yolks. Combine well and set aside for an hour. Then add a half pound of finely grated chocolate, 2 teaspoons of lemon juice and fold in gently the whites of 12 eggs, stiffly beaten. But first make sure to have finished a bottom layer of butter dough, put it into a tart pan, curl the edges nicely around the pan and put the beaten batter in and bake it. If you do not want the cake so large, then you can just take half of everything.

22. Eleanor T. Fordyce, "Cookbooks of the 1800s," in *Dining in America—1850–1900*, ed. Kathryn Grover (Amherst: University of Massachussets Press, 1987), 88.

23. An American recipe for pound cake from 1776 reads: Take a pound of butter, beat it in an earthen pan with your hand one way, till it is like a fine thick cream; then have ready twelve eggs, put half the whites; beat them well, and beat them up with the butter, a pound of flour beat in it, a pound of sugar, and a few caraways. Beat it all well together for an hour with your hand, or a great wooden spoon, butter a pan and put it in, and then bake it an hour in a quick oven. Julianne Belote, *The Compleat American Housewife 1776* (Concord: Nitty Gritty Publications, 1974), 104.

An American cupcake recipe from 1832 reads, Cup cake is about as good as pound cake, and is cheaper. One cup of butter, two cups of sugar, three cups of flour, and four eggs, well beat together, and baked in pans or cups. Bake twenty minutes, and no more. Mrs. Child, *The American Frugal Housewife, dedicated to those who are not ashamed of economy*, 12th ed. (Cambridge, Mass.: Applewood Books, 1834), 71. Pound cakes traditionally called for one pound each of flour, butter, and sugar, which was easy to remember; Mrs. Child's cupcakes use a 1–2–3–4 variation on that theme, which is also not too taxing.

24. Anon., *Koge Bog: Indeholdendis et hundrede fornødene stycker/ som ere/ om Brygning / Bagning/ Kogen/ Brendevijn oc Miød at berede-saare nytteligt udi Hussholding / u* (Copenhagen: Salomone Sartorio, 1616).

25. Anon., *Koge-Bog: Indeholdendis et hundrede fornødene stycker/ som ere/ om Brygning/ . . .* (Copenhagen, 1637).

26. Norbert Elias, *The Civilizing Process: Sociogenetic and Psychogenetic Investigations*, trans. Edmund Jephcott, ed. Eric Dunning, Johan Goudsblom, and Stephen Mennell (Oxford: Blackwell, 1994), 138.

27. Looft, *Den Kongelige Danske, Koge-, Bage, og Sylte-Bog.*

28. Anon., *Kogebog for mindre Huusholdninger, indeholdende over 100*

Anviisninger til paa en billig og nem Maade at Tillave god og velsma-gende Mad (Copenhagen: Jul Strandbergs Forlag, 1866).

29. Carl Ginderup, *Det danske Køkken* (Copenhagen: Ernst Bojesens, 1888).

30. Kristine Marie Jensen, *Frk. Jensens Kogebog* (Copenhagen: Det Nordiske Forlag, 1901).

31. See Gold, "The Danish Reform Era," especially chapter five. See also Byron J. Nordstrom, *Scandinavia since 1500* (Minneapolis: University of Minnesota Press, 2000), 128.

FIRST INTERMEZZO

1. Carl Müller, *Nye Koge-Bog for den retskafne Huusmoder med Figurer, som vise en net og ordentlig Serverings-Maade*, 2nd ed. (Copenhagen: Gyldendal, 1785), end pieces.

2. Anon., *Underviisning for unge Fruentimmere, som selv ville besørge deres Huusholdning, og have Opsigt med Kiøkken, Kjelder og Spisekam-mer, af egen Erfaring meddeelt af en Huusmoder*, vol. 1 (Copenhagen: M. Liunges Forlag, 1795), part 13, 123–25.

3. Conradine Hasberg, *Kogebog for Land- og Byhuusholdninger* (Kolding: J. M. Eibeschütz's Officin i Fredericia, 1857), 196–203.

4. Maria Rasmussen, *Kogebog for By- og Landhuusholdninger*, 2nd ed. (Kolding: J. L. Wisbech, 1864), 232.

5. Nielsine Nielsen, *Husvennens Koge- og Mælkeribog. Fuldstændig Vejledning til al Husgierning for Husmødre af Bondestanden* (Copenhagen: N. C. Roms Forlagsforretning, 1885), 17–18.

6. Ane Marie Mangor, *Kogebog for smaa Huusholdninger, indeholdende Anviisning til forskjellige Retters og Kagers tillavning, med angiven Vægt og Maal*, 40th ed. (Copenhagen: Thieles Bogtrykkeri, 1910), 292–95.

SECOND COURSE

1. "Spoon food" would include any type of food served with a spoon, for example, in liquid, porridge, or mashed form.

2. Anon., *Koge Bog* (1616).

3. Anna Weckerin, *En artig oc meget nyttelig Kogebog* (Copenhagen: Peter Hake, 1648), 266.

4. Wigant, *En Høy-Fornemme Madames Kaagebog*, 1703, 35. 1 pot = 1 liter

5. A. Svendsen, *Oeconomisk Sundheds-Kogebog, eller fuldstændig Anviisning til at tillave alle muelige Slags velsmagende Retter, der befordre og vedligeholde Sundheden* (Copenhagen: A. Soldins Forlag, 1800),

13.

6. J. C. Pelt, *Kogebog, hvori findes den bedste Maade at lave Kiødsupper og andre Supper, kogt Høns, Ænder og Giæs, Stege, Sauser, m.m.* (Copenhagen: Frans Nicolai Pelt, 1799), 5.

7. Mangor, *Kogebog for smaa Huusholdninger* (1837), 79–80.

8. Anon., *Koge Bog* (1616), recipe no. 99.

9. Anon., *En nye proberet og af mange approberet Kaage- Bage- og Sylte-Bog, indeholdende adskillige Retter af Supper, Posteyer, Fricaseer, Raguer, Souser og Fiske-Souser, samt alle Slags Bakkelser paa adskillige Maader, Sylte-Tøyer, Scaleyer med videre*, 2nd ed. (Copenhagen: Johan Jørgen Høpffner, 1754), 13.

10. Christiane Rosen, *Oeconomisk Huusholdnings-Bog*, vol. 2 (Copenhagen: C. A. Bording, 1818), 10.

11. Laura Adeler, *Illustreret Kogebog for By og Land, med over 600 Anvisninger til Madlavning, Bagning og Syltning*, 1st ed. (Copenhagen: H. Hagerups Forlag, 1893), 64–65.

12. See the fourth course (pages 00–00) for a detailed discussion of this point.

13. Anon., *Underviisning for unge Fruentimmere*, foreword.

14. Another example can be found in Jane Austen's *Pride and Prejudice*, first written in 1796–97 although not published until 1813. When Mr. Collins first visits the Bennets at Longbourn, "he begged to know to which of his fair cousins the excellence of its cooking was owing. But here he was set right by Mrs. Bennet, who assured him with some asperity that they were well able to keep a good cook, and that her daughters had nothing to do in the kitchen" (chapter 13). Although Mrs. Bennet is shown ordering dinners and otherwise managing the household, she has passed none of these skills on to any of her five daughters.

15. Svendsen, *Oeconomisk Sundheds-Kogebog*, 210.

16. Ibid.

17. Ibid., 212.

18. Ibid., title page.

19. Rosen, *Oeconomisk Huusholdnings-Bog*, vol. 1, 9.

20. Ibid., 13.

21. What Americans today call white bread, Danes call French bread. Early Danish cookbooks referred to this bread as wheat bread, because the basic flour was wheat rather than rye. However, "wheat bread" has a somewhat different connotation in America today, so I am hesitant to use that term. Further confusing the nomenclature is the fact that early Danish wheat bread used flour ground from the entire grain, rather than first processing the grain and then grinding it. "Whole grain bread" has an entirely different meaning today.

22. Jensen, *Frk. Jensens Kogebog*, 295.

23. Even today, it should be noted, there are bakeries every few blocks in Danish cities; one is never far from a baker.
24. T. Sarah Peterson, *Acquired Taste: The French Origins of Modern Cooking* (Ithaca, NY: Cornell University Press, 1994), 163 ff., 199–202.
25. The English sailed off with the Danish navy in 1807, which led to Denmark's alliance with Napoleon until the bitter end. Sweden, which had switched sides to join the Grand Coalition against Napoleon, thus was able to take Norway from Denmark in 1814, with the concomitant loss of much of the Danish merchant marine. Tranquebar and the Danish holdings in Ghana were sold to England in 1845 and 1850; the Virgin Islands were sold to the United States in 1917.
26. Anon., *Koge Bog* (1616).
27. Müller, *Nye Koge-Bog for den retskafne Huusmoder.*
28. Mangor, *Kogebog for smaa Huusholdninger.*
29. Erikke Barfoed, *Kogebog for store og smaa Huusholdninger* (Faaborg: Forfatterindens Forlag, 1863).
30. "Had it not been for the Fall, then the earth itself would have produced such well-tasting roots, herbs, fruit and plants that people would not have to cook them and the intentional seasoning with herbs would not be necessary." Anon., *Koge Bog* (1616), introduction.
31. Adeler, *Illustreret Kogebog*, preface.
32. Jensen, *Frk. Jensens Kogebog*, 175.
33. Jean-Louis Flandrin, "From Dietitics to Gastronomy: The Liberation of the Gourmet," in *Food: A Culinary History from Antiquity to the Present*, ed. Jean-Louis Flandrin and Massimo Montanari (New York: Penguin Books, 2000), 419–20.
34. Felipe Fernández-Armesto, *Near a Thousand Tables: A History of Food* (New York: The Free Press, 2002), 148.
35. *McCall's Cook Book* (New York: Random House, 1963), 3.
36. For an exploration of this literature and the changing ideals of womanhood, see Gold, *Educating Middle Class Daughters*, chapter three.

SECOND INTERMEZZO

1. Anon., *Koge Bog* (1616).
2. Christiane Rosen, *Den tænkende Huusholder* (Copenhagen: S. A. Nissen, 1824), 1–7; excerpts from chapter 1.
3. "Tre indenlandske Krydderier." This is a nice, albeit unintended, pun in English. The Danish word *indenlandske* literally translates as "inside the country," and is the direct opposite of "foreign," thus "home" or "domestic," both of which have a double meaning in

English. The Danish *indenlandske*, however, refers only to the country or land and has nothing to do with the home or house.

4. Ane Marie Mangor, *Kogebog for smaa Huusholdninger*, 14th ed. (Copenhagen: Thieles Bogtrykkeri, 1865), iii–iv.

5. Jensen, *Frk. Jensens Kogebog*, i–iii.

THIRD COURSE

1. Anon., *Koge Bog* (1616).
2. Müller, *Nye Koge-Bog for den retskafne Huusmoder*, foreword.
3. Anon., *Underviisning for unge Fruentimmere*, vol. 1, foreword.
4. Müller, *Nye Koge-Bog for den retskafne Huusmoder*, foreword.
5. "Three Domestic Spices" first appeared in the 1860 version of Mangor's cookbook. It was not a part of the original 1837 version but was taken from the handwritten dedication which Helsingør mayor Jacob Baden Olrik wrote to his daughter in 1853 and adopted by Mangor as representing her own attitudes. See Regina Vegenfeldt and Lilian Kornerup, *Danske kogebøger 1616–1974, med et tillæg 1975–1977*, 2nd ed. (Hamlet, 1978), 24.
6. Ibid., 23.
7. Ibid., 26.
8. Jensen, *Frk. Jensens Kogebog*, ii.
9. Coventry Patmore wrote a poem with this title in 1854, in which he details the perfection of his wife's attributes. The phrase was popularized by Virginia Woolf in a speech she gave in 1931, "Professions for Women," in which she said that "[k]illing the Angel in the House was part of the occupation of a woman writer." See Virginia Woolf, "Professions for Women," in *Virginia Woolf: Women and Writing*, ed. Michèle Barrett (New York and London: Harcourt Brace Jovanovich, 1980), 60. This essay was originally published in 1942 in *The Death of the Moth*.
10. Jensen, *Frk. Jensens Kogebog*, i–iii.
11. This is my list but based on reading John Smail, *The Origins of Middle-Class Culture: Halifax, Yorkshire, 1660–1780* (Ithaca, NY: Cornell University Press, 1994), and Leonore Davidoff and Catherine Hall, *Family Fortunes: Men and Women of the English Middle Class, 1780–1850* (Chicago: University of Chicago Press, 1987).
12. The complete section reads:
   There is no need to discuss the fact that the cook [female] or cook [male] must be clean and keep their pots, pans, kettles and other utensils always clean; everyone knows that themselves. Because if food is prepared and cooked in a dirty pot or pan, even were it only a spoon soup, it immediately takes on a dirty and bad taste. Or if you see a dirty kitchen boy or girl, think how they

handle the food, how dirt falls off his arms into the pot he is stirring, etc., then one has a disgust and tedium with his food. Therefore, everything ought to be clean; put dirt, hair and such on a plate and keep it for yourself. Put the clean food on another plate and serve it to the good people. Anon., *Koge Bog*, 1616, chapter 5.

13. Carl Müller, *Den danske Huusmoder, med hosføiede nye Kogebog for Borgere og Landalmuen* (Copenhagen: Gyldendal, 1793), 2, 10, 42.

14. Francis Collingwood and John Woollams, *Nye og fuldstændig Huusholdningsbog for dristige Huusmødre eller Anviisning til alle Sorter fine, velsmagende, men tillige solide Retters Tillavning, samt om Bagværk, Syltning, Marinering etc.* (Copenhagen: A. Soldins Forlag, 1796), 2. This quote is a translation from the Danish version. The original English reads, "The first and most important of all these [general observations] is *cleanliness*, not only in their own persons, but also in every article used in the kitchen" (emphasis in original). The English title is *The Universal Cook, and City and Country Housekeeper. Containing All the Various Branches of Cookery* (London: R. Noble, for J. Scatcherd and J. Whitaker, 1792).

15. Von Rumohr, *Joseph Königs Veiledning til Kogekunsten*, 5–6.

16. Ibid., 163–64.

17. Ibid., 165.

18. Ibid., 188.

19. Anon., *Kogebog for mindre Huusholdninger* (Kolding: J. L. Wisbech, 1864).

20. Halvorsen, *Kogebog* (1865), 1–3.

21. Petra Jacobsen, *Kogebog, indeholdende Husmoderens Pligter og hvorledes en Husholdning kan føres net og billigt* (Copenhagen: C. W. Stincks Boghandel, 1873), iii–iv.

22. Ginderup, *Det danske Køkken*, 13.

23. Von Rumohr, *Joseph Königs Veiledning til Kogekunsten*, 43.

24. Melchior Adam Weikard, *Kjernen af Diæten for Huusmødre og Huusfædre*, trans. Dr. J. C. Tode (Copenhagen: P. M. Liunges Forlag, 1799), 333–34.

25. Elias, *The Civilizing Process*, 51–52.

26. Mary Douglas, *Purity and Danger: An Analysis of the Concepts of Pollution and Taboo*, 2nd ed. (London: Routledge, 1984), 2.

27. Ibid., 36.

28. Jonas Frykman and Orvar Löfgren, *Culture Builders: A Historical Anthropology of Middle-Class Life*, trans. Alan Crozier (New Brunswick: Rutgers University Press, 1987), 163–64.

29. Ibid., 164–66.

30. Ibid., 214.

31. Ibid., 215.

THIRD INTERMEZZO

1. Rosen, *Oeconomisk Huusholdnings-Bog*, vol. 1, 9–11.
2. Ibid., 14. One *lod* = 15.6 grams = 1/2 oz.
3. Mangor, *Kogebog for smaa Huusholdninger*, 14th ed. (1865), 245–47.
4. Ibid., 247
5. Jensen, *Frk. Jensens Kogebog*, 325. One *kvint* = 5 grams; one pail = 1/4 liter.
6. Ingeborg Suhr, *Mad: Kogning, Bagning, Stegning, Syltning, El-Køk-ken, Trykkogning, Frysning, Ernæringslære, Varekundskab*, 24th ed. (Copenhagen: Gjellerup, 1965), 385.

FOURTH COURSE

1. Charles Emil Hagdahl, *Illustreret Kogebog*, trans. André Lütken (Copenhagen: P. G. Philipsens Forlag, 1883), 23.
2. Barbara Welter, "The Cult of True Womanhood, 1820–1860," *American Quarterly* 18 (1966): 151–74.
3. Alice Clark, *Working Life of Women in the Seventeenth Century* (1919; repr., London: Routledge and Kegan Paul, 1982); Louise A. Tilly and Joan W. Scott, *Women, Work, and Family* (New York: Holt, Rinehart and Winston, 1978), see part I; and Davidoff and Hall, *Family Fortunes*, 272–89.
4. Hagdahl, *Illustreret Kogebog*, 17–24.
5. Ibid., 21.
6. Ibid., 20.
7. Nordstrom, *Scandinavia since 1500*, 237–38.
8. Anon., *Koge Bog* (1616).
9. Weckerin, *En artig oc meget nyttelig Kogebog*, introduction.
10. Müller, *Nye Koge-Bog for den retskafne Huusmoder*, foreword.
11. Rosen, *Oeconomisk Huusholdnings-Bog*, vol. 1, 1–2.
12. Louise Beate Augustine Friedel, *Nye og fuldstændig Confectyr-Bog eller grundig Underviisning til selv at forfærdige alle muelige Slags Con-ditorievare. En Haandbog til Brug for Huusmødre, Mande- og Fruen-timmer-Kokke*, translated from German (Copenhagen: A. Soldins Forlag, 1795).
13. J. K. Høet, ed., *Euphrosyne*, vol. 1 (Copenhagen: A. Soldins Forlag, 1796), 380.
14. Collingwood and Woollams, *Nye og fuldstændig Huusholdningsbog*, 3. The original English reads:
    The fire must be prepared according to the weight and size of what is to be roasted. If it be any thing small or thin, a brisk fire will be necessary, in order that it may be done quick; but if it be a large joint, it will require a strong fire that has

lain some time to cake. . . . Take care to keep the meat at a proper distance from the fire; because, if it once gets scorched, it will make the outside hard, and will prevent the fire from having a proper effect on the meat, so that it will appear to be thoroughly cooked, while it may be nearly raw within side. Collingwood and Woollams, *The Universal Cook, and City and Country Housekeeper*, 2.

15. Rosen, *Den tænkende Huusholder*, 1–12.
16. Müller, *Den danske Huusmoder*, 2.
17. Von Rumohr, *Joseph Königs Veiledning til Kogekunsten*, 12–14.
18. Müller, *Den danske Huusmoder*, 2–3.
19. Linda K. Kerber, "Daughters of Columbia: Educating Women for the Republic, 1787–1805," in *The Hofstadter Aegis: A Memorial*, ed. Stanley Elkins and Eric McKitrick (New York: Alfred A. Knopf, 1974), 55–56.
20. Linda K. Kerber, "The Republican Mother and the Woman Citizen," in *Women's America: Refocusing the Past*, ed. Linda K. Kerber and Jane Sherron De Hart, 5th ed. (New York: Oxford University Press, 2000), 117.
21. Rasmussen, *Kogebog for By- og Landhuusholdninger*, foreword.

FIFTH COURSE

1. Von Rumohr, *Joseph Königs Veiledning til Kogekunsten*, 59.
2. Anon., *Nye fuldstændig Kaage-Bog* (Copenhagen: Friderick Christian Pelt, 1755), title page).
3. Samuel Conrad Schwach, "Om Ædikke at lave af Ribs, som skal blive ligesaa god som den Udenlandske Viin-Ædikke," *Maanedlige Afhandlinger til En og anden Forbedring i Huusholdning*, no. 7 (July 1762): Introduction, 221, 203–4.
4. See Boyhus, "Kogekunst og Kogebøger," 26.
5. Müller, *Nye Koge-Bog for den retskafne Huusmoder*, foreword.
6. Ibid.
7. Müller, *Den danske Huusmoder*, 16, 42–43.
8. Anon., *Underviisning for unge Fruentimmere*, vol. 3, preface.
9. Ibid., 83.
10. Weikard, *Kjernen af Diæten for Huusmødre og Huusfædre*, 130, 214.
11. Svendsen, *Oeconomisk Sundheds-Kogebog*, 104–5.
12. K. H. Seidelin, *Den danske Husmoders Køkken-Katekismus eller fuldstændig Kogebog hvori læres den bedste Maade at tillave alle brugelige Retter: Skyer, Koulier, Souser, Kjød- og Fiskeretter* (Copenhagen: K. H. Seidelin, 1801), iii.
13. The offending lines read "Learn from examples: freedom's growth does honor to the prince; despotism makes his grave," quoted in Gold, "The Danish Reform Era, 1784–1800," 229–30.

14. Ole Hyldtoft, *Danmarks Økonomiske Historie, 1840–1910* (Århus, Denmark: Systime, 1999), 111.
15. *"For hvert et tab igen erstatning findes! / Hvad udad tabes, skal indad vindes."* This phrase has been erroneously attributed to E. M. Dalgas, founder of the Danish Heath Society, and considered to refer to the process of heath drainage and utilization, which literally expanded the available Danish land. See Søren Toftgaard Poulsen, "Heden i kunst, litteratur og folkelig fortællekunst," *Skov-og Naturstyrelsen*, Danish Ministry for Energy and the Environment at www.sns.dk/udgivelser/2001/87-7279-316-3/kap11.htm, accessed on June 26, 2006.
16. Müller, *Den danske Huusmoder*, 3.
17. Feldbæk is clearly using the term "bourgeois consciousness" in a political sense, that is, as the development of a political entity such as the state, country, or fatherland. In the preceding courses, I have used the same term in a more social sense, that is, as the development of bourgeois traits such as order, moderation, and cleanliness. Although the focus is slightly different, the two are not unrelated in that they involve the same groups of people and develop at the same time. Ole Feldbæk, "Borgerskabets Danskhed 1720–1800," in *På sporet af dansk identitet*, ed. Flemming Lundgreen-Nielsen (Copenhagen: Spektrum, 1992).
18. Anon., *Nye fuldstændig Kaage-Bog*, title page.
19. Ole Feldbæk and Vibeke Winge, "Tyskerfejden 1789–1790: Den første national konfrontation," in *Dansk Identitetshistorie*, 4 vols., ed. Ole Feldbæk (Copenhagen: C. A. Reitzel, 1991), vol. 2, 107, 106.
20. Ole Feldbæk, "Fædreland og Indfødsret: 1700–tallets danske identitet," in *Dansk Identitetshistorie*, vol. 1, 205.
21. Müller, *Den danske Huusmoder*, 16; Seidelin, *Den danske Husmoders Køkken-Katekismus*, preface.
22. See, for example, Patricia R. Stokes, "Gendered Nations: Nationalisms and Gender Order in the Long Nineteenth Century—International Comparisons," (Berlin, Germany: Conference Report, Technical University of Berlin, March 25–28, 1998 [www.hsozkult .geschichte.hu-berlin.de/beitrag/tagber/gender.htm, accessed on November 16, 1998]), and Ida Blom, Karen Hagemann, and Catherine Hall, eds., *Gendered Nations: Nationalisms and Gender Order in the Long Nineteenth Century* (Oxford: Berg, 2000).
23. See, for example, Edward Said's discussion of the "division of men into 'us' (Westerners) and 'they' (Orientals)." Edward Said, *Orientalism* (New York: Vintage Books, 1979), 45.
24. C. Jacobsen, *Nye Koge-Bog eller Anviisning til at koge, bage, stege, indsylte, henlægge, indslagte, anrette, o.s.v.* Odense: S. Hempel, 1815, foreword.

25. Collingwood and Woollams, *Nye og fuldstændig Huusholdningsbog*, foreword.

26. Anon., *Huusmoderen eller Anviisning for unge Fruentimmer, som selv ville besørge deres Huusholdning, eller veilede i Bestyrelsen af samme* (Copenhagen: C. Steens Forlag, 1842), iii.

27. Bishop, *Illustreret Kogebog for store og smaa Huusholdninger* (Copenhagen: Rittendorff and Aagaards Forlag, 1855–1856), vol. 1, 4–5.

28. Anon., *Nyeste Kogebog for Middelstands-Huusholdninger eller Anviisning til fiin og simpel Madlavning after angiven Maal og Væg* (Odense: Miloske Boghandel, 1849), 1.

29. Ane Marie Mangor, *Kogebog for Soldaten i Felten* (Copenhagen: Thieles Bogtrykkeri, 1864), 9–10.

30. Mangor, *Kogebog for smaa Huusholdninger* (1837), 81; Mangor, *Kogebog for smaa Huusholdninger*, 14th ed. (1865), 86.

31. Mangor's 1837 cookbook contained the following potato recipes: potato flour dumplings, stewed potatoes, mashed potatoes, fried mashed potatoes, browned (sugared) potatoes, potato pudding, potato cake, and potato balls (a kind of cake). In addition to these, the 1865 cookbook also contained two kinds of potato soup, potato porridge, two additional potato puddings, and a recipe for plain boiled potatoes.

32. Anon. *Nye og fuldstændig Koge-Bog*, vol. 2 of *Underviisning for unge Fruentimmere*. Copenhagen: P. M. Liunges Forlag, 1796.

33. My 1963 *McCall's Cook Book* has recipes for Apple-Peanut-Butter Sandwiches, Zesty Peanut-Butter Sandwiches (includes sweet pickle relish), and Peanut-Butter 'n' Bacon Sandwiches, but no simple pb&j (*McCall's Cook Book*, 529–30).

34. Rasmussen, *Kogebog for By- og Landhuusholdninger*.

35. Ane Marie Mangor, *Kogebog for smaa Huusholdninger*, 40th ed. (1910).

36. Henrik Larsen, "Vi holder fast ved måltiderne," *Politiken*, May 22, 1999, 2.

SIXTH COURSE

1. See Aalborg Akvavit Web site at www.akvavit.dk/composite-306. htm (in English) and www.akvavit.dk/composite-59.htm (in Danish), accessed on June 26, 2006.

2. The official flag days are New Year's Day, Easter, the day of the German Occupation (April 9, half-mast until noon), Liberation Day (May 5), Constitution Day (June 5), Valdemar's Day (June 15), Christmas, and several other Christian holidays and royal birthdays. (For more on the official flag days, visit the official Danish web site at http://denmark.dk/portal/page?_pageid=374,520391&_

dad=portal&_schema=PORTAL, accessed on June 26, 2006.) Unofficially, Danes fly the *Dannebrog* all the time. They fly it for birthdays, weddings, anniversaries, any holiday, and just because the sun is out and they are at home. Peter Gundelach, professor of Sociology at the University of Copenhagen, believes that in comparison with many other peoples, Danes are "wild" about flying their flag. Danes consider it "natural" and "cosy," as quoted in Ole Damkjær, "Danskeden på Fremmarch," *Berlingske Tidende*, June 5, 2001, 5.

3. Inge Adriansen, *National symboler i det danske rige 1830–2000*, 2 vols. (Copenhagen: Museum Tusculanum, 2003), vol. 2, 531, 170.

4. Denmark's Potato Council, "Danmarks Kartoffel Råd" at www.kartoffelraad.landbrug.dk, accessed on June 26, 2001.

5. Else-Marie Boyhus, "Nye Kartofler," *Berlingske Tidende*, June 6, 1999.

6. Ibid.

7. Aalborg Akvavit, "Stik fingeren i jorden, og hæve glasset," www.aalborgakvavit.dk/composite-59.htm., accessed June 26, 2006.

8. Asta Bang, *Open Sandwiches and Cold Lunches*, 5th ed. (Copenhagen: Jul. Gjellerups Forlag, 1955), 34–35.

9. Denmark's Potato Council, "Kartoflens Historie" at www.kartoffelraad.landbrug.dk/museet/kartoflens_historiet.htm, accessed on June 26, 2006.

10. Søren Mørch, *Den ny Danmarkshistorie 1880–1960*, 3rd ed. (Copenhagen: Gyldendal, 1997), 319.

11. Hyldtoft, *Danmarks Økonomiske Historie, 1840–1910*, 215.

12. Eugen Weber, *Peasants into Frenchmen: The Modernization of Rural France, 1870–1914* (Stanford: Stanford University Press, 1976), 486.

13. Hans Kyrre, *Kartoffelens Krønike*, 2nd ed. (Copenhagen: Udvalget for Folkeoplysnings Fremme, G. E. C. Gad, 1938) 25–40 *passim*.

14. Larry Zuckerman, *The Potato: How the Humble Spud Rescued the Western World* (New York: North Point Press, 1998), 6.

15. Looft, *Den Kongelige Danske Koge, Bage, og Sylte-Bog*, 89.

16. Müller, *Nye Koge-Bog for den retskafne Huusmoder*, 204–5.

17. Müller, *Den danske Huusmoder*, 16.

18. Anon., *Underviisning for unge Fruentimmere*, 1798–1799, vol. 3, 158.

19. Christian Reventlow, "Tale," *Minerva* IV, no. 2 (1788): 1–7.

20. Torkel Baden, *Beskrivelse over den paa Godset Bernstorff . . . iverksatte nye Indretninge i Landbruget* (Copenhagen: Nicolaus Møller, 1774), 57–58.

21. After 1784, the Danish government was run by Crown Prince Frederik (the future King Frederik VI), because his father, King Christian VII, was demonstrably insane.

22. For a discussion of the reforms, see Fridlev Skrubbeltrang, *Agricultural Development and Rural Reform in Denmark*, trans. Reginald

Spink, vol. 22, *FAO Agricultural Studies* (Rome, Italy: Food and Agricultural Organization of the United Nations, 1953), and Gold, "The Danish Reform Era, 1784–1800."

23. Gr. Begtrup, *Beskrivelse over Agerdyrkningens Tilstand i Danmark*, 5 vols. (Copenhagen: A. and S. Soldins Forlag, 1803–1808), vol. 1, 345.

24. Ibid., vol. 2, 675.

25. Henrich Callisen, *Physisk Medizinske Betragtninger over Kiöbenhavn*. (Copenhagen: Frederik Brummers Forlag, 1807), vol. 1, 372, 390–91.

26. Rosen, *Oeconomisk Huusholdnings-Bog*, vol. 3, 50.

27. Bishop, *Illustreret Kogebog for store og smaa Huusholdninger*, vol. 2, 411–18.

28. E. A. Scharling, *Fornuftig Madlavning og Husbrug eller om hensigtsmæssig Valg og Tilberedning af Næringsmidler*, an adaptation of *Forstmester Asbjørnsens Bog Fornuftigt Madstel* (Copenhagen: "Selskabet for Naturlærens Udbredelse," Thieles Bogtyrkkeri, 1866), 16, 54.

29. Hagdahl, *Illustreret Kogebog*, 596.

30. Ibid.

31. Ulla & Søster, *Den bedste Gave for Smaapiger* (Copenhagen: V. Thaning and Appels Boghandel, 1889).

32. Kyrre, *Kartoffelens Krønike*, 40.

33. Jensen, *Frk. Jensens Kogebog*, 150.

34. See Appadurai, "How to Make a National Cuisine," and B. W. Higman, "Cookbooks and Caribbean Cultural Identity: An English-Language Hors D'oeuvre," *New West Indian Guide* 72, no. 1 and 2 (1998) for discussions of how cookbooks can help shape national identity.

35. Appadurai, "How to Make a National Cuisine," 19–20.

36. Quoted in Martin Clark. *Modern Italy, 1871–1995*. 2nd ed. (New York: Longman, 1996), 30. D'Azeglio was briefly prime minister of Savoy, succeeded by Count Cavour. Cavour is often, erroneously, given credit for this quote.

37. Benedict Anderson, *Imagined Communities: Reflections on the Origin and Spread of Nationalism* (London: Verso, 1983), 15.

38. Ernest Gellner, *Thought and Change* (Chicago: University of Chicago Press, 1964), 150, 168.

39. Anderson, *Imagined Communities*, 13–14, 40.

40. Eric Hobsbawm and Terence Ranger, eds., *The Invention of Tradition* (Cambridge: Cambridge University Press, 1983).

41. Ibid., 1. One of the best examples is the British creation of ceremonies to represent and reflect their authority in India, for example, the designation of Victoria as "Empress of India," and the elaborate rituals established for "Imperial Assemblages" and "Imperial Durbars," which brought English officials and Indian potentates together in a manner calculated to underscore British dominance. See Ber-

nard S. Cohn's "Representing Authority in Victorian India" in Hobsbawm and Ranger, *The Invention of Tradition*, 165–209.

42. Hobsbawm and Ranger, "Introduction" in *The Invention of Tradition*, 9.

43. See Eric Hobsbawm, "Mass-Producing Traditions: Europe, 1870–1914," in Hobsbawm and Ranger, *The Invention of Tradition*, 236–307.

44. This flag is "the symbol not only of the European Union but also of Europe's unity and identity in a wider sense." See http://europa.eu.int/abc/symbols/emblem/index_en.htm, 2001, accessed on July 12, 2001.

45. Eric Hobsbawm, *Nations and Nationalism since 1780: Programme, Myth, Reality*, 2nd ed. (Cambridge: Cambridge University Press, 1992).

46. Feldbæk, *Dansk Identitetshistorie*; Lundgreen-Nielsen, *På sporet af dansk identitet*.

47. On the invention of national costumes, see Ida Blom, "Gender and Nation in International Comparison," in Blom, Hagemann, and Hall, *Gendered Nations*.

48. Interestingly, although Inge Adriansen fully understands the use of unofficial as well as official national symbols in the creation of a monocultural national identity, she completely ignores food in her discussion, which includes such other unofficial elements as landscape, flowers, and animals. Adriansen, *Nationale Symboler*, see especially, vol. 2, section 4, 357–404.

49. Peterson, *Acquired Taste*, 163–202.

50. Sidney W. Mintz, *Tasting Food, Tasting Freedom: Excursions into Eating, Culture, and the Past* (Boston: Beacon Press, 1996), 97.

51. Michael Symons, *A History of Cooks and Cooking* (Urbana and Chicago: University of Illinois Press, 2000), 103–5.

52. See Hobsbawm and Ranger, *The Invention of Tradition*. Hobsbawm argues in the introduction that some symbols are "entirely new," created by "semi-fiction . . . or by forgery" (7), but his examples are still based on some element of reality, however distorted.

53. Boyhus, "Nye kartofler."

54. Tine Damsholt, "Om begrebet 'folk'," *Kulturens nationalisering*, ed. Bjarne Stoklund (Copenhagen: Musuem Tusculanums Forlag, 1999), 32.

55. Majken Schultz quoted in "Foghs image-kampagne kan blive boomerang," *Politiken*, April 3, 2006 available at *www.politiken.dk/VisArtikel.iasp?PageID=446641*, and personal communication with the author, April 14, 2006.

56. Ivan Larsen, "Husk at hejse flaget," *Havebladet*, no. 2 (November [sic, should read April] 2006), 26, 28.

57. Henning Looft, "Råd om indkøb og lægning af kartofler i 2006," *Havebladet*, no. 2 (April 2006), 15.

58. Carsten Bjørk Olsen, "Danmarks Kartoffel Råd," *Havebladet*, no. 1 (February 2006), 12.

59. Palle Ove Christiansen, "Peasant Adaptation of Bourgeois Culture: Class Formation and Cultural Redefinition in the Danish Countryside," *Ethnologia Scandinavica* 8 (1978): 98–152. See 99, 128, 147.

60. The "change of system" in 1901 was the first time the Danish king acknowledged that the majority party in the lower house of parliament (*Folketinget*) had the right to form a government.

61. "The significance of the holy icons is demonstrated by the universal use of simple pieces of coloured fabric—namely flags—as the symbol of modern nations and their association with highly charged ritual occasions or acts of worship." Hobsbawm, *Nations and Nationalism since 1780*, 72.

62. "King Christian stood by the high mast," written by Johannes Ewald in 1779, is considered by many as the royal, rather than the national, anthem. The other anthem, "There is a lovely land," was written by Adam Oehlenschläger in 1819. See Bent Rying, ed., *Denmark: An Official Handbook*, 14th ed. (Copenhagen: Danish Ministry of Foreign Affairs, 1970), 22. There has been some talk recently of changing the anthem to "In Denmark, I was born," written by Hans Christian Andersen in 1850, but the chances of this happening are considered to be slim.

63. Ibid.

64. It is highly doubtful that the National Liberal Party, which had organized the demonstration, would have indeed been willing or able to institute a revolution in Denmark, but they did beg the king not to drive them "to the self-help of confusion (*Fortvivlesens Selvhjælp*)."

65. Nordstrom, *Scandinavia since 1500*, 237–38; Bent Rying, ed., *Denmark: An Official Handbook*, 13th ed. (Copenhagen: Danish Ministry of Foreign Affairs, 1964), 503. In 1938, agricultural goods made up 71 percent of Danish exports, and industrial goods accounted for 27 percent. By 1962, the ratio was reversed; agricultural goods were down to 41 percent of Danish exports and industrial goods had gone up to 52 percent. Rying, *Denmark: An Official Handbook*, 13th ed. (1964), 503

66. Nordstrom, *Scandinavia since 1500*, 214–19.

67. "Rigsdagstidende," (Copenhagen: 1891). See Carol Gold, "The Origins of the Danish Welfare State in the 1890's," paper presented at the American Historical Association annual meeting, Dallas, TX, 1977.

68. Ministry of Foreign Affairs of Denmark, "Traditions and Food," http://denmark.dk/portal/page?_pageid=374,520391&_dad=portal&_schema=PORTAL (accessed June 25, 2003).

SIXTH INTERMEZZO

1. Gold, *Educating Middle Class Daughters*, see especially chapters 4 and 5.
2. Copenhagen City Directories published annually, from 1837 to 1848. Widow L. B. Thiesen, ed., *Veiviser eller Anviisning til Kjøbenhavns, Christianshavns, Forstædernes og Frederiksbergs Beboere for Aaret* . . . (Copenhagen: Boghandler L. B. Thiesen's Enke, 1837–1848).

SEVENTH COURSE

1. Anon., *Koge Bog* (1616), recipe number X
2. Weckerin, *En artig oc meget nyttelig Kogebog*, 136.
3. Wigant, *En Høy-Fornemme Madames Kaagebog*, 78.
4. Müller, *Nye Koge-Bog for den retskafne Huusmoder*, 27.
5. Rosen, *Oeconomisk Huusholdnings-Bog*, vol. 1, 2nd ed., 140.
6. Mangor, *Kogebog for smaa Huusholdninger*, 1st ed. (1837), 45.
7. Sørine Thaarup, *Kogebog for By- og Landhuusholdninger, eller Anviisning til at koge, stege, slagte, sylte, nedlægge, salte, bage, brygge, tilvirke Ost m.v.* (Copenhagen: V. Pio's Forlag, 1868), 146–47.
8. Adeler, *Illustreret Kogebog for By og Land*, 51–52.
9. Jensen, *Frk. Jensens Kogebog*, 78–79.
10. Bang, *Open Sandwiches and Cold Lunches*, 66.
11. Ibid., 67.
12. Mette Skougaard, *Bondens køkken: Madlavning og måltider i 1800-tallets landbosamfund* (Copenhagen: Nationalmuseet, 1984), 52.
13. Wigant, *En Høy-Fornemme Madames Kaagebog*, 111.
14. Anon., *Underviisning for unge Fruentimmere*, vol. 1, 153–54.
15. Rosen, *Oeconomisk Huusholdnings-Bog*, vol. 1, 2nd ed., 104–5.
16. Concerning the word, *frikadeller*, there is a presumed connection between the terms *fricassé*, *fricandeau*, and *frikadeller*, all of which have to do with chopping and mixing things together. The Danish dictionary from 1802 defines *fricassee* as, "a dish with finely chopped meat which is cooked in water, with flour, butter and vegetables." *Dansk Ordbog udgiven under Videnskabernes Selskabs Bestyrelse*, vol. 2 (Copenhagen: Johan Frederik Schultz, 1802).
17. Wigant, *En Høy-Fornemme Madames Kaagebog*, 111.
18. Anon., *Underviisning for unge Fruentimmere*, vol. 2 (Copenhagen: P.M. Liunges, 1796), 153.
19. Ibid., 153–54.
20. C. Jacobsen, *Nye Koge-Bog*, 61.
21. Ibid., 100.
22. Rosen, *Oeconomisk Huusholdnings-Bog*, vol. 1, 104–5.

23. Mangor, *Kogebog for smaa Huusholdninger* (1837), 75–76.
24. Anon., *Nyeste Kogebog for Middelstands-Huusholdninger*, 56.
25. Jensen, *Frk. Jensens Kogebog*, 228.
26. Suhr, *Mad*, 175–76. I have chosen Suhr's book for modern examples as a classic cookbook still in print. It was first published in 1909, a groundbreaking work that included weights, measures, cooking and preparation times, as well as information on nutrition and calories. See Hanne Søndergaard, "Ingeborg Suhr Mailand (1871–1969)" at *www.kvinfo.dk/side/170/bio/1338/*, accessed on June 26, 2006.
27. Ibid., 171.
28. Anon., *Koge Bog* (1616), recipe number 99. This is the only beef recipe in this cookbook.
29. Wigant, *En Høy-Fornemme Madames Kaagebog*, 110.
30. Looft, *Den Kongelige Danske Koge, Bage og Sylte-Bog*, 141–42.
31. Pelt, *Kogebog*, 5.
32. Rosen, *Oeconomisk Huusholdnings-Bog*, vol. 2, 10.
33. Mangor, *Kogebog for smaa Huusholdninger* (1837), 90–91.
34. Adeler, *Illustreret Kogebog*, 65.
35. Jensen, *Frk. Jensens Kogebog*, 194.
36. Boyhus, "Kogekunst og kogebøger," 13.
37. Looft, *Den Kongelige Danske Koge, Bage og Sylte-Bog*, 89.
38. Müller, *Nye Koge-Bog for den retskafne Huusmoder*, 204–5.
39. Anon., *Underviisning for unge Fruentimmere*, vol. 2, 41.
40. Christian Olufsen, "Kartoflers bedste Kogningsmaade," *Oeconomiske Annaler*, 1 (1797): 65–66.
41. Anon., *Underviisning for unge Fruentimmere*, vol. 3, 158.
42. Pelt, *Kogebog*, 8–10.
43. Rosen, *Oeconomisk Huusholdnings-Bog*, vol. 1, 132.
44. Rosen, *Oeconomisk Huusholdnings-Bog*, vol. 2, 104–5.
45. Rosen, *Oeconomisk Huusholdnings-Bog*, vol. 3, 108.
46. Rosen, *Oeconomisk Huusholdnings-Bog*, vol. 4, 116–17.
47. Mangor, *Kogebog for smaa Huusholdninger* (1837), 134.
48. Ibid., 135.
49. Ibid.
50. Ibid.
51. Wilhelmine Christensen, *Nyeste Koge- og Kagebog* (Aalborg: Den Reeske Boghandels Forlag, 1849), 86–87.
52. Bishop, *Illustreret Kogebog*, vol. 2, 415.
53. Ibid., 416.
54. Nicoline Schmidt, *Kogebog saavel for smaa, som store Huusholdninger* (Copenhagen: Fr. Woldike Forlags-Expedition, 1865), 172–73.
55. Ginderup, *Det danske Køkken*, 242–43.
56. Jensen, *Frk. Jensens Kogebog*, 150.
57. Suhr, *Mad*, 273.

58. This constituted a meal I ate at a *kro*, or country inn, in Hillerød, during the summer of 1963.
59. Anon., *Underviisning for unge Fruentimmere*, vol. 3, 158.
60. Schmidt, *Kogebog saavel for smaa, som store Huusholdninger*, 172–73.
61. Anon., *Koge Bog* (1616), recipe number 65.
62. Weckerin, *En artig oc meget nyttelig Kogebog*, 162.
63. Wigant, *En Høy-Fornemme Madames Kaagebog*, 35.
64. Anon., *En liden proberet Kaage- Bage- og Sylte-Bog, som ikke tilforn er trykt* (Copenhagen: H. Kongl. Maj. og Univ. Bogtr. Johan Jørgen Høpffner, 1740).
65. Anon., *Nye Fuldstændig Kaage-Bog*, 317–18.
66. Anon., *Underviisning for unge Fruentimmere*, vol. 2, 248.
67. Rosen, *Oeconomisk Huusholdnings-Bog*, vol. 4, 119.
68. Ibid., 188–89.
69. Mangor, *Kogebog for smaa Huusholdninger* (1837), 36–37.
70. Rasmussen, *Kogebog for By- og Landhuusholdninger*, 26.
71. Adeler, *Illustreret Kogebog*, 34.
72. Jensen, *Frk. Jensens Kogebog*, 293.
73. Suhr, *Mad*, 49.
74. Adeler, *Illustreret Kogebog*, 34.
75. Else-Marie Boyhus, *Grønsager: en køkkenhistorie* (Copenhagen: Gyldendal, 1996), 17.
76. Niels Kayser Nielsen, *Madkultur: opbrud og tradition* (Århus, Denmark: Forlaget Klim, 2003), 147. It is practically impossible for foreigners to get their tongues around this combination of letters and sounds, and Danes delight in teasing foreigners by asking them to pronounce the name of this dish.
77. Ibid., 152.

chocolates

BIBLIOGRAPHY

DANISH COOKBOOKS

Adeler, Laura. *Illustreret Kogebog for By og Land, med over 600 Anvisninger til Madlavning, Bagning og Syltning.* 1st ed. Copenhagen: H. Hagerups Forlag, 1893.

Anon. *Allernyeste Kogebog for unge Huusmødre.* Odense: den Miloske Bog- og Papirhandel, 1852.

———. *Den altid færdige Kok. En Kaagebog, hvorudi vises, hvorledes man skal tillave alleslage Retter, saavel kaagte som steegte.* Haderslev: Bogtrykkeriet, ca. 1760 (as cited in Vegenfeldt and Kornerup, 1978).

———. *Den Hurtige Kok, det er: En meget nyttig og fordeelagtig Kaage-Bog.* [Copenhagen], 1759.

———. *Den kloge Mands Haand-Bog, som indebefatter adskillige Huusraad og Lægemidler, samt Sundhedsregler for Aarets tolv Maaneder.* Copenhagen: Lauritz Christian Simmelkiær, 1775.

———. *En kort Undervisning om Hussholdning. Jeg vil holde Huss oc tage mig en Hustru.* Copenhagen: Laurentz Benedicht, [1572].

———. *En liden artig Konst Bog.* Copenhagen: I. N. Lossius, 1733.

———. *En liden proberet Kaage- Bage- og Sylte-Bog, som ikke tilforn er trykt.* Copenhagen: H. Kongl. Maj. og Univ. Bogtr. Johan Jørgen Høpffner, 1740.

———. *En nye proberet og af mange approberet Kaage- Bage- og Sylte-Bog, Indeholdende adskillige Retter af Supper, Posteyer, Fricaseer, Raguer, Souser og Fiske-Souser, samt allt Slage Bakkelser paa adskillige Maader, Sylte-Tøyer, Scaleyer med videre.* 2nd ed. Copenhagen: Johan Jørgen Høpffner, 1754.

———. *Huusmoderen eller Anviisning for unge Fruentimmer, som selv ville besørge deres Huusholdning.* Copenhagen: C. Steens Forlag, 1842.

———. *Kogebog,* 1750.

———. *Kogebog.* Copenhagen: Sally B. Salomon, 1858.

———. *Kogebog for mindre Huusholdninger.* Kolding: J. L. Wisbech, 1864.

———. *Kogebog for mindre Huusholdninger, indeholdende over 100 Anviisninger til paa en billig og nem Maade at tillave god og velsmagende Mad.* Copenhagen: Jul Strandbergs Forlag, 1866.

———. *Koge Bog: Indeholdendis et hundrede fornødene stycker/ Som ere/ om Brygning/ Bagning/ Kogen/ Brendevijn oc Miød at berede/saare nytteligt udi Hussholding/ u.* Copenhagen: Salomone Sartorio, 1616.

———. *Koge-Bog: Indeholdendis et hundrede fornødene stycker/ Som ere/ om Brygning/ Bagning/ Kogen/ Brendevijn oc Miød at berede/saare nytteligt udi Hussholding/ u.* Copenhagen, 1637.

———. *Medicinsk-diætetisk Brudegave for Nyegifte og for Ynglinge og Piger, som ere i Begreb med at træde ind i Ægtestanden.* Translated by Johan Wilhelm Fischer. Copenhagen: J. M. Stadthagens Forlag, 1797.

———. *Nye fuldstændig Kaage-Bog, eller grundig Underrætning og Anviisning, hvorledes man efter den nyeste Franske Maneer og Gout, . . .* Copenhagen: Friderik Christian Pelt, 1755.

———. *Ny Kogebog for større og mindre Husholdninger, tilligemed Anviisning til Syltning, Saltning, Vadsk, hurtig Bleg, samt nogle Husraad.* Copenhagen: C. H. Bielefeldt, 1861.

———. *Nye og fuldstændig Koge-Bog, indeholdende en tydelig Anviisning til at koge, bage, sylte, tillave Geleer, Iser, Compoter og andre Conditor-Sager . . . af en Huusmoder.* Vol. 2, *Underviisning for unge Fruentimmer.* Copenhagen: P. M. Liunges Forlag, 1796.

———. *Nyeste Kogebog for Middelstands-Huusholdninger eller Anviisning til fiin og simpel Madlavning efter angiven Maal og Vægt.* Odense: Miloske Boghandel, 1849.

———. *Oeconomia eller Nødvendige Beretning og Anledning, hvorledes en gandske Huusholdning paa det nytteligste og beste (saa fremt Gud Allermægtigste giver Sin Velsignelse) kan anstillis.* Copenhagen: Johann Nielaus Lossius, 1733.

———. *Underviisning for unge Fruentimmer, som selv ville besørge deres Huusholdning, og have Opsigt med Kiøkken, Kjelder og Spisekammer, af egen Erfaring meddeelt af en Huusmoder.* Vol. 1. Copenhagen: P. M. Liunges Forlag, 1795.

———. *Underviisning for unge Fruentimmer, som selv ville besørge deres Huusholdning, indeholdende adskillige udvalgte Kunst-Stykker eller Oekomoniske Haandgreb ved Krydderiernes og andre i Huusholdningen brugende Tings Indkjøb.* Vols. 3–4. Copenhagen: P. M. Liunges, 1798–1799.

———. *Veiledning i Brugen af det nye Madlavnings Apparat eller Kogebog for saadanne Retter, der kan behandles paa det Apparat, der er brugt ved Kogningsforsøgene paa Veterinair- og Landbohøiskolen.* Copenhagen: Flinchs Forlag, 1868.

B *de, Anna Margaretha. *Den erfarne Raadgiverinde for huuslige Fruentimmer eller Anviisning til vigtige Kundskaber og Fordele i Huusholdningen.* Copenhagen: A. Soldins Forlag, 1796.

Balling, Emanuel. *Huusmoderen, eller den værdige Landboeqvinde.* Copenhagen, 1792.

Bang, Asta. *Open Sandwiches and Cold Lunches.* 5th ed. Copenhagen: Jul. Gjellerups Forlag, 1955.

Barfoed, Erikke. *Kogebog for store og smaa Huusholdninger.* Faaborg: Forfatterindens Forlag, 1863.

Behrends, Enke. *Den lille Kogebog med 48 Anviisninger.* Copenhagen: forlagt af, samt tykt hos Behrends Enke, 1857.

Berendt, Vivi, ed. *Madam Mangor's Kogebog, Bogklubudgave.* Copenhagen: Vinten, 1988.

Berg, N. J. *Om Fødemidler A. Til Almuens Oplysning.* Christiania: efter Regjeringens Foranstaltning, trykt paa offentlig Bekostning, 1808.

Bishop. *Illustreret Kogebog for store og smaa Huusholdninger, indeholdende c. 2000 Recepter og Anviisninger m.m., Gjennemseet af en dansk Huusmoder.* 2 vols. Copenhagen: Rittendorff og Aagaards Forlag, 1855–1856.

Brandt, Mogens, ed. *Madam Mangors Bedst.* Copenhagen: Hans Reitzel, 1966.

Christensen, Wilhelmine. *Nyeste Koge- og Kagebog.* Aalborg: Den Reeske Boghandels Forlag, 1849.

Collingwood, Francis, and John Woollams. *Nye og fuldstændig Huusholdningsbog for dristige Huusmødre eller Anviisning til alle Sorter fine, velsmagende, men tillige solide Retters Tillavning, samt om Bagværk, Syltning, Marinering etc.* Copenhagen: A. Soldins Forlag, 1796.

Dahl, Juliane. *Praktisk Kogebog for enhver Huusholding.* Copenhagen: A. Levys Forlag, 1855.

Eibe, Line. *Kogebog for smaae og store Huusholdninger, indeholdende Anviisning til en Mængde forskjellige Retters og Kagers Tillavning, samt Syltning og Slagtning.* Copenhagen: Bog og Papirhandler F. H. Eibe, 1848.

F., Madamme. *Fuldstændig Kogebog for mindre Huusholdninger, indehold-ende 202 Anviisninger i Madlavning, Syltning, Bagning, Brygning, Slagtning, Mælens Behandling osv.* Aalborg: Magnus A. Schultz's Boghandel, 1868.

Friedel, Louise Beate Augustine. *Nye og fuldstændig Confectyr-Bog eller grundig Underviisning til selv at forfærdige alle muelige Slags Condito-rievare. En Haandbog til Brug for Huusmødre, Mande- og Fruentim-mer-Kokke.* Copenhagen: A. Soldins Forlag, 1795.

Fristrup, Clara Margrethe. *Fuldstændig Kogebog, samt Anviisning til at bage og sylte, saavel for smaa som store Huusholdninger.* 2nd ed. Copenhagen: A. G. Solomon, 1840.

Ginderup, Carl. *Det danske Køkken.* Copenhagen: Ernst Bojesens, 1888.

Hagdahl, Charles Emil. *Illustreret Kogebog.* Translated by André Lütken. Copenhagen: P. G. Philipsens Forlag, 1883.

Halvorsen. *Kogebog,* 1865.

Hansen, Jomfrue C. *Den danske Kokkepige, eller: almindelig Huushold-ningsbog indeholdende: letfattelig Anviisning til velsmagende, men tillige solide Retters Tillavngin [sic].* Copenhagen: Jacobsen, 1841.

Hansen, Lorenz, *Huusholdnings Haandbog for Aaret 18—, til nøjagtig og rigtig Beregning af alle i en Huusholdning aarlig forekommende Indtægter og Udgifter.* Fridericia, 1804.

Harsdorffer, Georg Philip. *Den Valske Forsnider lærendis hvorledis Mand skal kunsteligen i Stykker skiære och skikkeligen forlegge allehaande Spise.* Copenhagen: Daniel Paulli, 1676.

Hasberg, Conradine. *Kogebog for Land- og Byhuusholdninger.* Kolding: J. M. Eibeschütz's Officin i Fredericia, 1857.

Holmqvist, Johanne. *Kartoffel-Bogen: Kartoflen anvendt paa 246 Maader.* Vol. 1, *Husmoderens Blad's Special-Kogebøger.* Copenhagen: Husmo-derens Blads Forlag and J. H. Schultz, 1903.

Høegh-Guldberg, Fru Caroline. *Almindelig Kogebog for alle Stænder og særlig for Husmødre og vordende Husmødre.* 2 vols. Copenhagen: G. S. Wibes Bogtrykkeri and Forlagt af J. H. Schubothes Boghandel, 1866.

Høet, J. K., ed. *Euphrosyne.* Copenhagen: A. Soldins Forlag, 1796–1803.

Jacobi, Marie Elisabeth. *Nye og fuldstændig Koge-Bog indeholdende en tydelig Anviisning til at koge, bage, sylte, . . . tilligemed Regler for Anretningen.* Copenhagen: J. G. C. Hartier, 1815.

Jacobsen, C. *Nye Koge-Bog eller Anviisning til at koge, bage, stege, indsylte, henlægge, indslagte, anrette, o.s.v.* Odense: S. Hempel, 1815.

Jacobsen, Jfr. J. *Koge- og Syltebog for unge Damer, som selv ville bestyre deres Huusholdning.* Copenhagen: H. E. Rissen, [1860].

Jacobsen, L. *Kogebog for store og smaa Huusholdninger, indeholdende Anviisning til en Mænge forskellige Retters Tillavning, samt Kogning, Bagning, Syltning, Slagtning og Nedsaltning.* Copenhagen: Univer-sitetsboghandler C. A. Reitzel, 1851.

Jacobsen, Petra. *Kogebog, indeholdende Husmoderens Pligter og hvorledes en Husholdning kan føres net og billigt.* Copenhagen: C. W. Stincks Boghandel, 1873.

Jensen, Kristine Marie. *Frk. Jensens Kogebog.* Copenhagen: Det Nordiske Forlag, 1901.

Lassen, Christine. *Praktisk, nøjagtig og økonomisk Kogebog for Familier, særlig af den Mosaiske Tro.* Copenhagen: J. L. Wulffs Forlag, 1897.

Looft, Marcus. *Den Kongelige Danske og i Henseende til alle slags Maader fuldstændige Koge-, Bage-, og Sylte-Bog, eller Syv Hundrede og Ti Anviisnings-Regler indrettet for Herskaber og fornemme Familier saavelsom for Alle og Enhver.* 1st ed. Copenhagen: Johann Gottlob Rothe, 1766.

Madsen, A. V. *Kogebog for den danske Husmoder.* 2 vols. Copenhagen: Boghandler Th. Sandrup, 1871–1872.

Mangor, Ane Marie. *Fortsættelse af Kogebog for smaa Huusholdninger, indeholdende Anviisning til at tillave forskjellige Retter, Kager, Compotter og Salater m.m. efter angiven Vægt og Maal.* Copenhagen: Thieles Bogtrykkerie, 1842.

———. *Kogebog for smaa Huusholdninger, indeholdende Anviisning til forskjellige Retters og Kagers tillavning, med angiven Vægt og Maal.* 1st ed. Copenhagen: Thieles Bogtrykkeri, 1837.

———. *Kogebog for smaa Huusholdninger.* 14th ed. Copenhagen: Thieles Bogtrykkeri, 1865.

———. *Kogebog for smaa Huusholdninger.* 40th ed. Copenhagen: Thieles Bogtrykkeri, 1910.

———. *Kogebog for Soldaten i Felten.* Copenhagen: Thieles Bogtrykkeri, 1864.

Maren. *Kogebog for Tjenestepiger.* Copenhagen: Sally B. Salomon, Brunichs Efterfølger, 1849.

Marin, François. *Les Dons de Comus eller Indledning og Undervisning udi Koge-Kunsten, . . .* Vol. 1. Translated by J. H. Alling. Copenhagen: L. L. Heiden, 1762.

Møller, J. L. *Kogebog paa Vers.* 2nd ed. Copenhagen: C. A. Reitzel, 1830.

Müller, Carl. *Den danske Huusmoder, med hosføiede nye Kogebog for Borgere og Landalmuen.* Copenhagen: Gyldendal, 1793.

———. *Nye Koge-Bog for den retskafne Huusmoder med Figurer, som vise en net og ordentlig Serverings-Maade.* 2nd ed. Copenhagen: Gyldendal, 1785.

Nielsen, Anne. *Kortfattet Kogebog for enhver Huusholdning.* Odense: Den Hempelske Boghandel, 1861.

Nielsen, H. V. *Allernyeste Kogebog indeholdende Anviisning til at lave saavel alle simple i en borgerlig Huusholdning brugelige Retter.* 2nd ed. Copenhagen: Den beekenske Boghandlings Forlag, 1823.

Nielsen, Karen. *Dansk Kogebog samt Bage-, Slagte- og Syltebog.* Copenhagen: Flindt and Nielsen Forlag, 1898.

Nielsen, Margrethe Sophie. *Veiledning i Kogekunsten for Huusmødre og Huusholdersker, indeholdende Tillavningen af næsten to hundrede udsøgte Retter.* Copenhagen: N. G. F. Christensens Enkes Bogtrykkeri, 1829.

Nielsen, Nielsine. *Husvennens Koge- og Mælkeribog. Fuldstændig Vejledning til al Husgierning for Husmødre af Bondestanden.* Copenhagen: N. C. Roms Forlagsforretning, 1885.

Olufsen, Christian. "Kartoflers bedste Kogningsmaade." *Oeconomiske Annaler,* 1 (1797): 65–66.

———. *Nye Oeconomiske Annaler.* Copenhagen: J. H. Schubothe, 1812–1820.

———. *Oeconomiske Annaler.* Copenhagen: K. H. Seidelin, 1797–1810.

Pelt, J. C. *Kogebog, hvori findes den bedste Maade at lave Kiødsupper og andre Supper, kogt Høns, Ænder og Giæs, Stege, Sauser, m.m.* Copenhagen: Frans Nicolai Pelt, 1799.

———. *Nye Koge-Bog om Supper, Fiske, Stege og Sauser m.m.* Copenhagen: Boghandler Pelts Forlag, 1801.

Petersen, Hans Henrich. *Nye original dansk Koge-Bog for Fruentimmer, som selv forestaae deres Køkken eller vil have Tilsyn ved dets Bestyrelse.* Copenhagen: Johan Fred. Schultz, Kongelig og Universitets Bogtrykker, 1806.

———. *Nye original dansk Koge-Bog for Fruentimmer, som selv forestaae deres Køkken eller vil have Tilsyn ved dets Bestyrelse.* 2nd ed. Copenhagen: Andreas Seidelin, 1824.

Rasmussen, Maria. *Kogebog for By- og Landhuusholdninger.* 2nd ed. Kolding: J. L. Wisbech, 1864.

Rosen, Christiane. *Den tænkende Huusholder.* Copenhagen: S. A. Nissen, 1824.

———. *Oeconomisk Huusholdnings-Bog.* Vol. 2. Copenhagen: C. A. Bording, 1818.

———. *Oeconomisk Huusholdnings-Bog.* Vol. 3–4. Copenhagen: C. A. Bording, 1821.

———. *Oeconomisk Huusholdnings-Bog.* Vol. 1. 2nd ed. Copenhagen: C. A. Bording, 1821.

Rostrup, Christine. *Fem Hundrede Recepter i Kogekunsten, eller Veiledning for Bestyrere af Herskabskjøkkener, som og til Huusholdningsbrug.* Copenhagen: Forfatterindens Forlag, 1844.

Rudmose, Emma Mathilde Agnes. *Kogebog for landlige Huusholdninger, nærmest til Vejledning for den mere dannede Deel af Bondestanden.* 2 vols. Copenhagen: Meulengracht, 1846.

Rumohr, C. F. von, ed. *Joseph Königs Veiledning til Kogekunsten.* Copenhagen: Gyldendal, 1832.

Scharling, E. A. *Fornuftig Madlavning og Husbrug eller om hensigtsmæssig Valg og Tilberedning af Næringsmidler,* adapted from Forstmester Asbjørnsens Bog *Fornuftigt Madstel.* Copenhagen: "Selskabet for Naturlærens Udbredelse," Thieles Bogtyrkkeri, 1866.

Schmidt, M. Rødsted, ed. *Huusholdningsbog, en Anviisning for unge Koner og Piger til selv i enhver Henseende at kunne bestyre deres Huus.* Veile: S. Hertz, 1843.

Schmidt, Nicoline. *Kogebog saavel for smaa, som store Huusholdninger.* Copenhagen: Fr. Woldike Forlags-Expedition, 1865.

Schwach, Samuel Conrad, ed. *Maanedlige Afhandlinger til en og anden Forbedring i Huusholdning.* Christiania: Bog-Trykkeriet i Christiania, 1762.

Seidelin, K. H., ed. *Den danske Husmoders Køkken-Katekismus eller fuldstændig Kogebog, hvori læres den bedste Maade at tillave alle brugelige retter: Skyer, Koulier, Souser, Kjød- og Fiskeretter.* Copenhagen: K. H. Seidelin, 1801.

Suhr, Ingeborg. *Mad.* Copenhagen: Jul. Gjellerups Forlag, 1909.

———. *Mad: Kogning, Bagning, Stegning, Syltning, El-Køkken, Trykkogning, Frysning, Ernæringslære, Varekundskab.* 24th ed. Copenhagen: Gjellerup, 1965.

Svendsen, A. *Oeconomisk Sundheds-Kogebog, eller fuldstændig Anviisning til at tillave alle muelige Slags velsmagende Retter, der befordre og vedligeholde Sundheden.* Copenhagen: A. Soldins Forlag, 1800.

Thaarup, Sørine. *Kogebog for By- og Landhuusholdninger, eller Anviisning til at koge, stege, slagte, sylte, nedlægge, salte, bage, brygge, tilvirke Ost m. v.* Copenhagen: V. Pio's Forlag, 1868.

Ulla and Søster. *Den Bedste Gave for Smaapiger.* Copenhagen: V. Thaning and Appels Boghandel, 1889.

Ussing, Eulalia. *Nyeste Kogebog for store og smaa Huusholdninger.* Ribe: paa eget Forlag, 1860.

Weckerin, Anna. *En artig oc meget nyttelig Kogebog / udi kvilcken korteligen er befattet / hvorledis adskillige slags konsterige Rætter / være sig aff tamme eller vilde Diur / tamme eller vilde Fugle / ferske eller tørre Fiske; sampt adskillige slags Backelse Tærte / Marcipaner / Postejer / oc saadant meere beredis skal.* Translated by Povel Iverssøn Kolding. Copenhagen: Peter Hake, 1648.

———. *Fuldkommen Kaage-Bog udi hvilcken er befattet hvorledis adskillige slags velsmagende Rætter/ item Backelse/ Tærter/ Postejer og saadant meere beredis skal.* Translated by Paul Iverssøn Kolding. Copenhagen: Daniel Paulli, 1675.

Weikard, Melchior Adam, Imperial Russian Counselor of State and Court Doctor. *Kjernen af Diæten for Huusmødre og Huusfædre.* Translated by Dr. J. C. Tode. Copenhagen: P. M. Liunges Forlag, 1799.

Wigant, Anna Elisabeth. *En Høy-Fornemme Madames Kaagebog.* Copenhagen: Christian Geertzen, 1703.

———. *En Høy-Fornemme Madames Kaage-Bog, paa Manges Begieren og Efterspørgsel, anden Gang Oplagt, og med en Register til en hver Ræt Forfattet.* 2nd ed. Copenhagen: Johann Christoph Groth, 1731.

OTHER SOURCES

OTHER SOURCES

Aalborg Akvavit. http://www.aalborgakvavit.dk/composite-7.htm (Danish); -269.htm (English).

Adriansen, Inge. *National symboler i det danske rige 1830–2000.* Vol. 2. Copenhagen: Museum Tusculanum, 2003.

Alenius, Marianne, ed. *Digternes Paryk: studier i 1700-tallet—festskrift til Thomas Bredsdorff.* Copenhagen: Museum Tusculanum, 1997.

Anderson, Benedict. *Imagined Communities: Reflections on the Origin and Spread of Nationalism.* London: Verso, 1983.

Appadurai, Arjun. "How to Make a National Cuisine: Cookbooks in Contemporary India." *Comparative Studies in Society and History* 30, no. 1 (1988): 3–24.

Appel, Charlotte. *Læsning og bogmarked i 1600-tallets Danmark.* Copenhagen: Det Kongelige Bibliotek, Museum Tusculanums Forlag, 2001.

Aron, Jean-Paul. "The Art of Using Leftovers: Paris, 1850–1900." In *Food and Drink in History: Selections from the Annales,* edited by Robert Forster and Orest Ranum. Baltimore: Johns Hopkins University Press, 1979.

Baden, Torkel. *Beskrivelse over den paa Godset Bernstorff . . . iverksatte nye Indretninge i Landbruget.* Copenhagen: Nicolaus Møller, 1774.

Barrett, Michèle, ed. *Virginia Woolf: Women and Writing.* New York and London: Harcourt Brace Jovanovich, 1980.

Barthes, Roland. "Toward a Psychosociology of Contemporary Food Consumption." In *European Diet from Pre-Industrial to Modern Times,* edited by Elborg Forster and Robert Forster. New York: Harper Torchbooks, 1975.

Begtrup, Gr. *Beskrivelse over Agerdyrkningens Tilstand i Danmark.* 5 vols. Copenhagen: A. and S. Soldins Forlag, 1803–1808.

Belote, Julianne. *The Compleat American Housewife 1776.* Concord, CA: Nitty Gritty Publications, 1974.

Bentley, Amy. *Eating for Victory: Food Rationing and the Politics of Domesticity.* Urbana: University of Illinois Press, 1998.

Berriedale-Johnson, Michelle. *The British Museum Cookbook.* Translated by Jette Røssel (see Røssel 1992 for Danish title). London: British Museum Publications, 1987.

Bjørn, Claus. *Dengang Danmark blev moderne: eller historien om den virkelige danske utopi.* Copenhagen: Fremad, 1998.

Blom, Ida. "Gender and Nation in International Comparison." In *Gendered Nations: Nationalisms and Gender Order in the Long Nineteenth Century,* edited by Ida Blom, Karen Hagemann, and Catherine Hall. Oxford: Berg, 2000.

———. Karen Hagemann, Catherine Hall, eds. *Gendered Nations:*

Nationalisms and Gender Order in the Long Nineteenth Century.
Oxford: Berg, 2000.

Boyhus, Else-Marie. *Grønsager: en køkkenhistorie.* Copenhagen:
Gyldendal, 1996.

————. *Historisk Kogebog.* 4 vols. Copenhagen: Wormianum, 1975–1979.

————. "Kogekunst og Kogebøger: Fem Eksempler 1581–1793." *Bol
og By*, no. 2 (2002): 9–33.

————. "Nye kartofler." *Berlingske Tidende*, June 6, 1999.

Braudel, Fernand. *Capitalism and Material Life, 1400–1800.* Translated
by Miriam Kochan. New York: Harper Colophon, 1973.

————. *The Structures of Everyday Life: The Limits of the Possible.* 3 vols.
Translated by Sian Reynolds. New York: Harper and Row, 1981.

Callisen, Henrich. *Physisk Medizinske Betragtninger over Kiöbenhavn.*
Copenhagen: Frederik Brummers Forlag, 1807.

Chaudhuri, Nupur. "Shawls, Jewelry, Curry, and Rice in Victorian
Britain." In *Western Women and Imperialism: Complicity and Resistance*, edited by Nupur Chaudhuri and Margaret Strobal. Bloomington: University of Indiana Press, 1992.

————, and Margaret Strobal, eds. *Western Women and Imperialism:
Complicity and Resistance.* Bloomington: University of Indiana Press,
1992.

Child, [Lydia]. *The American Frugal Housewife, dedicated to those who are not
ashamed of economy.* 12th ed. Cambridge, MA: Applewood Books, 1834.

Christiansen, Palle Ove. "Peasant Adaptation of Bourgeois Culture:
Class Formation and Cultural Redefinition in the Danish Countryside." *Ethnologia Scandinavica* 8 (1978): 98–152.

Clark, Alice. *Working Life of Women in the Seventeenth Century.* London:
Routledge and Kegan Paul, 1982.

Clark, Martin. *Modern Italy, 1871–1995.* 2nd ed. New York: Longman,
1996.

Coe, Sophie D., and Michael D. Coe. *The True History of Chocolate.*
London: Thames and Hudson, 1996.

Cohn, Bernard S. "Representing Authority in Victorian India." In
The Invention of Tradition, edited by Eric Hobsbawm and Terence
Ranger. Cambridge: Cambridge University Press, 1983.

Collingwood, Francis, and John Woollams. *The Universal Cook, and
City and Country Housekeeper. Containing All the Various Branches of
Cookery.* London: R. Noble, for J. Scatcherd and J. Whitaker, 1792.

Counihan, Carole M. "Female Identity, Food, and Power in Contemporary Florence." *Anthropological Quarterly* 61, no. 2 (April 1988): 51–62.

Damkjær, Ole. "Danskeden på Fremmarch." *Berlingske Tidende*, June 5,
2001, 1, 5.

Damsholt, Tine. "En national turist i det patriotiske landskab." *Fortid
og Nutid*, no. 1 (1999): 3–26.

————. "Fædrelandskærlighed og borgerånd: En analyse af den patriotiske diskurs i Danmark i sidste del af 1700-tallet." PhD diss., University of Copenhagen, 1996.

————. "Om begrebet 'folk'." In *Kulturens nationalisering: et etnologisk perspektiv på det nationale*, edited by Bjarne Stoklund. Copenhagen: Musuem Tusculanums Forlag, 1999.

Danish Lutheran Churches in British Columbia. *Best of Danish Heritage Cookbook and More*. 2d ed. No place or publisher, 2004.

Davidoff, Leonore. *The Best Circles: Society Etiquette and the Season*. London: Croom Helm, 1973.

Davidoff, Leonore, and Catherine Hall. *Family Fortunes: Men and Women of the English Middle Class, 1780–1850*. Chicago: University of Chicago Press, 1987.

Davis, Natalie Zemon, and Arlette Farge, eds. *Renaissance and Enlightenment Paradoxes*. Vol. 3, *A History of Women in the West*, edited by Georges Duby and Michelle Perrot. Cambridge, MA: The Belknap Press of Harvard University Press, 1993.

Denmark's Potato Council. "Danmarks Kartoffel Råd." http://www.kartoffelraad.landbrug.dk.

Denmark's Potato Council, "Kartoflens Historie." http://www.kartoffelraad.landbrug.dk/museet/kartoflens_historiet.htm.

Douglas, Mary. "Deciphering a Meal." In *Implicit Meanings: Essays in Anthropology*, edited by Mary Douglas. London: Routledge and Kegan Paul, 1975.

————. *Purity and Danger: An Analysis of the Concepts of Pollution and Taboo*. 2nd ed. London: Routledge, 1984.

Elias, Norbert. *The Civilizing Process: Sociogenetic and Psychogenetic Investigations*. Translated by Edmund Jephcott; edited by Eric Dunning, Johan Goudsblom, and Stephen Mennell. Oxford: Blackwell, 1994.

Elkins, Stanley, and Eric McKitrick, eds. *The Hofstadter Aegis: A Memorial*. New York: Alfred A. Knopf, 1974.

European Union. "The Symbols of the EU." http://europa.eu.int/abc/symbols/index_en.htm.

Fannie, Farmer. *The Boston Cooking-School Cookbook*. Boston: Little Brown and Co., 1896.

Feldbæk, Ole. "Borgerskabets Danskhed 1720–1800." In *På sporet af dansk identitet*, edited by Flemming Lundgreen-Nielsen. Copenhagen: Spektrum, 1992.

————. "Clash of Cultures in a Conglomerate State: Danes and Germans in 18th Century Denmark." In *Clashes of Cultures: Essays in Honour of Niels Steensgaard*, edited by Jens Christian V. Johansen, Erling Ladewig Petersen, and Henrik Stevnsbog. Odense: Odense University Press, 1992.

————, ed. *Dansk Identitetshistorie*. 4 vols. Copenhagen: C.A. Reitzel, 1991.

————, and Vibeke Winge. "Tyskerfejden 1789–1790: Den første national konfrontation." In *Dansk Identitetshistorie*, vol. 2, edited by Ole Feldbæk. Copenhagen: C. A. Reitzel, 1991.

Fenton, Alexander, and Eszter Kisbán, eds. *Food in Change: Eating Habits from the Middle Ages to the Present Day*. Glascow, Scotland: John Donald Publishers, in association with the National Museums of Scotland, 1986.

Fernández-Armesto, Felipe. *Near a Thousand Tables: A History of Food*. New York: The Free Press, 2002.

Flandrin, Jean-Louis. "From Dietitics to Gastronomy: The Liberation of the Gourmet." In *Food: A Culinary History from Antiquity to the Present*, edited by Jean-Louis Flandrin and Massimo Montanari. New York: Penguin Books, 2000.

————, and Massimo Montanari, eds. *Food: A Culinary History from Antiquity to the Present*. New York: Penguin Books, 2000.

Fordyce, Eleanor T. "Cookbooks of the 1800s." In *Dining in America: 1850–1900*, edited by Kathryn Grover. Amherst, MA: University of Massachussets Press, 1987.

Forster, Elborg, and Robert Forster, eds. *European Diet from Pre-Industrial to Modern Times*. New York: Harper Torchbooks, 1975.

Forster, Robert, and Orest Ranum, eds. *Food and Drink in History: Selections from the Annales*. Baltimore: Johns Hopkins University Press, 1979.

Friis, Lilli. "Æde og Drikke." In *Dagligliv i Danmark i det syttende og attende århundrede*, vol. 1, edited by Axel Steensberg. Copenhagen: Nyt Nordisk Forlag Arnold Busck, 1969.

————. "Nydelse og næring." In *Dagligliv i Danmark i det syttende og attende århundrede, 1720–1790*, vol. 2, edited by Axel Steensberg. Copenhagen: Nyt Nordisk Forlag, 1971.

Frykman, Jonas, and Orvar Löfgren. *Culture Builders: A Historical Anthropology of Middle-Class Life*. Translated by Alan Crozier. New Brunswick: Rutgers University Press, 1987.

Gabaccia, Donna R. *We Are What We Eat: Ethnic Food and the Making of Americans*. Cambridge, MA: Harvard University Press, 1998.

Gellner, Ernest. *Thought and Change*. Chicago: University of Chicago Press, 1964.

Gold, Carol. "The Danish Reform Era, 1784–1800." PhD diss., University of Wisconsin-Madison, 1975.

————. *Educating Middle Class Daughters: Private Girls Schools in Copenhagen, 1790–1820*. Copenhagen: The Royal Library, Museum Tusculanum Press, 1996.

————. "The Origins of the Danish Welfare State in the 1890's." Paper presented at the American Historical Association annual meeting, Dallas, TX, December 27–30, 1977.

Goldschmidt, Hanne, and Birgit Siesby. *Til bords indenfor murene:*

Københavnske minder om mennesker og mad. Copenhagen: Selskabet for dansk jødiske historie, C.A. Reitzels Forlag, 1988.

Goody, Jack. *Cooking, Cuisine and Class: A Study in Comparative Sociology.* Cambridge: Cambridge University Press, 1982.

Grover, Kathryn, ed. *Dining in America: 1850–1900.* Amherst, MA: University of Massachusetts Press, 1987.

Havebladet, nos. 1–2, Feb.–April 2006.

Higman, B. W. "Cookbooks and Caribbean Cultural Identity: An English-Language Hors D'oeuvre." *New West Indian Guide* 72, nos. 1 and 2 (1998): 77–95.

Hilden, Adda. "Fromme, stærke Kvinder: Lærerindeuddannelse, 1800–1950." In *Dansk Læreruddannelse 1791–1991,* 3: 1–303. Odense: Odense Universitetsforlag, 1993.

Hobsbawm, Eric J. "Mass-Producing Traditions: Europe, 1870–1914." In *The Invention of Tradition,* edited by Eric Hobsbawm and Terence Ranger. Cambridge: Cambridge University Press, 1983.

———. *Nations and Nationalism since 1780: Programme, Myth, Reality.* 2nd ed. Cambridge: Cambridge University Press, 1992.

———, and Terence Ranger, eds. *The Invention of Tradition.* Cambridge: Cambridge University Press, 1983.

Horstbøll, Henrik. *Menigmands Medie—det folkelige Bogtryk i Danmark 1500–1840.* Copenhagen: Museum Tusculanums Forlag, The Royal Library. 1999.

Humble, Nicola. "A Touch of *Bohème*: Cookery Books as Documents of Desires, Fears and Hopes." *Times Literary Supplement,* June 14, 1996, 15–16.

Hyldtoft, Ole. *Danmarks økonomiske historie, 1840–1910.* Århus, Denmark: Systime, 1999.

Johansen, Jens Christian V., Erling Ladewig Petersen, and Henrik Stevnsborg, eds. *Clashes of Cultures: Essays in Honour of Niels Steensgaard.* Odense: Odense University Press, 1992.

Kerber, Linda K. "Daughters of Columbia: Educating Women for the Republic, 1787–1805." In *The Hofstadter Aegis: A Memorial,* edited by Stanley Elkins and Eric McKitrick. New York: Alfred A. Knopf, 1974.

———. "The Republican Mother and the Woman Citizen." In *Women's America: Refocusing the Past,* edited by Linda K. Kerber and Jane Sherron De Hart. 5th ed. New York: Oxford University Press, 2000.

———, and Jane Sherron De Hart, eds. *Women's America: Refocusing the Past.* 5th ed. New York: Oxford University Press, 2000.

Kisbán, Eszter. "Food Habits in Change: The Example of Europe." In *Food in Change,* edited by Eszter Kisbán and Alexander Fenton. Glasgow: John Donald, 1986.

———, and Alexander Fenton, eds. *Food in Change.* Glasgow: John Donald, 1986.

Kyrre, Hans. *Kartoffelens Krønike.* 2nd ed. Copenhagen: Udvalget for Folkeoplysnings Fremme, G. E. C. Gad, 1938.

Larsen, Henrik. "Vi holder fast ved måltiderne." *Politiken,* May 22, 1999, 2.

Larsen, Ivan. "Husk at hejse flaget." *Havebladet,* no. 2 (November [April] 2006): 26, 28

Latham, Jean. *The Pleasure of Your Company: A History of Manners and Meals.* London: Adam and Charles Black, 1972.

Levenstein, Harvey. *Revolution at the Table: The Transformation of the American Diet.* New York: Oxford University Press, 1988.

Lewis, Bernard. "In the Finger Zone." *New York Review of Books,* May 23, 2002, 61–63.

Looft, Henning. "Råd om indkøb og lægning af kartofler i 2006." *Havebladet,* no. 2 (April 2006): 15

Lundgreen-Nielsen, Flemming. "Danskhed: hvorfor og hvorledes?" In *På sporet af dansk identitet,* edited by Flemming Lundgreen-Nielsen. Copenhagen: Spektrum, 1992.

———, ed. *På sporet af dansk identitet.* Copenhagen: Spektrum, 1992.

Mai, Anne-Marie. "Overvættes Læselyst: Om nogle kvindelige læsere i det danske 1700-tal." In *Digternes Paryk,* edited by Marianne Alenius. Copenhagen: Museum Tusculanum, 1997.

Mangor, Anne Marie. *Tante Cousine: En Familie-Skildring fra det forrige og dette Aarhundrede.* Copenhagen: Thieles Bogtrykkeri, 1852.

Markussen, Ingrid. *Til Skaberens Ære, Statens Tjeneste og Vor Egen Nytte.* Copenhagen: Institut for Dansk Skolehistorie, Danmarks Lærerhøjskole, 1991.

McCall's Cook Book, edited by the food editors at McCall's magazine. New York: Random House, 1963.

Mennell, Stephen. *All Manners of Food: Eating and Taste in England and France from the Middle Ages to the Present.* Oxford, England: Basil Blackwell, 1985.

———, Anne Murcott, and Anneke H. van Otterloo. "The Sociology of Food: Eating, Diet and Culture." *Current Sociology* 40, no. 2 (1992): 1–152.

Ministry of Foreign Affairs of Denmark. "National Flag." http://denmark.dk/portal/page?_pageid=374,520391&_dad=portal&_schema=PORTAL

Ministry of Foreign Affairs of Denmark. "Traditions and Food." http://denmark.dk/portal/page?_pageid=374,477813&_dad=portal&_schema=PORTAL.

Mintz, Sidney W. *Sweetness and Power: The Place of Sugar in Modern History.* New York: Viking, 1985.

———. *Tasting Food, Tasting Freedom: Excursions into Eating, Culture, and the Past.* Boston: Beacon Press, 1996.

———. "Time, Sugar & Sweetness." *Marxist Perspectives* 2, no. 4 (winter 1979–1980): 56–73.

Mørch, Søren. *Den ny Danmarkshistorie 1880–1960.* 3rd ed. Copenhagen: Gyldendal, 1997.

Nielsen, Niels Kayser. *Madkultur: opbrud og tradition.* Århus, Denmark: Klim, 2003.

Nordstrom, Byron J. *Scandinavia since 1500.* Minneapolis: University of Minnesota Press, 2000.

Oakley, Stewart. *A Short History of Denmark.* New York: Praeger, 1972.

Olsen, Carsten Bjørk. "Danmarks Kartoffel Råd." *Havebladet,* no. 1 (February 2006): 12.

Paston-Williams, Sara. *The Art of Dining: A History of Cooking and Eating.* London: The National Trust, 1993.

Pedersen, Ole Karup. *Dansk Landbrugsbibliografi.* Vol. 1 (indtil 1814). Copenhagen: Det kgl. danske Landhusholdningsselskab, 1958.

Peterson, T. Sarah. *Acquired Taste: The French Origins of Modern Cooking.* Ithaca and London: Cornell University Press, 1994.

Poulsen, Søren Toftgaard. "Heden i kunst, litteratur og folkelig fortællekunst." Danish Ministry for Energy and the Environment, http://www.sns.dk/udgivelser/2001/87-7279-316-3/kap11.htm.

Procida, Mary A. "No Longer Half-Baked: Food Studies and Women's History." *Journal of Women's History* 16, no. 3 (2004): 197–205.

Reventlow, Christian. "Tale." *Minerva* 4, no. 2 (1788): 1–7.

"Rigsdagstidende." Copenhagen, 1891.

Rombauer, Irma. *The Joy of Cooking.* New York: Bobbs-Merrill Company, 1936.

Rosen, Christiane. *Jfr. Christiane Rosens Levnets-Historie.* Copenhagen: S. L. Møllers Bogtrykkerie, 1836.

Røssel, Jette. *Den Antikke Kogebog.* Introduction by Bi Skaarup. Aarhus: Modtryk, 1992

Rotberg, Robert, and Theodore Rabb, eds. *Hunger and History: The Impact of Changing Food Production and Consumption Patterns on Society.* Cambridge: Cambridge University Press, 1985.

Rying, Bent, ed. *Denmark: An Official Handbook.* 13th ed. Copenhagen: Danish Ministry of Foreign Affairs, 1964.

———, ed. *Denmark: An Official Handbook.* 14th ed. Copenhagen: Danish Ministry of Foreign Affairs, 1970.

Said, Edward. *Orientalism.* New York: Vintage Books, 1979.

Schama, Simon. "Mad Cows and Englishmen." *The New Yorker,* April 8, 1996, 61–62.

Schultz, Majken. "Foghs image-kampagne kan blive boomerang." *Politiken,* April 3, 2006. http://www.politiken.dk/VisArtikel .iasp?PageID=446641.

Scully, D. Eleanor, and Terence Scully. *Early French Cookery: Sources, History, Original Recipes and Modern Adaptation.* Ann Arbor: University of Michigan Press, 1995.

Sered, Susan Starr. "Food and Holiness: Cooking as a Sacred Act

among Middle-Eastern Jewish Women." *Anthropological Quarterly* 61, no. 3 (July 1988): 129–39.

Skaarup, Bi. "Middag på Koldinghus." *Skalk*, no. 6 (1990): 12–22.

Skougaard, Mette. *Bondens køkken: Madlavning og måltider i 1800–tallets landbosamfund*. Copenhagen: Nationalmuseet, 1984.

Skrubbeltrang, Fridlev. *Agricultural Development and Rural Reform in Denmark*. Translated by Reginald Spink. Vol. 22, *FAO Agricultural Studies*. Rome, Italy: Food and Agricultural Organization of the United Nations, 1953.

Slettbo, Jørgen. "Mad og Drikke." In *Dagligliv i Danmark i det nittende og tyvende århundrede*, edited by Axel Steensberg. Copenhagen: Nyt Nordisk Forlag Arnold Busck, 1963.

Smail, John. *The Origins of Middle-Class Culture: Halifax, Yorkshire, 1660–1780*. Ithaca: Cornell University Press, 1994.

Smith, Bonnie G. *Changing Lives: Women in European History since 1700*. Lexington, MA: D. C. Heath and Co., 1989.

Steensberg, Axel, ed. *Dagligliv i Danmark i det syttende og attende århundrede*. 2 vols. Copenhagen: Nyt Nordisk Forlag Arnold Busck, 1969–71.

———. *Dagligliv i Danmark I det nittende og tyvende århundrede.* Copenhagen: Nyt Nordisk Forlag Arnold Busck, 1963.

Stokes, Patricia R. "Gendered Nations: Nationalisms and Gender Order in the Long Nineteenth Century—International Comparisons." Berlin: Conference Report, Technical University of Berlin, March 25–28, 1998, www.hsozkult. geschichte.hu-berlin.de/ beitrag/tagber/gender.htm.

Stoklund, Bjarne, ed. *Kulturens nationalisering: et etnologisk perspektiv på det nationale*. Copenhagen: Museum Tusculanums Forlag, 1999.

Symons, Michael. *A History of Cooks and Cooking*. Urbana and Chicago: University of Illinois Press, 2000.

Tannahill, Reay. *Food in History*. New York: Stein and Day, 1973.

Theophano, Janet. *Eat My Words: Reading Women's Lives through the Cookbooks They Wrote*. New York: Palgrave, 2002.

———. "Household Words: Women Write from and for the Kitchen." Philadelphia: Van Pelt Dietrich Library, University of Pennsylvania, exhibition catalog, April 10–June 26, 1996.

Thiesen, Enke L. B., ed. *Veiviser eller Anviisning til Kjøbenhavns, Christianshavns, Forstædernes og Frederiksbergs Beboere for Aaret. . . .* Copenhagen: Boghandler L. B. Thiesen's Enke, 1837–1848.

Tilly, Louise A., and Joan W. Scott. *Women, Work, and Family*. New York: Holt, Rinehart, and Winston, 1978.

Vegenfeldt, Regina, and Lilian Kornerup. "Danske Kogebøger 1616–1974." MA thesis Danmark's Bibliotekskole, Copenhagen, 1976.

———. *Danske kogebøger 1616–1974, med et tillæg 1975–1977.* 2nd ed. Hamlet, 1978.

Weber, Eugen. *Peasants into Frenchmen: The Modernization of Rural France, 1870–1914*. Stanford: Stanford University Press, 1976.

Welter, Barbara. "The Cult of True Womanhood, 1820–1860." *American Quarterly* 18 (1966): 151–74.

Woolf, Virginia. "Professions for Women." In *Virginia Woolf: Women and Writing*, edited by Michèle Barrett. New York and London: Harcourt Brace Jovanovich, 1980.

Zuckerman, Larry. *The Potato: How the Humble Spud Rescued the Western World*. New York: North Point Press, 1998.

Ørting, Susan. "Danske Kogebøger: En annoteret fortegnelse over danske kogebøger fra 1616–1880." MA thesis. Copenhagen: Danmark's Bibliotekskole, 1974.

Østergaard, Uffe. "Peasants and Danes, the Danish National Identity and Political Culture." *Comparative Studies in Society and History* 34, no. 1 (January 1992): 3–27.

INDEX

Economy
  Danish, 101, 133, 176
  household, 59, 62, 65, 67, 82,
    87, 101, 122
education, 18–19, 119, 136, 177
Elias, Norbert, 73, 181n26
empire, 45–46, 99–100, 103, 106–
    7, 174, 177, 184n25
  map of, 91–92
  Norway, 46, 92, 95, 99–100,
    107, 184n25
  U.S. Virgin Islands, 46, 106,
    184n25
Enlightenment, European, 42–43
Estrup, J. B. S., 133
European Union, 127–28, 134,
    193n44

Family structure, 177
Fannie Farmer, 16, 180n6
farmers, 14, 24–25, 64, 74–75, 83–
    84, 118–21, 129–34
  See also peasant
Feldbæk, Ole, 100–101, 189n17,
    193n46
Fernández-Armesto, Felipe, 52
flag days, 115–16, 130, 190–91
Flandrin, Jean-Louis, 184n33
folkehøjskole (people's high schools),
    84, 119
Fordyce, Eleanor T., 181n22
foreign terms and dish names,
    101–6
French bread, **183n21**
French kitchen, 45–46, 102–3, 105,
    128
Friedel, Louise Beate Augustine,
    85
Frøken Jensens Kogebog (Miss
    Jensen's Cookbook), 14–16,
    20, 24, 44–47, 64–66, 71
  cookbook introduction, 58–60
  frontispiece, 9
  recipes, 79, 124, 149–50, 154,
    158–59, 167, 173

frontispieces, 2–9
Frykman, Jonas, 73–74

Gellner, Ernest, 126
gender roles, 13, 53–54, 63, 70, 73,
    81–83, 86, 88, 101, 176–77
  German, anti–, 100–101
Ginderup, Carl, 23–24, 71–72
  frontispiece, 7
  recipe, 166
Gold, Carol, 180n12, 182n31,
    184n36, 188n13
Goody, Jack, 14, 18
government, 99–101, 106, 121, 132,
    134, 191n21, 194n60

Hagdahl, Charles Emil, 81–83, 123
Hall, Catherine, 185n11
Hansen, C., 104
Hasberg, Conradine, 52
  menu, 30–32
health and cooking, 42–43, 51, 56–
    57, 62, 68, 84, 95, 97–98,
    117, 169
Heiberg, Johanne Luise, 105
Heiberg, P. A., 98
Hobsbawm, Eric, 127, 193n52,
    194n61
Høet, J. K., 187n13
holidays, 116, 127, 190–91n2
Holst, H. P., 99
Huguenots, 119
Humble, Nicola, 11
Hyldtoft, Ole, 118, 188n14

Identity and identification
  class, 131
  cultural, 119, 134
  Danish, 12, 100–104, 115–34
  European, 128, 193n44
  farmers' cultural, 119, 131, 134
  French national, 119
  national, 12, 104, 115–34,
    192n34, 193n48
  women's, 82

Napoleonic Wars, 41, 46, 98–99,
134
national anthem. *See* anthems,
national
national cuisine, 120, 125, 128
national identity. *See* identity
nationalism, 12, 82, 94–109, 126–
30, 176–77
Nielsen, H. V., 15
Nielsen, Nielsine
menu, 32–33
Nielsen, Niels Kayser, 174
nobility, 4, 23–24, 36, 45, 95, 103,
120–21, 125, 136, 159
See also aristocracy; class: upper
Nordstrom, Byron J., 187n7,
194nn65–66
Norway, 46, 92, 95, 99–100, 107,
184n25
numeracy, 12, 21–22, 177

Olsen, Carsten Bjørk, 194n58
Olufsen, Christian,161
"otherness," 102

Patmore, Coventry, 65, 185n9
peasantry, 24–25, 52, 73–75, 84,
117–25, 129–31, 134, 138
See also class: lower; farmers
Pelt, J. C.
recipes, 39, 157, 162–63
Peterson, Sarah, 128, 184n24
political parties, 25, 119, 133
Danish National Liberal Party,
98–99, 194n64
Social Democratic Party, 133
Venstre (Liberal or Agrarian
Party), 129, 133
popular (*folkelig*) culture, 119, 124, 131
potato council, Danish, 115–16, 130
potato culture, 122, 125
potatoes, 12, 107, 115–134, 146–47,
168–69, 190n31
recipes, 118, 124, 160–168
Poulsen, Søren Toftgaard, 189n15

prescriptive literature, 12–13, 25,
52–54, 94, 124–25, 176

Ranger, Terence, 127
Rasmussen, Maria, 88–89, 108–9,
172
menu, 32
recipes
beef à la mode, 156–59
beef and English beef, 39, 40
changes in, 146–74
chocolate cake, 180–81n21
cinnamon cakes, 22
cup cakes, 181n23
frikadeller, 151–55
herring, 147–50
potatoes, 118, 124, 160–68
pound cake, 181n23
red pudding (*rødgrød*), 38, 169–73
roast, 86, 187–88n14
rye bread, 76–77
soup, fried fish, 38
spoon food, 37, 52
wheat bread, 78
white bread, 77–80
reform era, 24, 84, 121
religion, 18–20, 47, 55–56, 61–62,
64, 81, 116, 190–91n2
confirmation, 18–19
Reventlow, Count Christian, 120–21
Rombauer, Irma, 16, 180n7
Rosen, Christiane, 15–16, 19, 21,
40, 43–45, 67–69, 84–88,
104–5, 122, 151
autobiography, 135–143
cookbook introduction, 56–57
recipes, 76–77, 148, 153, 157,
163–64, 171
rural enlightenment, 84, 199
Rying, Bent, 194nn62–63

Scharling, E. A., 123
Schleswig and Holstein, 46, 98–
99, 106, 115, 126
map of, 93

LIBRARY OF CONGRESS
CATALOGING-IN-PUBLICATION DATA

Gold, Carol, 1942-
Danish cookbooks :
domesticity and national identity, 1616-1901 / by
Carol Gold — 1st ed.
p. cm. — (New directions in Scandinavian studies)
Includes bibliographical references and index.
ISBN-13: 978-0-295-98682-1 (pbk. : alk. paper)
ISBN-10: 0-295-98682-4 (pbk. : alk. paper)
1. Food habits—Denmark—History.
2. Cookery—Denmark—Social aspects.
3. Cookery, Danish—History. I. Title.
GT2853.D4G66 2007
394.1'2—dc22   2007002324